Praise for

All Over the Map

A National Bestseller

"One thing Ron James has always been is a writer. And the journals he kept along the way helped him write his new book, *All Over the Map*. The book is full of Ron's encounters with memorable strangers from the road as well as his childhood growing up in Nova Scotia. And have I mentioned his use of language? It is jaw-dropping." —Tom Power, Q, CBC

"In these times of anxiety and social combat over COVID-19, laughter is closer to medicine than merriment, and *All Over The Map* provides plenty. . . . While the rants and wisecracks are still there in spades, quite a few of [James'] words on paper are kindly and persuasive, and you feel at home with him. He's a good writer." —*Winnipeg Free Press*

"This book is more than just another funny memoir. It's an eloquent and beautiful tribute to this great country of ours and the wonderful people who populate it, written by one of Canada's greatest comedians. Hilarious, poignant and perceptive, the stories will stay with you long after your laughter has subsided. Read slowly. You'll miss it when it's gone." —Mark Critch, author of *An Embarrassment of Critch's* and *Son of a Critch*

"Ron James offers a hilarious tour through some of the unfunny realities of life as a Canadian comedian—enough to make a grown-up laugh and cry, cringe and think." —Linden MacIntyre, award-winning author of *The Winter Wives* and *The Bishop's Man*

"A wild ride of a book. I laughed out loud. I also think the people should know that the ending . . . is the funniest ending to a memoir I have ever, ever read in my life. The book is worth getting just for that alone." —Mutsumi Takahashi, CTV News, Montreal

All Over the Map

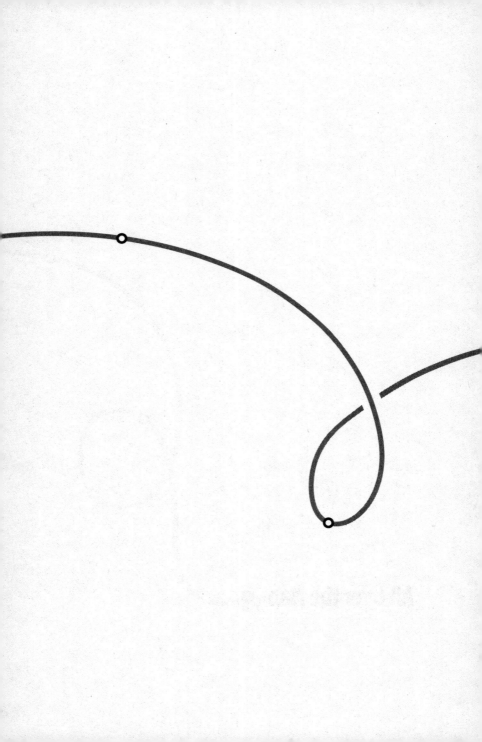

RON JAMES

ALL OVER THE MAP

Rambles and Ruminations from the Canadian Road

ANCHOR CANADA

Anchor Canada paperback published 2022
Doubleday Canada hardcover published 2021

Excerpt on page vii from "The Country of the Young" by Al Purdy, *Beyond Remembering: The Collected Poems of Al Purdy*, edited by Sam Solecki, 2000, Harbour Publishing, www.harbourpublishing.com

Library and Archives Canada Cataloguing in Publication
Title: All over the map : rambles and ruminations from the Canadian road / Ron James.
Names: James, Ron, 1958- author.
Identifiers: Canadiana 20200212052 | ISBN 9780385671156 (softcover)
Subjects: LCSH: James, Ron, 1958- | LCSH: Comedians—Canada—Biography. | LCGFT: Autobiographies.
Classification: LCC PN2308.J35 A3 2022 | DDC 792.702/8092—dc23

Cover design: Andrew Roberts
Cover photograph: Ed Kowal

Printed in the USA

Published in Canada by Anchor Canada,
a division of Penguin Random House Canada Limited,
a Penguin Random House Company

www.penguinrandomhouse.ca

10 9 8 7 6 5 4 3 2 1

Penguin
Random House
ANCHOR CANADA

To June, Cayley and Gracie,
who were always there
when I went elsewhere.

Go ahead, chase fame. See what that does to your soul.

Follow your bliss.

—Joseph Campbell

Look here
You've never seen this country
it's not the way you thought it was
Look again

—Al Purdy

CONTENTS

FOREWORD

All Over the Map is a travelogue through time; a road trip between one comedian's ears, taking pit stops in the past and present, that embraces the mysteries of people and place.

That comedian is me, by the way, and I wouldn't be writing the book were I not one—I'd be busy in the lab with other nuclear physicists, playing with boron.

That's a lie. You need good marks in math to be a nuclear physicist, and I repeatedly flunked that subject in school, because I'd rather talk than think. I'd also rather hit the road, looking for laughs, than deal with a nuclear meltdown in a cooling tower any day . . . so there's that, too.

By the way, when I write "mysteries of people and place," I don't mean the run-of-the-mill mysteries, like "Are sasquatches real, and if so, why does the only existing film footage of them look like a neighbour running through a backyard in a hair suit they sewed in their man cave?" Or "Was the last recorded sighting of the serpent

Ogopogo—which legend says swims in British Columbia's Lake Okanagan—authentic, or the result of the claimant enjoying a magic mushroom–induced afternoon? (Perfectly plausible. I certainly saw my fair share of giant lizards after scarfing a mittful of shrooms at a folk festival or two back in the day. Believe me, a trio of seven-foot salamanders singing backup for Valdy in 1978 was a vision a twenty-year-old kid could have done without.)

Perhaps the most enduring of Canadian mysteries is: "How many mosquitoes, over what period of time, does it take to drain you dry of blood while you're attempting to fill your bucket with the blueberries you're picking north of Temiskaming? (Actually, it's 729,623, in under five minutes. How about that? Maybe I *am* good at math.)

At the risk of pushing the envelope into hypothetical realms of the fantastical, the mystery I'm referring to is the tactile connection of spirit to place. It's the soul note that connects you to the authentic. I heard it ringing Sunday-morning clear when touring cities, towns and whistle stops along 7,821 kilometres of our nation's connective tissue: the Trans-Canada Highway. The hidden boons accrued in a call to adventure answered, occurred when I crossed paths with fellow pilgrims who, unprompted, shared their stories that in the telling, delivered a currency far greater than a payday's treasure.

Whether in coffee shops, hotels, planes, street corners, food courts or bars, when these strangers started talking, I'd just listen. When they were done and disappeared to where they'd come from, I wrote it all down so I wouldn't forget. I'm glad I did, because those conversations took place well before we were forced to close off the real world we actually walked through in exchange for the digital one we don't. They happened before everything changed. They happened before a worldwide pandemic shifted our psychic paradigm, dramatically altering daily life, crippling economies, gutting government infrastructure and, at this writing, leaving 3.6 million global casualties in its wake.

The performing arts suffered a particularly devastating blow. Throughout the global village, those places where practitioners of the myriad disciplines that comprise the profession once plied our trades—theatres, stadiums, bars, clubs, concert halls—were shuttered to protect audiences and performers alike from an invisible enemy ten times more contagious than the common flu. This killing of *authentic* social contact made social media's *inauthentic* contact a mandatory lifeline. What for me had once been a live audience seated in theatres, suddenly became an *unseen* audience, seated somewhere in cyberspace. With everyone housebound, Zoom became cyberworld's ubiquitous delivery system. Where I'd once stood onstage hearing laughter, I now stood in my living room . . . hearing, well . . . nothing at all! (Given the contemptibly quiet crowds I'd weathered in my first few years in stand-up, the irony wasn't lost on me. You gotta love it when life comes full circle, eh?)

Streaming gigs live from my living room certainly kept my mojo workin' and threw a few bucks in my kitty, yet every performance felt as if I was delivering my set to fellow earthlings from a space capsule orbiting the Nebulon galaxy. Authentic connection is not the medium's strong suit.

My Covid-enforced dependence on technology can't be entirely blamed on the virus, though. I'd already become prisoner to the dopamine release that a smart phone's "ping" delivers to the neocortex. With each one, the brain's receptors experience such an orgasmic hit of adrenalin it's a wonder there's not a discharge of fluids! The thing about receiving a dose of dopamine, though, is that in less than an hour, you'll be wanting another one. Its buzz is fleeting. Ephemeral. Empty calories. A soul note, on the other hand, is not just a passing sensation, but one of permanence. It echoes through time, by setting its anchor way down deep to where spirit abides. It's what those fellow pilgrims I chatted with felt compelled to share and I felt privileged to hear. That makes this their book as much as it does mine.

I started writing *All Over the Map* three years ago in my Old Town Toronto condo, never imagining that I'd be writing the second draft during an Atlantic Bubble–mandated quarantine—cocooned in a sanctuary by the sea that made my Nova Scotia province of origin the safest place *in . . . the . . . world* during the summer of 2020—to ride out the plague. During the fourteen days indoors, neighbours and friends brought me food or reached out via text, asking what was needed. Their kindness personified the unifying phrase: "We're all in this together."

This wasn't unique to the East Coast, either. Despite all the mixed messages the public received from authorities as to how to beat the virus—and the virulent idiocy of the anti-maskers with their conspiratorial belief that COVID-19 was a Bilderberg/New World Order/ illuminati star chamber–orchestrated *plan*-demic supported by evil Big Pharma, George Soros, Beijing billionaires, Russian oligarchs, Bill Gates and his Silicon Valley minions busy planting microchips in our bloodstream for mind control shenanigans, a couple of Masons named Bill and Reg playing shuffleboard at the Okotoks Legion and that pair of giant lizards beneath the White House living on a diet of Republican babies snatched by Hillary Clinton riding a broomstick— Canadians for the most part prioritized the common good. We wore masks, washed our hands and kept our social distance as we fought to "flatten the curve" of globalism's first plague, the impact of which will be felt for generations. Provided, of course, the Martians don't invade first. Which, given the consistently bizarre geopolitical plot twists in our planet's daily narrative, would not surprise me in the least. By the time the paperback edition of this book hits the stands, the entire planet could be under alien bondage with me doing hard labour in the zinc mines of Thompson, Manitoba guarded by Martians with ray guns. (I'm sorry. Do outer space invaders even use ray guns? They probably just stare at your forehead until it explodes, right? Okay. I stand corrected. So, no ray guns. Apologies for the 1930s Buck Rogers–level of reference for Martian weaponry, but the only science fiction I read is an occasional op-ed in the *National Post* by Conrad Black, and that's just for the sesquipedalian rush of it all. By the way, I bet Conrad Black *is* a Martian.)

Even with the majority of Canadians following protocols at the start of the pandemic, the ineptitude of Canada's political class was staggering when it came to managing it. Our national travesty saw 81 percent of deaths from COVID occur in elder care homes. The populist dominions of Doug Ford's Ontario and François Legault's Quebec led the nation in geriatric deaths. Privately run elder care facilities were the most notorious offenders. Owned by stone-cold corporate profiteers, these warehouses to the hereafter hired devalued workers to care for devalued lives who were as disposable as the diaper they were wearing that hadn't been changed in a week. Perhaps when these heartless totems of capitalist greed meet their Maker, their reward will be that crowded corner in a very special place in hell.

"Move over, Bernie Madoff—Mike Harris and Chartwell's board of governors just arrived!"

By the pandemic's second wave, the frustratingly slow procurement of vaccines by Canada may have showcased our prime minister's skills at reading a teleprompter, but when inoculation rates put our G20 nation thirty-third in the world, I bet there were plenty days Trudeau had wished he'd stayed a snowboarder in Whistler. At one point we were behind Slovenia! In layman's terms, that meant Melania Trump's third-cousin Igor got the jab before our essential workers!

But when the third wave arrived, carrying a host of lethal variants, it hit with a tsunami's impact. Canada's most populous province, Ontario, suffered a near collapse of its public health care system and a mind-boggling projected loss of 15,000 lives a day, all thanks to the science-defying arrogance of Premier Doug "Big Daddy" Ford and his cabal of Conservative henchmen, whose mismanagement of everything from vaccine roll-out to paid sick leave was nothing short of criminal. I swear the man had a better grasp of supply and demand when he was a community college drop-out selling hash from the trunk of his father's Cadillac!

Yet during COVID's initial assault, the communal response of Canadians stood in stark contrast to that colossus to our south. The next-door neighbour we once knew and admired slipped its moorings, drifting into far more dangerous waters of the Rubicon we were all crossing over. That will happen when you choose to follow the petulant diatribes of an intellectually compromised paranoid POTUS, whose pathological narcissism, moronic dictates and unmitigated cruelties were enabled by a cabal of lickspittle sycophants, fawning toadies, billionaire kleptocrats and delusional legions of evangelical Christians whose blind obedience to that American id run amok made a mockery of everything the Saviour stood for. Whatever happened to love thy neighbour as thyself? Someone should have told them when "me" trumps "we" everyone loses. When the richest, most technologically advanced nation on Earth couldn't even put personal protective equipment into the hands of front-line workers when it had once succeeded in putting a man on the moon, I figured the *least* they could have done was try to put their president up there!

Thankfully, the oozing cyst on America's body politic was removed by Joseph R. Biden. Yet two weeks before the new president's inauguration, the poison festering in the bowels of a Republican Party evacuated its rancid effluvia into the streets of Washington, metamorphosing into a flesh-and-blood mob of mouth-breathing batshit-crazy conspiracy-addled zealots in MAGA hats hell bent on death and destruction in their Capitol building and looking to put the coup in koo-koo.

And that was only 3,000 of the 74 *million* Americans who still believe the election was stolen. Good ol' Uncle Joe may personify the "better angels of man's higher nature" but besides wrestling a pandemic to the mat, making America *sane* again will be the toughest task.

I mention all this because I couldn't discuss a life spent as a foot soldier in the trenches of Canadian show business without a nod to the allure of America's. The war wounds incurred pursuing an acting career in the attrition-littered arena of Los Angeles another lifetime ago taught me a fundamental lesson: the individual is responsible for his or her own happiness. Unfortunately, that clarion call to self-empowerment courtesy of the Enlightenment, has, over the past forty years, fallen hostage to neoliberalism's feverish pursuit of mammon, where the road to "happiness" has been hijacked by a Gordon Gekko level of greed whose hunger for acquisition could never be satiated. Once "more is never enough" became the mantra America chanted, even getting by in the Land of Plenty was seen as losing . . . and I was barely doing that in the early '90s.

Ironically, not grabbing the grail I'd sought in that Los Angeles of long ago proved instrumental in siring a radical shift in my perspective. After three years, I realized the creatively fulfilling life I wanted would not be hand-delivered by someone else but had to be sought for and fought for by me. Once I returned to Canada, I decided to put that epiphany into action. If something came of it, bonus! If not, given the debt I'd incurred chasing Hollywood's golden goose, I'd better start turning a buck soon or else I'd have to sell a kidney.

Hitting the road in search of employment is nothing new for those of us born to the Maritimes. "Going where the work is" has been as integral to that region's identity as staying put. We're tartan nomads, driven beyond the familiar for a better run at a new day.

Even though I've called Toronto home for more than forty years, learned my stock in trade and raised a family here, that other somewhere I'm from is encoded in my DNA. Because no matter how far we roam, Maritimers never really leave "back home." Our need to return every summer is not dissimilar to that of the wily Pacific salmon—stay with me—which, after a lifetime spent swimming strange waters, suddenly finds its internal compass at the mercy of Earth's magnetic pull, bearing it back to its river of birth.

Perhaps our annual return is an attempt to reclaim something that's been lost. To reconnect with the place where, once upon a time, you genuinely *belonged*. To feel a continuity of spirit with those now gone, whose presence once coloured the tapestry of your life. The ability to channel the timeless feels all the more possible in landscapes of the familiar.

Just a heads up . . . the content of this book does on occasion bounce around a bit, as you've no doubt already noticed. Think of your reading experience as playing a pinball game with a man suffering attention deficit hyperactivity disorder (ADHD) in charge of the flippers. It's the way my mind works. A diagnosis a couple of years ago gave a name to what I'd experienced for a while: serotonin and norepinephrine do a daily tap dance on the floor of my frontal lobes, making my ability to concentrate on one subject at a time somewhat of a challenge. Multi-tasking is another man's forte. On the other hand, standing onstage in front of a thousand people, my synapses cutting and pasting two hours of content at the speed of thought from a combination of memory and spontaneously created material, is not an issue. Apparently, that ability is an attribute of the ADHD-afflicted.

It's a peculiar superpower though. Sometimes I wish I had the talent to hold my breath underwater for ten minutes instead, so I could be a Polynesian pearl diver. How cool would that be?! I would never have been forced to battle blizzards a yeti wouldn't wander as I drove through Rocky Mountain passes to a gig. Instead, I'd be running a pearl-diving business from a beachside shack in Bora Bora. Mind you, *were* I a pearl diver, I would have to contend with tiger sharks, one of the more notorious man-eaters of the South Pacific. They regularly grow to thirteen feet in length, sporting a head full of sharp-as-obsidian serrated teeth, as they prowl Oceania's shallow warm waters and bays, looking to satiate the bottomless appetite of the apex predators that they are. (See what I mean?)

On the following pages, you'll also find reflections on nature's fury and the humbling wonders I've been privy to while chasing a living crisscrossing the vast expanse of the Big Wide Open. There are opinions about the industry I'm in and some recounting of experiences I've had in some television shows that I've done.

The nano-second pace of change during these years of the plague may mean some of the observations about current events have an even shorter shelf life than is usual for topical content. So here's hoping they aren't too irrelevant by the time the book reaches your hands. (Then again, if the Martians have invaded in the meantime, my concern is a moot point anyway, so there's that.)

Memories of failure, fear, loss, change, redemption and challenge are here too, with occasional pit stops taken to times long gone when life was spent amongst those I'm from in a world that was, whose heartline hum I feel beating still.

Chapter One

CROSSING THE THRESHOLD

I was behind the wheel of my '99 Toyota 4Runner, overlooking Lake Superior, that vast inland sea the Ojibwa call Gitchi-Gami, when a logging truck came barrelling full tilt round a hairpin turn with all the malevolence of a bad dream. We were suddenly jousting for dominance on an empty stretch of the Trans-Canada Highway, running through the heart of the Canadian Shield scoured granite-hard by retreating glaciers you'd swear had just left yesterday. I'm willing to wager that Joseph Campbell wasn't driving this ribbon of widow-making asphalt when the wizened sage coined his galvanizing phrase: "Follow your bliss."

Nevertheless, I was doing exactly that: a stand-up comedian bound for eight one-night stands, playing towns strung sentinel lonesome round the frozen lip of Lake Superior. Surrounded on all sides by jaw-dropping, iconic geography that would have given the Group of Seven a collective woody, I was doing my best to dodge a cannonading steel leviathan threatening to bounce me off its Peterbilt logo into the afterlife, where my dubious end would be marked by one of those ubiquitous white crosses coyotes happily hop the highway to piss on. I was so far out on the edge of forever that if our world ended tomorrow, it wouldn't register up there until a week later!

Moose rule that country, and they have developed a taste for highway road salt with all the feverish addiction a junkie has for Afghani smack. At any moment, I expected to collide with six hundred kilos of stunned ungulate, standing clueless in the middle of the highway . . . licking it. The impact would have most certainly sent that swamp donkey caterwauling arse-over-antlers through the windshield, rendering me comatose in a blur of fur, blood and bone.

As my now-gone father used to warn, "It's not the moose landing on your lap that'll kill you, Ronnie. It's their flailing hooves beating your face to a pulp once they're *in* the car does that!" I was in no rush to test Dad's claim, having once seen a substantial hoofprint on the forehead of his third cousin once removed.

Speaking of moose, after my show in Atikokan, Ontario, an audience member handed me a seven-and-a-half-pound sirloin tip moose roast. I remember thinking that America may have a multi-million-dollar Hollywood star system, where talent can ride a comet-worthy career trajectory from obscurity to forty-foot-tall neon billboards advertising your latest film in every corner of the known world, but you know you're on the right showbiz road in Canada when locals in towns beyond the pale are paying you in butchered game. You just don't get post-show perks like that when you're playing Vegas. When someone hands you a brown paper bag dripping with blood in *that* town, it's probably got the head of a Teamster in it!

Atikokan, the canoeing capital of Canada, is an iron-hard outpost of 1,500 souls, perched on the edge of boreal forest, home to a labyrinth of waterways that bandy-legged voyageurs once paddled to reach the heart of a wild continent back in a fur-trading day when beaver was king.

What kid who canoed at summer camp didn't fantasize about being a voyageur? Living a life paddling the wilderness in a birchbark canoe full of your crusty habitant pals, all of you smelling ripe as an old diaper, with nary a care in the world. In actuality, it was a will-killing, ball-busting gig. When you weren't running Class V rapids capable of pulverizing your vertebrae to the consistency of tapioca pudding, you were portaging seventy-five pounds of pemmican through mosquito-infested *terra incognita*, shackled to servitude by corporate overlords in Montreal, all for a feudal wage. (Though they were still paid better than most Canadian comedians are for a gala set at Just for Laughs today!)

Outside Atikokan, I bunked at the only nice hotel on the tour, the White Otter Inn, sitting beside the Voyageur Route of the Trans-Canada Highway. An elderly bartender there told me that as a kid growing up in town, he'd seen Dan Blocker—the guy who played Hoss on the long-running 1960s television series *Bonanza*—stocking up on supplies for summertime fishing trips he was taking in-country. Other showbiz notables of the day would drop in from time to time too, he said, should they happen to be gigging a short plane flight away in Michigan. He swore the likes of Dean Martin, Jerry Lewis and other Rat Pack pals were seen stepping from a plane loaded down with hooch and hookers, headed for a luxurious fishing camp that catered to Las Vegas royalty. Now *there's* a vision of the Canadian wilds we never saw on *Hinterland Who's Who* when we were growing up: a taciturn, monosyllabic Ojibwa fishing guide, watching the Nutty Professor cast for muskie from the boat with a Vegas showgirl on his lap while yelling, "Nice lady!" and scaring the fish.

Rivers were Canada's roads once, snaking through a forest primeval, carrying commerce to wild dominions eons before RE/MAX was a cottage country catchphrase. I was following lines on maps born as corridors in some Clovis-point dreamtime, when First Peoples stumbled windward, bent and bowed, in search of meadows green with game. Next came explorers, trappers and settlers, escaping the rat-choked, scab-picking, syphilitic alleyways of the Old World for the pine-scented, fresh-air freedoms of the New. Mind you, after one winter of tooth-spitting, gum-bleeding eighteenth-century Montreal scurvy, you'd be damn near whimsical for a case of Parisian clap!

If life is all about the journey and not the destination, that seminal winter tour was my first step across the threshold into a wider world of wonders that, twenty-five years later, I'm still giving thanks for.

Before I made the move to Los Angeles in 1990, my approach to career had been the usual co-dependent actor/agent relationship, where you *hope* they will score you an audition so you can *hopefully* score whatever role they sent you out for. That approach exhausted itself during the relentless pursuit of too-few-and-far-between paydays; a gruelling run compounded by Biblical calamities of riots, floods, fires and earthquakes. Nothing alters perspective quite like a 6.7 seismic how-do-you-do that gets you and your loved ones huddling beneath the kitchen table as the ground below your shaking townhouse turns to Jell-O.

Lesson learned: there is a price to pay for Paradise.

After three years of chasing a moving target, I was done down there. I was done with agents. I was done waiting for a break. I was done being broke. (Well, not quite.) I was done waiting for my life to start. And I was most certainly done waiting for someone else to start it for me. It was time to set a new compass bearing.

Upon my return to Canada, I shifted the paradigm. Instead of being an actor who depended on others to feed me and mine, I became a comedian who fed them himself. Picking the best eight minutes worth of "bits" from a one-man show I'd written about my three years in Los Angeles, called *Up and Down in Shaky Town: One Man's Journey Through the Californian Dream*, at thirty-eight I started over and stepped onstage at a comedy club called the Laugh Resort, for that ego-crushing crucible called "amateur night."

To this day, the memory spooks. Those eight minutes scare you spitless *and* buck naked shitless as the glaring solo spot threatens to burn a hole straight to your soul with a merciless determination befitting the judgmental eye of God. That's why those of us who answered the call do it . . . because we *have* to.

Five years were spent honing my act, playing Canada's laughably lean club circuit for a paltry wage, until mouths to feed and a mortgage to pay bade me move beyond the parochial limitations of the Big Smoke and blaze a trail playing small-town theatres in lands beyond the pale. Granted, the theatres I played weren't exactly Carnegie Hall. In fact, they weren't even theatres! They were smoke-choked Legions, community centres, church basements and school gymnasiums, all housing a quality of acoustics only a mime could love. Still, there was an authenticity to it all. It was tactile. It had a real you could feel.

Back then, many comedians and their agents were prone to the prejudice that trying to break into "soft-seat" theatres in Canada wasn't worth the effort. Where's the career trajectory in playing a high-school auditorium on a Friday night in Dryden, Ontario? (Well, none actually . . . but the gig paid three times more for one show than the Toronto clubs did for five, so there's that.) "Why bother with Canada?" went the mantra, when the incantatory juju of that American woman's siren song said a life flush with riches beyond the realm of reason was but a hop across the US border and a green card away.

Everyone believed that when it came to stand-up comedy, validation in the Land of Liberty was the only option worth pursuing. I begged to differ—naively perhaps, but if people in a host of other professions never had to leave to actualize their livelihoods, why should a comedian? Most importantly, that inaugural tour ignited my faith that a worthy stand-up career could be built in Canada. So, I stayed here stringing my trap line from Corner Brook to Courtenay-Comox, and over several years as the gigs increased and crowds grew, I came to realize that hearing one thousand people laughing in a country I call home sounds *exactly* the same as hearing one thousand people laughing in a country I don't.

Working homegrown stages didn't depend on the pursuit of a predominant myth every Canadian comic once embraced: that a killer set at Montreal's internationally renowned Just for Laughs festival would lead to a career in the States. That once the appointed and anointed saw you catch lightning in a bottle at the world's biggest comedy festival, you'd be plucked from obscurity and suddenly find yourself surrounded by a team of perpetually tanned Los Angeles handlers and managers so secure in their assessment of what's funny, they never laughed. As if by teleportation, you'd awaken to a eucalyptus-scented breeze on a sunny southern California morning, signed to a lucrative network development deal where you'd live under glorified house arrest in a charming bungalow on the Warner Bros. lot, dreaming up television shows while you kicked a bag of money around the floor. In actuality, the odds of that happening were so infinitesimal, you'd have had better luck finding Oak Island gold.

It's easy to understand why we believed this was possible. Comedic status in Canada has always been measured by whether or not you're successful elsewhere. Ask any of us who have seen that look of pity cross a certain kind of Canadian's face when they ask whether we perform in the States and we answer no. Their reaction says, "Well, I *guess* you're doing okay, despite that big hairy ear growing out of your forehead."

Yet, even after a very rewarding seven-year run across Canada, with three specials to my name and more in the works, the thought of taking another run at America still percolated. But I finally committed to keeping my feet firmly planted in Canada thanks to an encounter with my comedy hero at a Just for Laughs post-show party in 2007. It was none other than that Glaswegian wizard . . . Mr. Billy Connolly.

If a person can have a religious experience laughing themselves into a state of grace, then watching this man's first HBO special in 1991, during a soul-sucking year-long run of unemployment in Los Angeles, was most definitely mine. This uncensored force of nature threw himself from one end of the stage to the next, delivering a rollicking, profane and fearless ninety-minute set as he extolled the virtues of his fractured tribe. Billy's performance elevated me to that alternate state of awareness I imagine alien abductees must walk forever, after they've been beamed back to the cornfield they'd been snatched from. (It's always a cornfield.) Nothing is ever the same again. I remember thinking, *That's my tribal song, too!* And I felt I'd be sinning against my purpose in life if I didn't try to sing along. Simply put, it was a calling.

Standing tall above the schmoozing Montreal crowd, filled with comedians, hangers-on, managers and agents, Billy—with his shoulder-length white locks, General Custer–like goatee and a cigar pinched between his teeth—looked every inch the hermitic sage wandering pilgrims would seek for words of wisdom. I was hoping his insight might help me step beyond what I had been told countless times: that my Canadian content severely limited my chances of achieving a *real* career.

Despite Billy's affable nature, I was hesitant to approach, aware of the boundaries famous people prefer you'd respect when you see them in public. Fans can be intrusive. Forceful. Unpredictable. I presume that's why film festivals erect red ropes at their star-studded premieres. Should the likes of Brad Pitt or Scarlett Johansson, say, ever decide to step *beyond* the boundary and mingle with the crowd, the pack's euphoria could easily shift into a feeding frenzy worthy of *The Walking Dead* and before you know it, there's blood on the ground and an actor's lost a finger.

I stood before Billy on the receiving end of a piercing stare that said he did not suffer fools. I spoke.

"The only reason I'm here," I said, "is because fifteen years ago, I saw your HBO special when I was church-mouse poor and out of work in LA. It was my Saint-Paul-on-the-road-to-Damascus comedic epiphany."

He laughed and said, "I hope you don't open with that!"

I mustered my courage and, with all earnestness, asked, "How did a working-class welder from the Glasgow docks become an internationally renowned comedian?"

He plucked the cigar he had pinched between his teeth and, with a fiery-eyed defiance, barked, "That's a question about fame! To hell with fame! Just do what you do and sing your song!"

Lesson learned: sages confirm what pilgrims already knew in the first place.

This alchemist of the calling whom I watched, mesmerized, as he spun gold from straw during a blistering two-and-a-half-hour set at Hamilton Place later that same year, knew that to pursue fame was to court the Promethean fire. What mattered to him was the pure joy of performance. You could see it in every concert of his. This tartan shaman tapped into the life force! Every performer worth their salt is tuned to that frequency, but success breeds fame and fame fuels the engine of celebrity—and no one does celebrity quite like America. It's why our national media feeds on theirs, because the phrase "Canadian celebrity" is a glaring oxymoron. You don't get a street named after you in Scarborough for starring in three seasons of *The Littlest Hobo*.

Because Canada has no star system, we have also mostly dodged Scientology's pernicious ruse of using Hollywood celebrities to recruit future disciples. It's one thing to hear a pitch from that über movie star "gone clear," Dianetics deity Tom Cruise, on how a cruel interplanetary warlord named Xenu dropped billions of his people into an active volcano from DC-8s 75 million years ago, but I'll bet the house not many of my countrymen in search of a messiah are going to join a cult because buddy from *Murdoch Mysteries* told them to.

I'd met celebrities at Toronto's iconic Old Firehall during my days as a rookie actor on the Second City mainstage, when the cast of *SCTV* would hire me on occasion. That group of comedic illuminati were dedicated, consummate actors/writers already at the top of their game in 1983. Although they were certainly accommodating and professionally welcoming, to say I was intimidated in their company is a glaring understatement. Chatting up Eugene Levy while he's fine-tuning an impression of a drunken Henry Kissinger for a Joe Flaherty–hosted *Maudlin o' the Night* sketch, as Andrea Martin threads the needle on an Edith Prickley bit, while Marty Short runs up and down the halls channelling an uncannily obnoxious and accurate Howie Mandel impression—for eight hours *prior* to shooting—was not encouraged. Know your boundaries, kid. You learned your lines, hit your mark, hopefully didn't suck, cashed the cheque and paid the rent. I realize now, I was witness to a remarkably talented cast whose groundbreaking series had miraculously harnessed the zeitgeist, creating a standard of comedy that still stands the test of time forty years later.

In 2017, I was asked to perform a ten-minute audience warm-up set for the shooting of *SCTV*'s Netflix special, directed by Martin Scorsese and moderated by Jimmy Kimmel, at Toronto's historic 2,500-seat Elgin Theatre. That stage, along with its sister theatre the Winter Garden, once welcomed luminaries of the vaudeville circuit like Buster Keaton, as well as far lesser-known acts such as . . . "Wanda! The Seal with a Human Brain!"

You read that correctly. I tried to imagine the owner travelling the dirt roads of that gruelling North American vaudeville circuit of 1910 with a seal as a sidekick. Did it ride beside him on the bus with the other acts as they watched him throw a glass of salt water in the seal's face every half hour? Seals have to be wet or they die, don't they? Where do you find seal food in the Midwest? As far as I know, there's not a lot of herring to be found in Toledo, Ohio. I'm sure a seal wouldn't settle for a grilled cheese if the diner was out of squid. Tell me that wouldn't make a great film? If Clint Eastwood could make two movies with an orangutan in a truck, then surely a barking seal on a bus could fly. No? Let the idea germinate for a bit, and I'm sure you'll see its potential.

I'd last performed at the Elgin in 2003, when Conan O'Brien came to town for three sold-out shows after America's fear of SARS had

ravaged Toronto's film and tourism industries. It's not an exaggeration to say the city lost its collective mind. Nothing gets Torontonians
damp in the pants faster than American recognition. I was getting
messaged from people I hadn't heard from in thirty years, asking me
for a ticket.

"I could get you a kidney quicker!" I barked.

The night of the *SCTV* taping, the Elgin was humming with the
electric anticipation of a jam-packed audience come to honour their
homegrown Emmy Award–winning comedy heroes. Meanwhile
backstage, the real showbiz machine was in gear . . . Hollywood was
here! The *SCTV* cast were gracious and warm, all exuding a generosity of spirit devoid of the standoffish attitude one might associate with
their status. I'd logged more than a few kilometres looking for laughs
since they'd hired a kid for half a dozen sketches in the early 1980s,
and for once, I believed the invitation had been honestly warranted.

Jimmy Kimmel entered, surrounded by a coterie of carcinogeni-
cally tanned LA handlers, all wearing dismissive, nonplussed looks
unique to the perpetually unimpressed. I'd bet good money they
wouldn't raise so much as an eyebrow of expression even in the presence of a talking, card trick–performing cat riding a unicycle. In a
roped-off area stood the most influential and revered director of our
age, Martin Scorsese himself. This diminutive presence of such
peaceful disposition stood in direct juxtaposition to his cinematic
pedigree, whose palette of lyrically orchestrated violence made it
hard to imagine him giving directions to Robert De Niro and Joe
Pesci in that infamous *Goodfellas* scene, where they put the serious
boots to the head of Billy Batts in their bar. There was a side of me
that wanted to slip into the De Niro impression I'd honed over the
past thirty years and yell, "Marty!! When do I get my close-up?!" But,

having been schooled in a respect for boundaries, I thought otherwise. (Besides, there was also a chance Scorsese's personal security detail—who, my imagination assumed, were blending in as that couple of thick-necked IATSE union dudes in the corner—were also very handy with their boots.)

You have to understand, it's not every day a working Canadian comic is involved in an event like this. I love the road and every town or city played, but my touring world is so far removed from the rarefied air of high-stakes showbiz, I might as well be a medieval juggler working market day during the annual shaving of the simpletons. (I'm not sure they actually had those days, so apologies to whatever simpleton was simple enough to buy this book and is now simply offended.) Prior to getting the invite from *SCTV*, I was actually feeling fortunate for having just sold out two shows in Sarnia . . . on weeknights!

If readers will indulge me a tangent . . . for those living east or west of Ontario, Sarnia is known as Chemical Valley, thanks to the sixty or more chemical plants, fertilizer facilities and oil refineries whose industries daily dump a devil's brew of carcinogens into the air and water. Locals seem to take it in stride, though. Granted, the bartender at a certain watering hole may be sporting a mysterious seven-pound cauliflower growth on his chin . . . that changes colour with the seasons . . . but that's a small price to pay for a truck in the driveway and a job at Dow Chemical. Besides, there's really no need to worry: union health benefits would cover the removal of any facial tumours incurred as a result of slopping up an industrial-sized spill of ethylbenzene that's already melted some poor bastard's feet off clear to the shins.

My Elgin set went exceptionally well. The laughs roared up from the seats with the fury of rogue waves. It felt redemptive, especially since I'd been fired from the Second City mainstage thirty-five years prior. The invite came from the man who did it, impresario Andrew Alexander. To be asked to deliver a set before this august body of talent hit the stage was testimony to his faith in my abilities. Even though he'd been the one to hand me my pink slip, he knew the improviser I tried to be in 1983 wasn't the stand-up I'd become.

Second City was the best place for any eager young actor to learn the craft of character-driven ensemble comedy, where scene structure and spontaneity worked in tandem to create, as high priestess of the form, Viola Spolin, put it, "something wonderful right away."

Yet, despite Second City's indisputable opportunities for creative growth, a sword of Damocles hung over the place, where whispered names of the unceremoniously fired stood as portents of how quickly you could be "disappeared." Oblivious to the fate about to befall them, one minute, an actor was in the cast, and the next, their backstage dressing room booth was occupied by a hungry wannabe who'd been watching the show every night from their perch at the back of the theatre in vulture's corner, when they weren't at home sticking pins in a voodoo doll that resembled the actor who just got the boot.

After five years and three shows with the organization, the sword fell on me. Given how light I'd become in the nightly improv sets, (from whose scenes we built each new show), it came as no surprise. Feeling that I wasn't pulling my weight, a gnawing insecurity took hold, fuelling an anxiety that stifled an innate comedic intuition that, up to this point, had served me well my entire life.

Suffice it to say, every time I opened my mouth I felt I should shut it, and every time I shut it, I felt I should speak up. To quote my father, "Jesus Murphy, Ronnie! A man wouldn't know whether to shit or go blind!"

Among those of us who started together in the Touring Company, pressure to succeed in the major leagues of Toronto's mainstage compromised what had once been a have-your-back brothers-in-arms camaraderie, earned in the fight for laughs surviving tough gigs in ugly rooms and long drives on winter roads in a crowded van, where we vacillated between being a mirthful gang of ribald young satirists and a seething crew of battle-crusted veterans expressing contempt for whatever idiosyncrasies might manifest themselves in the close quarters of a vehicle gone ripe with a winter's worth of stale marijuana smoke, Big Macs, and a vegan member's sneaky flatulence. (The only difference between that van and the submariners of *Das Boot* is that we weren't speaking German.)

As eager disciples of the form, we had progressed from beginner to advanced in Second City's improv classes. If you passed their twice-yearly auditions, you won entrance to the Touring Company where this aforementioned van sat parked outside the front doors of Toronto's historic Old Firehall Theatre at 110 Lombard Street. Once aboard and on the road, you were now a card-carrying member of a club that was the first step to youthful ambition realized. Unless of course, after two weeks, two months or too long for your own good, you still stunk up a scene, had no comedic timing, couldn't improvise to save your life, were way too weird even for a comedy troupe, missed your onstage cues or got on everyone's nerves in the van by telling boring stories that lacked punchlines. In that case, during one interminable drive back to Toronto through another February midnight after suffering another hellish gig spent moiling for comedy gold north of "Why Were We Ever Booked in This Hillbilly Holler in the First Place?", you'd be thrown from the moving vehicle and left to suffer the vicissitudes of a cruel season, when, come spring, what was left of your bones would be ground to potash by enterprising farm-hands and sold to the nurseries that dot the fertile soil of the Holland Marsh. Or worse . . . just ignored.

The bonus of suffering Ontario's winter roads was a summertime residence at Deerhurst Resort, in the heart of Muskoka cottage country. In 1981, Deerhurst was hardly the sprawling corporate retreat it would later become, but getting paid to hone your funny in what was really the Canadian Catskills before audiences of vacationing Torontonians was as good as it gets.

Our cast rented a defunct turn-of-the-century hotel called Portage Station that in its late-nineteenth-century salad days of parasols, top hats and Victorian manners, catered to affluent passengers arriving on the Muskoka steamship lines. By the time of our tenure, it had sat empty since its short-lived role as a liquor licensed summertime party palace, which in its late twentieth-century incarnation catered to the caramel tanned Topsider wearing aryan eyed sons and daughters of Muskoka blue bloods, who when they weren't fraternizing with the locals they'd forget about in September, were incurring DUIs for rolling Daddy's beamer in the ditch on the dirt road drive home. The place came complete with an institutional-sized kitchen and a dance floor with a working disco ball that we'd turn on and laugh at in praise of our bizarre good fortune. Our stately white elephant sat on a hill with a commanding view of a lake surrounded by forest, where young lovers could steal away to hidden glades in those elfin woodlands and shag with the zeal of docile house cats recently gone feral. Life was good.

We performed at Deerhurst Resort twice a week all year long for whatever corporate group was on retreat (and once for a lone pair of newlyweds who, we assumed, couldn't afford a trip to Vegas), diligently making the Wednesday and Saturday drive for our 8 p.m. show, regardless of what hellacious weather nature was throwing our way. In that neolithic age of travel, the only place to grab a meal on Highway 11 during our 11 p.m. drive back to Toronto was a forlorn service station and adjoining small diner run by a grumpy man and his sad wife. When the seven of us entered, jabbering non-stop, sporting our ravenous post-show "food faces", the couple eyed us much in the way one would if surprised by euphoric outpatients who had suddenly shown up in your kitchen right before bedtime, talking loudly, touching stuff, and eating your Frosted Flakes.

I'm back at the Elgin now. (Stay with me.) I remember making a point of keeping my set "universal," so it could be understood by any Americans in attendance unacquainted with our nation's regional idiosyncrasies, such as the size of the potholes on the streets of Inuvik in spring, or the impact of a chinook's dropping barometric pressure on manic-depressives in Lethbridge. Actually, my keeping it universal was for the benefit of Torontonians, too. When you consider your city to be the centre of the universe, knowing the price of a dozen eggs in Pangnirtung is not a priority.

(Truth be told, I'm so Canadian, most *Canadians* don't know what the hell I'm talking about!)

After my Elgin set I was standing in the wings watching the show when the head of Netflix, Ted Sarandos, came up to me and said, "That was a great set." I thanked him and said, "You've certainly seen a lot of comedy."

"Yes, I have," he replied, looking down at me from his six-foot, seven-inch height with a paternal smile unique to those with a net worth of six *billion* dollars. "And that was a great set," he said again.

As a minion scurried him away, while throwing a surly, proprietary stink eye back at me, I figured that at sixty years of age, I'd finally gotten my big break. It would only be a matter of time before Netflix rolled out the welcome mat.

Lesson learned: age might only be a number, but in television, if that number's over fifty, it's a number that carries COVID.

Judging a Canadian performer's worth against American standards is unfair, but perfectly understandable, especially when 80 percent of our population lives so close to the border, we're practically looking up Lady Liberty's skirt! The incantatory spell of her siren song has for generations heralded the promise of dreams made manifest. At least in my business. After all, America invented television. They knew, and still *do* know, entertainment. They set the standard. Granted, Canadian television might be light years from where it was in the 1970s but still, back then *The Beachcombers* coming on CBC on Sunday night just meant *The Wonderful World of Disney* was over!

It was the same for our leaders as well. During America's golden era of postwar prosperity in the early 1960s, when President Kennedy and Jacqueline Bouvier Kennedy were the shining, sexy young couple of Camelot, just next door in dour Canada, jowly John "The Farmers' Friend" Diefenbaker and his main squeeze, Olive, were stepping over cow pies at a tractor pull in Girvin. Sure, eight years later a cape-and-fedora-sporting Pierre Trudeau dating Jill St. John may have bought us some cred with the paparazzi, but the die had been cast.

We grew up watching American comedians whose subversive voices inspired an entire generation of stand-ups. No way could the

likes of Richard Pryor, George Carlin or even the Smothers Brothers
have developed in our "peaceable kingdom." Nor could the man I'd
talked to at JFL, Billy Connolly. No Canadian television network
would have given that comedic force of nature a ninety-minute special, out of which he spends twenty minutes imitating farting sled
dogs. (I love how he doubles down on the bit, too—pushing it farther
and farther and revelling in the unapologetic, unbridled puerile joy
of it all, while trumpeting an operatic impression of Arctic canines
passing their raw, seal-meat-supper-powered ass gas into the wind.
Google the clip. In fact, watch *any* clip of Billy Connolly. If you don't
think he's funny, throw this book away right now!)

These socially disruptive voices simply could not have developed
here, because the cultural illuminati and network gatekeepers during
the era that made them could be prudes when it came to comedy.
And not just in television, either. Even live acts suffered at the hands
of puritanical censorship. It's why the trail-blazing, uncompromis-
ingly profane and hilarious comedy team of brothers MacLean and
MacLean had to fight a charge of immoral content all the way to the
Supreme Court of Canada in 1977, all because they dropped a fusillade of f-bombs in their act, which an adult audience had paid *expecting* to hear! It's not like Mr. Dressup pulled a drunken Finnegan out
of the Tickle Trunk and the first thing the puppet did was take a whiz
onstage. (I know puppets don't pee; I'm just making a metaphoric
allusion to describe how surprised an audience would be had they
paid to see these totems of innocence fully expecting innocuous rep-
artee between the duo—lauding access to colouring books and cray-
ons on a rainy day as a soothing cure for the mumps for instance—but
instead, were subjected to an inebriated Finnegan defiantly taking
the act in a surprising new direction.) Even though adults had made

an adult decision to hear the brothers MacLean, a Sault Ste. Marie prosecutor with political ambitions and a sense of propriety far more conservative than the comedy duo's fans thought their act would do irreparable harm to the moral fibre of society, perhaps even incite a level of anarchy resulting in everything from a rise in teenage pregnancies to a drop in softwood prices. So, he pressed charges. But the brothers won. Twice.

Angry iconoclasts are distrusted in a country whose motto is "Peace, order and good government." That call to arms says, "Be nice, follow the rules and keep the noise down." On the other hand, America's motto—"Life, liberty and the pursuit of happiness"—amounts to "This way for hookers and blow, bro!" That's why so many Canadian-born comedians headed for the States. Not for hookers and blow, I mean, but to rock the apple cart in a country with 365 million people. Not thirty-seven million. You can have half the population of America hating your act and the other half loving it . . . which is still roughly *five times* the population of Canada. That's some decent wiggle room.

So, before you think I've sold my allegiance to America, I haven't. I was merely giving context to why Canadian comedians head south. (I know, it's a stretch.)

There's another reason these comedy legends could never have built their acts here. It's because the origins of our two nations were diametrically opposite. Canada wasn't sired by the smoke and fire of revolution, while America was. When her Thirteen Colonies gave England the boot in 1776 by raising an army of fighting farmers who beat the Yorkshire pudding out of a professional British one, she canonized a distrust of authority stoked by stirring catchphrases from their deified Founding Fathers such as "Give me liberty or give me death" . . . a sentiment actualized during COVID by the many who refused to wear a mask.

Canada's founding fathers, on the other hand—if you can give such immortal status to a gang of mutton-chopped lawyers harbouring such deference for the monarchy that they'd have bronzed one of Queen Victoria's turds to use as a paperweight—took a far more measured approach when they *legislated* our country into being. Where Canada was a benign delivery from the womb of Mother Britain, America's was a crack baby breech birth that chewed off its own umbilical cord.

To the untrained eye, it would appear Canada is clinically short on rebels, when in reality, that role has been played by Indigenous leaders who have fought settler privilege and the colonial mandate of expansion since before Confederation. During the nineteenth century, leaders such as Chief Poundmaker and Chief Crowfoot of the prairie Assiniboine and Sioux, to the fearless Mohawk of the Oka standoff, the Heltsiuk of Bella Bella who saved the Great Bear Rainforest from Enbridge pipelines, and the Wet'suwet'en of British Columbia, who refused company bulldozers entry to their lands, thus galvanizing a nationwide Indigenous blockade of railway lines, were bona fide Canadian rebels standing in defiant opposition to the status quo. Honouring the treaties and Supreme Court decisions signed in good faith by the Crown would be a step in the right direction, but when influence-peddling corporate interests in collusion with government proxy hold all the aces in the deck, it's no wonder solutions seem impossible. I don't get it. Oil and mining companies can pollute the country with impunity and it's business as usual. When I was a homeowner and dared to burn a few fall leaves in my backyard, the SWAT team showed up!

Perhaps the most famous of these land defenders is Manitoba iconoclast Louis Riel, who fought the right fight for his Métis people in the North-West Rebellion of 1885. His reward was to be hanged by John A. Macdonald's Conservatives. One hundred and forty years later, and well into the twenty-first century, successive governments—Conservative *and* Liberal—have refused to pardon the man. You know you must have been doing something right when Ottawa hates your guts that long! Louis disrupted the white Anglo-Saxon status quo, and nothing pisses off old white dudes more than telling them they can't have it their way—which is what rebels do.

Of course, Riel didn't have to get laughs while he did it, though maybe his men laughed behind his back when he started talking to angels in the clouds and had the bright idea of moving the Vatican to Batoche, Saskatchewan. (Then again, anyone who has spent time in a Roman Catholic seminary as Louis did, shouldn't be surprised if they come out of the experience susceptible to hallucinations.)

But I'm getting ahead of myself.

In 1997, I'd heard of an event called Contact, a marketplace where performers of all stripes could set up a booth, advertise their act and do fifteen minutes of it for an auditorium full of people who had the authority to book you in their theatres and the clout to write a cheque. After my set, a dozen of them did just that—which was unusual, because theatres wanted nothing to do with comedians in those days. We were anathema to their more refined tastes.

The only experience Canadians had of seeing homegrown stand-up comedians on television in the mid-'90s was CBC's *Comics!* This series brought the art form into the nation's living rooms for the first time ever. *Comics!* was filmed in front of a live studio audience, and every comedian got a thirty-minute set that acted as a calling card for club owners and bookers, who could see an actual audience validate a comedian's performance with their laughter and applause. When few homegrown comedians were scoring a coveted eight-minute televised gala set at Just for Laughs, *Comics!* was giving us the incredible luxury of half an hour of national airtime.

Lorne Elliott's radio show *Madly Off in All Directions* did much the same, providing comedians with what Steve Patterson and CBC's *The Debaters* offer many today: national exposure and a payday.

The Comedy Network, with its promotional tag of "Time Well Wasted," had yet to be born, but when it was, parent company CTV handed rare ninety-minute specials to Ottawa-born bulletproof act, Jeremy Hotz, Brampton's own Russell Peters and myself. I shot my one-man show *Up and Down in Shaky Town*, and damned if CTV didn't play it every New Year's Day for seven years in a row! Nary a penny came my way in residuals, though, because in Canada, we're bought out for 100 percent of our fee, which means a show can be played in perpetuity—until Joggins, Nova Scotia, is once again attached to the Horn of Africa. But at least I could take vicarious pleasure in knowing I was helping some hurting buckos sweat their way through a hangover while they watched me do the "Liquor Barn" dance.

Truth is that more often than not, the moving target I never hit a lifetime ago in LA was far from the studios of Hollywood legend. My worlds were the vast casting houses I shared with dozens of other struggling members of the Screen Actors Guild, all of us desperate to land the bread and butter of the performing proletariat: television commercials. Everyone hoped to score a coveted and lucrative national campaign that would keep the bills from prowling round their mail slot like wolves over a litter of blind piglets in the snow. The first commercial I got down there saved us a winter of purgatorial gloom.

Do you remember those years when you were so broke, you had to scour the house for suitable Christmas gifts? I remember phoning my mother and asking, "So, you liked the pot holders, then, Mom? Yes, that's the way they make them in California . . . covered in crusty food with burn marks on them."

I'd moved down to do a television series created by a couple of talented Toronto Second City actresses, Deborah McGrath and Linda Kash. They'd sold it to Ron Howard's company, Imagine Entertainment, and it was syndicated nightly to independent channels across America. *My Talk Show* was a quirky, original concept set in a suburban home in the fictional town of Derby, Wisconsin, where a woman and her neighbours (including me) chatted up celebrity guests on a living room couch. At first, the guests were bona fide celebrities of the day, such as William Shatner, Martin Mull and Jim Belushi. But as the ratings took a nosedive, the show's booker—rebuffed, I assume, by agents who'd sooner see their A-list clients cutting a ribbon at the opening of an abattoir than chatting with us—began scouring showbiz purgatory for anyone who once had a modicum of television notoriety. Someone opened the gates at the "Where Are They Now?" compound, and every network personality from yesteryear who was still capable of functioning in public unescorted by orderlies got a day pass.

Werner Klemperer, who played Colonel Klink on *Hogan's Heroes* in the '60s, showed up, as did a Romanian plate spinner who'd gained fame on *The Ed Sullivan Show* and was still going to lunch on that appearance—thirty years later! They tried to get Bob Denver of *Gilligan's Island* fame, but were told, "There's not a chance. Besides, he's a very difficult guest."

No kidding he's "difficult"! Who wouldn't be the exact opposite in real life of that happy-go-lucky, sailor-hat-wearing, goofy man-child he played on a television show decades ago—a guy whose persona was forever fused in public memory thanks to endless reruns that never paid him a penny in residuals? That's not a career; that's a curse!

Chubby Checker also visited the set and lip-synched to "The Twist." That's right, *lip-synched*. In the hallway after shooting was done for the day, the man whose song had started a worldwide dance craze in 1960 after he sang it on Dick Clark's *American Bandstand* told me he used to work at a chicken-cutting plant. (Not the subject I'd open a conversation with, but to each his own.) He was an uncomfortably close talker too, whose pleading eyes, moist either with melancholy or medication, made me wish I wasn't an actor with his back to the wall offering no avenue of escape but a simple Sardinian shepherd leading his flock to pasture nurturing no dream of Hollywood glory.

I will bet good money that shamanic novitiates, well into the throes of an ayahuasca-induced hallucinogenic-shape-shifting vision quest, could never reach the level of surreality I did while listening with rapt attention to Chubby Checker's dissertation on his stolen American Dream.

"I noticed with all the choppin' of chickens we were doin'," said Chubby, "that we were throwin' away perfectly good chicken parts."

(I had a good idea that the parts he was referring to wouldn't even make the cut on the menu at Fat Jerry's House of Organ Meats.)

"After I got my big break, I left the plant, but the idea of doing something with all that wasted chicken stayed with me. One day I told my manager the idea. He said, 'You are crazy, man! That's why they throw it *away*! Ain't nobody gonna want to eat a bowl of chicken dicks!'

"Well," Chubby continued, "soon as my song was no longer number one, what did that no-good scoundrel do? But steal my idea and invent . . . mock chicken! That's right! *Mock chicken* is my idea! Chicken made with other parts of the chicken is . . . ?"

"Mock chicken," I answered.

He poked me in the chest. "You got it! Sonofabitch manager *stole* my idea! He got the credit for inventing mock chicken, became a billionaire, and Chubby," he lamented, arms outstretched at the injustice of it all, "he's still singing the 'Twist'!"

If that's not pathos, good reader, I'm Burton Cummings.

Vince Edwards, the actor who played neurosurgeon Dr. Ben Casey from 1961 to 1966 on ABC, also joined us, as if released from the kind of coma his television character was always pulling patients out of. I don't remember much about him, other than that his girlfriend was from New Brunswick, and when he found out I was born in the province next door, he made me say hello to her on the phone. We talked about the Magnetic Hill, McCain shoestring french fries, K.C. Irving's billions—and how the Bay of Fundy's infamous tidal *bore* is the most aptly named geographic phenomena in the world. (Look, it might be a big money maker for Moncton where tourists stand and wait for this expectant wall of water to come racing up an estuary that heralds the rise of the world's highest tides but sweet Jesus, people, I've made bigger waves in the tub after eating a breakfast burrito!)

Mostly, though, I remember the servile and sallow-faced executives from Imagine Entertainment who roamed the hallways before every show, poring over the previous night's Nielsen ratings sheet. Once the numbers began their fiery nosedive to oblivion, they stood in the shadows, wearing faces wracked with feigned concern, all the while wringing their manicured hands like Pontius Pilate looking for someone to crucify. Our bane was a particularly unctuous and insipid courtier, still sporting a disco dance-floor perm twenty years after its best-before date who wore a sweater wrapped round his neck like some dime-store Gatsby and called everybody "family." Right. So did Charles Manson.

On Tuesday, our cast photo was in *Newsweek*, accompanying a piece that lauded us as this year's "cult show to watch." On Thursday, we were cancelled. And on Monday, I was chest-deep in a hole on the actor Robert Urich's front lawn with a local pal's father's landscaping company, tugging at the roots of a rotted bush. The man who played Jake Spoon on the riveting mini-series *Lonesome Dove* walked out the front door dressed in knee-high leather riding boots with a polo helmet tucked under one arm while nonchalantly swinging a mallet made for the sport with the other. The dude looked every inch the baronial master of his San Fernando Valley domain ready for an afternoon engaged in the sport of kings. My pal greeted him with "Hi, Bob!" and pointing down to me said, "This is my friend Ron. He's an actor, too." "Really?" he responded with all the feigned interest a Hollywood star could muster while staring at a mud-smeared troll-in-a-hole. I would have happily taken a break from my digging to discuss the merits of the Stanislavski method and its impact on contemporary American cinema, but oddly enough, Jake Spoon didn't seem psyched for a chin wag. Go figure?

Suffice it to say that when the dust finally cleared, I found I hadn't made the kind of money you'd associate with American TV. In fact, I hadn't made the kind of money you'd associate with a manager of a mini-putt course. I was supposed to make three grand a week with sixty-five shows guaranteed, but after a palace coup at Imagine resulted in a new head of development replacing the *old* head of development who supported the show, a bloody gutting of our original group was under way, and out of an eight-person writing and acting team, three were left standing. What had been three thousand dollars a week at sixty-five shows guaranteed in 1990, became fifteen shows guaranteed at four hundred and fifteen bucks an episode. You read that right. Four *hundred* and fifteen. Taxes took 30 percent of that, and I *still* got audited by the IRS for the thirty-seven thousand dollars I made that year—correct again, *thirty-seven*—because the H&R Block accountant at the mall I had paid to do my taxes (who also played an accountant once in an episode of *Mannix*) put a decimal point in the wrong place. I know. Seems unfair.

The same year that the California aerospace industry bottomed out, taking sixty thousand jobs with it and throwing an entire state into recession, the IRS figured an actor from Canada who netted three hundred and fifty dollars a show after taxes on a now-cancelled series, whose family car was a second-hand '79 Dodge Colt that left an oil slick so thick on the floor of the garage that every time he pulled out of the driveway, there was a dying sea bird flopping in it, was the cause of the collapse.

Because of the plodding nature of bureaucracy, the IRS never notified me of my arrears until I was safely back in Canada. What had started out as two thousand dollars owing had now, thanks to interest, doubled to four.

The IRS agent and I spoke half a dozen times on the phone, and each time we did when I'd confidently inform him that, "You have no jurisdiction over me here," I swore I heard the ventricles in that bureaucrat's ice-cold heart crystallizing on the other end of the phone.

"We have ways of making life very difficult should you ever cross the border again," he warned.

The IRS has an elephant's memory and a fearsome reputation for pursuing their quarry with a Nazi hunter's zeal. Simon Wiesenthal with a team of Mossad agents and a list of of residents with German last names at an old folks' home in a hidden corner of Paraguay couldn't hold a candle to the dedicated hitmen of Washington's tax department when they were hell-bent on retribution. Not going to lie, a little shiver still goes up my spine every time I hand my passport to an American customs agent. I'm worried my long-gone tax infraction will show up on their computer screen and I'll be whisked into a soundproof room on the wrong side of Toronto's Pearson Airport, for a pistol-whipping courtesy of Homeland Security.

Every Canadian who chases Hollywood's grail has an experience uniquely their own. That just happened to be mine. Hats off to the perseverance of my fellow countrymen who also went south and managed to scratch out a career in a nation that knows no middle ground. In America, you're either winning or you're not. Victory is the only option. Anything less, and you've lost. So, after three years of trying to make something happen there, I returned to Canada and made something happen here.

But I didn't do it alone. Once upon a time I had a wife who really had my back. She said, "When we move home to Toronto, you can't do the same thing you've always done. You can't just wait for your agent to phone with an audition and hope you get it. You've got to approach your career differently." So, I did. Unfortunately, becoming a comedian wasn't what she'd anticipated, which is why I live alone now.

That's a shorter way of saying: The road became my priority and I returned from my tours an exhausted, emotionally depleted, cranky bastard who used up all his funny for paying audiences, so that once he crossed the threshold of his own home, he transformed into a moody, distant cur tucked into a corner reading another tome on the Battle of Stalingrad. Suffice it to say, a mechanic's car isn't always clean, and a comedian's home isn't always funny.

After a few years of booking rooms on my own, good fortune saw me fall into partnership with an exemplary producer of unimpeachable honesty, business acumen and integrity: Terry McRae of Shantero Productions. The Contact event got me booked for a night at the Academy Theatre in Lindsay, Ontario, a show that was supposed to be attended by townsfolk, as well as one hundred and fifty members of the Cadillac Club. I guess owning a Cadillac isn't enough; you also have to spend weekends and holidays amongst your Cadillac kin, all wearing jackets sporting Cadillac logos, with whom you'll share esoteric information on everything from finding spark plugs for your '61 El Dorado to how owning such a vehicle makes you so much better than the proles who can only afford a Dodge Neon.

This tribal allegiance is not terribly dissimilar from that of Civil War re-enactors. (It's very dissimilar, actually, and I'll admit the analogy's a stretch, but bear with me . . . *again*.) Like Cadillac Club people, Civil War re-enactors lead lives of normalcy during the week, but come Saturday, they'll be amongst their own, running through a field, clutching a period-piece rifle in 102-degree heat, dressed from tip to tail in mid-nineteenth-century regimental uniforms made of wool, so they can pretend they've caught a bullet in the breast at the Second Battle of Bull Run. Get this, though: once you're "shot," you've got to stay where you've fallen, under the blistering sun . . . *for the rest of the day*. Oh, what fun! If that's what it takes to feel a sense of belonging, I'd sooner live alone in a cave, subsisting on rainwater and toe jam.

In the re-enactor world, authenticity is everything. Meticulous attention to detail is paramount, from the make of their uniform buttons to using toothbrushes made of horsehair. I guess they draw the line at dysentery. (Wimps.) If getting as close as possible to authentically experiencing the horror of battle without time-travelling to 1863 is their real modus operandi, then I have a suggestion: shoot yourself in the foot, let gangrene set in and have a drunken buddy dressed as a battlefield surgeon saw it off in a cornfield under the hot sun, while you bite down on a piece of wood and pass out. There you go: time-travelling problem solved.

I just realized that anyone reading this book who belongs to a Cadillac Club has probably just drifted it across the room in a pique of anger. My sincere apologies. Dying of a fake suppurating chest wound is far more unusual a hobby than talking engine size with a Cadillac owner in a mall parking lot in Lindsay, Ontario—which, I guess, is where most of the Cadillac Club was the night I was performing, because only two of the clowns showed up. Counting the townsfolk who *did* come, that made forty-one. The theatre held six hundred. My take for the night was supposed to be eight hundred dollars, but with the loss the theatre took at the door, we agreed on four hundred.

A month later, Terry McRae and his son dropped in looking to see if the artistic director who ran the theatre had ever booked comedians. The artistic director held up my photo and said, "This guy is pretty good." Lesson learned: it's not always about the money.

I learned the hard way about the importance of a great producer after leaving Terry's company for bigger Toronto agencies . . .

twice, thinking they'd take me to "the next level"—whatever that was supposed to be. The decision was spawned by an ego-driven belief that where you're *at* isn't as good as where you *should be.* But, in fact, where I *was* was exactly where I have always wanted to be . . . just working!

Shantero and I started our first tour in April 1999 with half a dozen theatres along Ontario's Highway 401. We sold out the 1,000-seat Centrepointe Theatre in Nepean and added an encore date, too. I couldn't believe my good fortune! Terry did what no other promoter in Canada had the guts to do for a relatively unknown comic looking to play theatres: he put his own dollar on the line, took the risk, rented the theatres, landed local radio stations as sponsors and advertised aggressively on that medium and in print, never seeing a penny of federal largesse or corporate funding to fuel our engine. A work ethic worthy of biblical Job did that, and with forty years spent running acts this wide country over, that taciturn Scotsman, despite COVID's impact on live touring, is still in business.

When I first hit the road, the tech revolution was in its infancy, and it took me a while to get on board. (After all, I'm from a day where a hashtag was something you got from doing hash *knives.*) Not to disparage social media entirely, because I enjoy sharing photos on Instagram of meals I've made, rivers I've run, hikes I've taken and tomatoes I've grown . . . but I still don't know *why*. I don't know why it matters that someone in Salmon Arm, British Columbia, "likes" the garden I planted on the deck of my Toronto condo, but the dopamine it releases in the brain's pleasure centre does a great job of making me believe it *should.* ("Pleasure centre." Sounds like a sex club in Berlin where you'd catch chlamydia, COVID-19, Zika virus,

SARS, Ebola and a bad case of Bactrian camel ass rash just by ringing the doorbell. Out of curiosity, of course.)

The nanosecond pace of technological change made the sale of my specials on DVD obsolete overnight. From 2007 until 2013, I'd stay for an hour in the lobby after every show, autographing copies for patrons who'd purchased them. By 2015, this bit of extra income had suffered the dodo's fate. There are now a dozen boxes of my final four specials, shot between 2013 and 2017, holding up a wall in a Toronto storage space. Now I know how buddy felt who invested a family fortune in buggy whips, five years after Henry Ford flooded the market with Model Ts.

Here we are at the end of the chapter, and you're no doubt wondering, "Whatever happened to that logging truck?" (I didn't forget.) Well, with half the boreal forest's worth of logs strapped to its carriage and its ass end swaying into my lane, I cut hard for the shoulder.

As it blew past at an unholy clip, barely a sliver of Eucharist away from introducing me to dead relations, I let loose with:

"Slow down, ya bastard! You're carrying wood. It will keep!"

Chapter Two

TWO DAYS IN SASKATCHEWAN

A cold and sepulchral ice fog smothers the coulees of the Qu'Appelle Valley while the vacant eye of a reluctant sun makes a feeble attempt at breaking through the grey mantle of sky. If the ceiling were any lower, it would be in my lap. Squinting through the car's windshield, I swear I see antlered silhouettes of mule deer moving wraithlike in the distance. Hitting one would most certainly turn this ergonomic nightmare of tin and plastic I've rented from Avis into a piece of abstract art.

The Yellowhead Highway is streaked with bloodstains where many of the ungulates have met their Maker, leaving nothing but a smear of deer between the double lines and a pair of spindly legs poking up at unnatural angles from a mound of pink meat and fur on the soft shoulder.

I'm always travelling this corner of the country when winter has the land in a hammerlock and the sweetgrass smells of a prairie summer seem as far away as Chief Poundmaker's childhood. Every Canadian comic hits the road when it's under frigid siege, and people are looking for a night of laughs to take the edge off the long haul towards spring. They know from experience that there's an undeniable visceral charge you get from watching stand-up performed live, cocooned with others in a packed theatre, as opposed to watching it on TV, alone at home in your pajamas. (That observation can't help but feel bittersweet as I write these words in April 2021. With live performance forced into the realm of cyberspace, we've become acutely aware how important a *shared* experience really is.) For a few hours, stand-up puts strangers seated shoulder to shoulder all on the same page channelling the same life force. Laughter releases a cascade of endorphins through their collective nervous systems, lightening the load of the daily struggle. Or, as a cab driver in Sault Ste. Marie once said to me, "It's a vacation for the soul, Ronnie."

Stand-up creates an umbilical relationship between audience and comedian. It is symbiotic, proving that laughter is an affirmation of what it means to be human. After all, we're the only species in the animal kingdom that *can* laugh! (As much as I love meerkats, you never see them getting together as a group beneath the monkey tree to watch one of their own imitate the time he saw a hyena get gored in the arse by a warthog.)

As mentioned, I'm fortunate enough to have a competent producer in my corner, one with an impeccable pedigree and unimpeachable reputation. Unlike other producers who are content to book a tour, take their commission and then subcontract its execution to others, the indomitable Terry McRae (now joined by sons Patrick and Robin) not only books his theatres with a deposit a year in advance, garners sponsors and drives publicity with his one-stop shop, he also commits to driving every kilometre his acts do.

Thankfully, the man had the presence of mind to keep a map on his desk when he booked a tour. When I foolishly left his family's boutique operation for other outfits with star-studded rosters, their assurances that they would take me to "the next level," whatever *that* is in Canada, proved shamelessly long on promises and laughably short on substance. Upon signing with them, I entered a world of such cartographic ignorance, my tour must have been booked by a room full of drunken interns in blindfolds, seated at a table cluttered with empty shot glasses opposite a map of Canada on a wall riddled with darts they had thrown in imitation of a frat house drinking game. One February tour I took a pass on, designed with no regard for my personal safety, would have had me criss-crossing the Rocky Mountains through avalanche country for back-to-back gigs 640 kilometres apart along the killer Coquihalla Highway, a road that was surely designed by an optically compromised engineer who bought his degree at a Honduran flea market.

This is the sort of touring hell you suffer when you're an eager rookie in the Yuk Yuk's comedy mines, where the vast majority of Canadian comedians have honed their chops. They learn to weather brutal driving conditions, drunken patrons and paltry paydays, yet persevere, because stand-up is what they've been called to do. You've got to tip your hat to four comics in a no-name beater living on fast food and faith, bound for a one-nighter at a biker bar somewhere north of nowhere whose owner knows where the bodies are buried. They'll be bunking at a funky, down-at-the-heels motel whose cigarette butt–burned carpets reek from decades of sloppy sex, cheap whisky and the Pine-Sol the maids used in a futile attempt to scrub the stink of hopelessness away.

My early dues-paying years on the road had nothing on that level of suffering. For one thing, I travelled in a van with a cast of actors—because, well, I wanted to be one. What I didn't know then was that the basic job requirement for most actors is the ability to survive *not* being employed as one.

After graduating university, I landed a gig in a Wolfville, Nova Scotia–based puppet company. You read that right: puppets. Over the years, this well-run and very professional company has gone on to win many awards and global acclaim. But back then, we weren't flying to Beijing and Krakow, as they eventually would, for international puppet festivals where marionettes are revered and puppeteers drink for free in the company of municipal officials and art councils run by disillusioned communists. No, we were driving to elementary schools around Nova Scotia, performing in that equity-wage rite of passage known as "children's theatre."

The morning it all went horribly south, we were encircled by preschoolers in a very small, smothering-hot gymnasium after a night spent eating pickled eggs and drinking skunky draft in a New Glasgow Legion.

This particular production never involved puppets, which were reserved for older children who could survive the sight of an actor wearing a frightening face mask, standing seven feet tall in boots with wooden blocks on them, dressed as Gitchi Manitou of Mi'kmaq myth. (White people expropriating the cosmology of an Indigenous people never played on that company's conscience forty-two years ago. It was a much different day. However, had we played any First Nations reserves, I'm sure the locals living there would have enlightened us—and justifiably so—as to why we shouldn't.)

What we were performing that morning was a counting game for four- to six-year-olds. I played a character called Baby One, who ambled round the floor on knee pads, holding a rattle. I was twenty-two years old, with a bachelor's degree in history. "Pride goeth before a fall," they say. I clearly had none, so I was safe. I'm not sure if Laurence Olivier kicked his career into gear doing children's theatre, but in the days of early hunger hoping for a foothold in a precarious industry, I felt I had hit the jackpot.

My pal was playing . . . the Chicken. He never wore a full chicken suit, as our prop budget was limited. After all, we were supported by government grants in what was then called a "have-not" province. (I'm told that Canada's greatest Shakespearean actor, Colm Feore, had the full and pristine chicken suit during *his* years in children's theatre, but that's Ontario affluence for you.) The Chicken wore a mask fashioned from scuba headgear that had a red rubber glove glued to the top. Inside the fingers of the glove were cigar tubes, so that they would stand up straight like a rooster's comb, even though my pal was not a rooster, but the Chicken. (Given our demographic, costume gender accuracy was a moot point.)

The Chicken's face was entirely visible, and the pores on his forehead were leaking the swill we'd been quaffing the night before. The droplets were beading into a dank, cold sweat, as the nauseating reek of pickled eggs that had been quietly fermenting in our colons overnight began to silently sneak from their recesses and permeate every corner of that very small, equatorially stifling-hot gymnasium. The children seemed oblivious to the deadly attack of chlorine-level ass gas that, without a shadow of a doubt, would have buckled every troop to their knees in the trenches of Passchendaele. But not here. They were transfixed . . . on a chicken and a baby.

Everyone gets punchy after a long theatrical run, no matter what the play. I'm not saying a counting game for preschoolers can hold a candle to *Come from Away*, but I *am* willing to wager that even those incredibly talented actors, performing in the most heart-warming musical since the von Trapp family ran from Nazis in *The Sound of Music*, will, as we did, slowly start to lose their minds. More than likely, they'll stay the course, because they're all talented professionals of the highest order. I, on the other hand forty-two years ago, was not.

Children seated three rows deep on the floor surrounded us in a semicircle. One of the other actors had some scene-chewing monologue about the number three, and he'd just left the stage with a confident strut, exuding a self-serving satisfaction worthy of a young Peter O'Toole after delivering a show-stopping soliloquy in the West End. It's pretty hard to justify that level of ego when your entire audience has entered the gymnasium attached to each other's mittens.

Maybe that's why my pal started clucking louder than usual. Maybe it had dawned on him sometime the night before, when we were drunk in a Legion—*again*—that whatever plans he had of escaping this internment to become the next Robert Duvall were as gossamer-thin in delivering on that dream, as a desert mirage would be to a lost and dehydrated Englishman hallucinating a naked duchess with a tray of tea and crumpets.

The Chicken had hit what journalist Malcolm Gladwell would later describe as the "tipping point." It's the moment where the gloves come off, where what had once mattered no longer does. Another idea popularized by Malcolm is that one must dedicate a minimum of ten thousand hours to achieve proficiency at one's chosen craft. This morning would witness no such perseverance from the Chicken—nor his sidekick. Other puppeteers may assail the heights of the profession and become the willing muse of every marionette maker in Leipzig, but for us, that dream was dead.

What, at the start of our tour, had been a gentle, happy-go-lucky *cluck-cluck-cluck* any barnyard chicken would make while scratching in the dirt, on this notorious morning became a painful howl: *booo-deck! booo-deck!* It was nothing short of a *cri de coeur*, delivered with all the gusto a journeyman actor, still drunk at 9 a.m. and dressed as poultry, could muster. The young man had been cold-cocked by the realization that his hope of stardom had dematerialized before his eyes with all the indifference of a ghost at dawn. So, why fight it? With a dangerously flushed pallor and spit arcing in great sprays of gesticulation, the Chicken's wilful display of anarchy bade the Baby step "off book." (*Off book* is a theatrical term that means, you are no longer in need of the script because you've memorized all the lines for whatever role you're playing, which in my case was no lines at all.)

As the Chicken moved towards me with a louder and far more aggressive *booo-deck*, I upped my tormentor's ante. Licking the suction cup on the bottom of my rattle, I stuck it to my forehead, crossed my eyes for maximum effect and launched into a nonsensical garble of baby speak. Great paroxysms shook the Chicken's squatting body as he fought boldly to stay in character, but that battle proved futile. He was choking instead . . . but in a good way—the way you choke on your own spit when you're laughing your hole off!

I waddled round the gymnasium on padded knees, shaking the rattle that was stuck to my head, as cherubic faces of wide-eyed children exploded in fits of laughter, accompanied by the applause of their appreciative teachers. Don't tell *me* I can't play a room!

Not everyone was laughing, though. From behind the curtain, I saw the steely-eyed stare of the company's senior member. Beside him was the actor who'd just delivered the galvanizing monologue on the number three—who, in his bloated moment of messianic bliss, believed he'd soon be the recipient of the David O. Selznick Lifetime Achievement Award from the Academy of Motion Picture Arts and Sciences. Soon as I got backstage (I mean, behind the black curtain suspended on poles beside the bathroom), the company's senior member hissed at me:

"I have never seen such unprofessionalism in my life!"

"Unprofessional? Give me a break," I replied, with the rattle still stuck to my forehead. "How can playing to a room full of preschoolers be considered remotely professional, when most of the audience still goes to the bathroom in their pants?" Which, forty-two years later, is exactly the standard I shoot for in my shows today!

Lesson learned: if the ushers aren't wiping the seats down after a show, I haven't done my job.

On the Trans-Canada Highway between Regina and Saskatoon, an iron effigy of the animal that once darkened the plains in a moving blanket of meat on the hoof sits beside an erratic dropped as a glacial afterthought when sheets of ice once receded to oblivion. Called a "buffalo stone," it commemorates an animal that once numbered eighty million strong and moved mighty as Jehovah from the treeline to Texas with nary a mini mall to block its passage. On their way to calving grounds in eons gone, they'd stop at boulders such as this to scratch their hairy rumps free of winter fur. (Because it's hard, I guess, to scratch your bum when you've got a hoof not a hand. Chalk another one up for man.)

I'm bound for a gig in Prince Albert, a town with little over thirty-five thousand people and the sweet, six-hundred-seat EA Rawlinson Centre. It's the last substantially populated community before rolling hills of aspen give way to northern boreal forest, peat bogs and moose pasture. Besides being home to three prisons, Prince Albert is also where jowly ol' John Diefenbaker, Canada's thirteenth prime minister, was raised. The legacy of this Conservative is a tarnished one, thanks to his decision in 1959 to cancel Canada's state-of-the-art supersonic fighter jet, the Avro Arrow. That decision resulted in the loss of fifteen thousand jobs and more or less scuttled our fledgling (but innovative) aerospace industry.

In fairness to the man who spent the latter years of his political life ostracized from power, mumbling to himself behind stone pillars in the Parliament Buildings, he did appoint the first woman to cabinet, and he passed Canada's Bill of Rights—whose scope and legal force were increased a decade later by Pierre Trudeau's Charter of Rights and Freedoms. Diefenbaker also "allowed" Indigenous people to vote . . . finally.

(By the way—Quebec didn't give Indigenous people the right to vote until 1969. That's right: two years *after* Expo 67. And to think it's francophone culture that plays the victim card.)

On occasion, I've been the recipient of condescending judgment from snotty urban cognoscenti as to why I'd perform way up in Prince Albert. Well, for one thing, it's a great theatre; for another, performers are essentially hunter-gatherers. We may not follow the buffalo for sustenance, but the metaphor is an apt one. Follow the herds / follow the gigs. Kill a buffalo / "kill" an audience. Get food / get paid. Eat buffalo meat on the prairie / eat rubbery chicken wings in a roadhouse bar post-show. Sleep, wake up in the morning and keep moving / sleep, wake up in the morning and keep moving . . . but forget a raincoat, sweater or scarf in the hotel room.

Compared to the almost twenty years I spent chasing a buck as an actor in Toronto and LA, waiting for the phone to ring with news of an audition for roles in an occasional film, commercial, or guest spot on some long-forgotten television show, a comedian's road allows for a connection with an audience that can't be manufactured, rigged or jigged. Great lighting and editing can't help when you're walking the high wire, pinned to a solo spot. Every comedian standing alone onstage, with nothing but a microphone and memory, channeling the energy of a packed, expectant house, experiences a fundamentally satisfying reward in knowing that whatever quotidian demands bedevil their audience's daily march through life's bright fury are for ninety minutes, to quote my 89-year-old Cape Breton-born mother, given "a kick in the arse with a frozen boot straight out the friggin' door."

Ticket sales are down in Prince Albert compared to my visit two years ago, when I did two sold-out shows. Maybe seeing my noggin on television once a week in the series has something to do with it? Maybe the numbers are dropping because there's more to keep people at home, rather than leave the house to brave a wind chill just to see a show? Maybe it's because the marketplace is glutted with acts like never before? There is certainly no doubt that, since the collapse of the American economy in 2008, every comedian's manager down there with a GPS has happened to discover a country north of them, that up until now, they never knew existed. Seems everyone but Peaches and Herb was touring an act that year.

Pulling my suitcase into the lobby of a Ramada Inn, I'm greeted warmly by the receptionist, Jocelyn, an elegant woman in her late forties whose co-worker is a younger woman with a five-year-old daughter she's raising herself. The woman has a tattoo on her arm to commemorate the death of a friend, and she tells me of time spent as a volunteer, chatting through plexiglass with lifers in the penal system. She is their only contact with the outside world, except for the hour a day they get for exercise in "the yard." After a day spent dodging mule deer, it feels good to share a communion of spirit, connecting to something deeper than the sole purpose of my visit.

Jocelyn tells me she's a single mom who raised three boys herself in a "tough town with plenty of crime."

"There's lots of drugs, murder and domestic violence. We're the last stop before the North, and you know the North—it's a wide-open halfway house with no curfew," she says, rolling her eyes. There are legions of criminals wandering our North, and despite the haunting beauty of its primal landscape and the hamlets and towns strung along the treeline, the region also attracts an odious detritus from "down South," come to prey on the despair born from isolation and unemployment, in a place where winter hangs around for seven months of the year.

"We don't need F-18s in the North," Jocelyn tells me. "We need social programs, with cops on the ground, nurses, schools and teachers. We need infrastructure." She says the crime in Prince Albert is getting out of hand, but when I tell her we raised our two daughters in Toronto, she says, "I'd hate to raise my children there! It's too big and dangerous!" Poor Toronto. It will never win in the eyes of the rest of the country.

There's a spine of resilience I admire in her straightforward, no-nonsense way of speaking. She is direct, forthright and refreshingly matter-of-fact. I'm still smarting from my recent separation and its emotional toll when she asks me how my wife deals with the long stretches I'm away from home. I tell her she doesn't anymore, because we're not together.

"When I was getting standing ovations, she was getting another load of laundry," I confess. "It's a creatively fulfilling life for me; for her, not so much."

She nods knowingly with a nuanced sigh unique to those who have weathered the emotional fray of love lost, whose scar tissue might sit tough around their heart, but not tough enough to harden it.

"A month after my divorce, my parents were killed in a car accident. I had three small boys to raise myself, with no family to rely on. I did it. Don't know how, but I did. They're all teenagers now. I have a cabin in Weyakwin. It's good for my soul to go there. In fact, it's not too far from where Johnny Cash, June Carter and John Jr. used to come to fish. Lots of locals in La Ronge still remember him. He was just real people."

I wonder if the Man in Black had a wandering eye for a lithe summertime-tanned Jocelyn walking past his table at a La Ronge diner. Trying hard not to stare, but losing the battle, I bet Johnny couldn't help but stop in mid-sentence to do just that, when he'd receive a sharp boot to the shins beneath the table and a reprimand from June saying:

"Eyes forward! You are *not* on the road now, Johnny!"

Jocelyn has bought her youngest something from Avon. I didn't know Avon still existed. (Avon Soap-on-a-Rope was a standard Christmas gift in the 1970s. I hadn't had that in my shower since "everybody was kung-fu fighting!") Her son's Christmas gift is a toaster emblazoned with a Montreal Canadiens logo, but when the toast pops up, burned into the bread is . . . a Toronto Maple Leafs logo. Maybe the coolest little gift ever! We share a good laugh. You don't get a moment like that at the front desk of a high-end Hilton in Vegas.

Nor do you get comped the King Henry Suite in a Ramada Inn that caters to travellers in a four-prison town. My themed suite had a plush indoor/outdoor royal blue carpet decorated with gold crowns, where in the middle sat a matching contoured blue velvet lounging couch. I assumed that was there in case enthusiastic occupants couldn't make it all the way to the four-poster king-sized bed, covered in a canopy rimmed with ornate gold-braided tassels. I guess nothing makes a former inmate forget ten years of incarceration faster than having a shag in a setting fit for a jester.

Most hotels on tour are airless, generic franchises lacking any attribute you could call remotely unique. However, there was once a hotel in Belleville, Ontario, that's long since burned down, whose rooms were named after the Fathers of Confederation—and the Sir George-Étienne Cartier room had a stripper's pole in it. It did! A stripper's pole! I'm willing to wager there was more bacteria on that adult novelty item than on a toilet seat in a shantytown rub 'n' tug! I know the French love their peelers, so given that Cartier hailed from Quebec, I assumed the pole was in keeping with the province's cultural appetite for lunchtime lap dances. I'm not sure if Cartier enjoyed the occasional lap dance, but there was no stripper's pole in the D'Arcy McGee suite. Just sayin'.

My show only brings in four hundred or so patrons. Small turnout, given the long drive, and I bemoan the turn of events, worried that the market has changed for good—as it probably has. All the same, you do your show, and on this night at the Rawlinson Centre, I deliver a tight two-hour performance without breaking a sweat and have an excellent time. Still, there's the worry that the money made wasn't worth the kilometres driven. It's something that's still gnawing at me the next day, when I head into the Safeway supermarket for a Starbucks.

While I'm putting cream in my coffee, a young Indigenous man extends his hand for a shake and speaks to me.

"Hey, Ron James. My family and I saw you a couple of days ago in Regina." Like most in Saskatchewan, his face is open and friendly, exuding the unpretentious affability unique to flatlanders. Sure, people might stumble with an Orwellian lethargy through winter's gloom on the downtown streets of Regina, but it being the seat of provincial government, I chalk that mood up to a life spent moiling in the bowels of bureaucracy, praying they'll not lose their marbles before their civil servant's pension provides clemency. That's when flatlanders make a beeline for a British Columbia retirement community where relentless winter doesn't break them so hard, they're found in May curled in a fetal position behind the couch, and wearing nothing but a Roughriders toque.

I once pulled in for breakfast at a roadside diner outside Lloydminster where half a dozen farmers were enjoying their morning coffee. They called me over to tell a joke, and although the last thing a comedian wants to hear is a joke, this one wasn't bad. "You can tell this one onstage in Regina: Why can't a government employee look out the window in the morning? 'Cause they'd have nothing to do in the afternoon." The table roared in agreement. I noted they were all farmers having coffee on a working day but decided not to share my observation.

I remember seeing the Indigenous kid and his family during a noisy breakfast at Regina's Delta Hotel, in a pictureless room with a brutal buffet. He was surrounded by a pair of brilliant red-haired older sisters, their husbands and little ones, a white-haired matriarch and her husband. Their dairy-fresh faces stood in contrast to the high cheek-bones and brown complexion of his heritage. It was Saskatchewan Roughrider game day, and the place was filled with fans bedecked in the colours of a team that personifies their prairie heart. During Roughrider game day at that hotel several years earlier, I bumped into a family stepping off the elevator. From the youngest child of ten to the parents themselves, all were wearing hollowed-out watermelons on their heads. Naturally, I asked why they were all wearing melons on their melons, and they stared quizzically as if there was something wrong with *me*.

We sit in the Safeway, enjoying our coffee. Initially, we talk of the game and Saskatchewan's collapse in the fourth quarter. Then the kid opens a door to his life and the universe drops another ruby in my lap.

"I love Don Burnstick, the Native comedian. He got me through an awful lot of pain. How to not let what others say define me but let *me* define me."

The kid tells me he has lived with racism every day of his life. "Up in Birch River, my dad ran a buffalo ranch. Twenty-five hundred head. Some of those bulls were three hands high. Heads like trucks. We steered clear of them during the rut and calving season. It's great meat! Just great. Always cook it on low heat, or else it will be too tough," he advises. "Mom used to comb the buffalo fur off their heads and put it in our boots. Some warm! Trust me, when it's minus-45, you want some buffalo fur in your boots. Ironic, eh? A Native kid working on a white man's buffalo farm!" He laughs, then just as quickly lapses into pensive reflection.

"I had to learn to stand tall. I had to make those kids at school not make me believe who they said I was. They used to call me 'chink,' because I look Asian. 'Hey chink. Chink!' they'd yell. I developed a temper. It was boiling in me. So, in grade seven, I started taking karate outside town, but only after three guys in my class pinned me against the fence after school. One of them, the ringleader, was a big, stupid hillbilly. His buddies had shovels. They held my arms, and he punched me hard in the stomach. I went down, and they kicked me. I started taking karate after that. I'm a second-degree black belt now. About six months after they beat me, I got him alone." He smiles with a satisfaction born from righteous retribution. "The dumb hillbilly.

"'Who's the brave one now without his pals? Let's go. One on one.'

"I could tell he was scared. He took a swing. I stepped back and planted a punch in his throat. He started to cry.

"'You want some more?' I asked him.

"The big baby reported me to the principal's office. The principal and the vice-principal wanted to expel me. I said, 'You try that, and I'll have the television cameras and newspapers here tomorrow. The mission statement of this school says, "Every child should feel safe." I don't.' They backed off."

"Did the kids back off, too?" I asked.

"No. My buddy and I were walking down the hill after school one afternoon. I see a bunch of kids at the bottom with bats and hockey sticks. I turned to him and said, 'This doesn't look too good. Have you got my back?'

"'Thur,' he says . . . 'cause he had a lisp. I say, 'Thur? This is no time to be calling me "thur."'"

"See? Don Burnstick makes everything funny.

"When I walked toward those kids, I turned around and he was gone. So, I ran that gauntlet of bullies myself. Thanks to them, I only have 20 percent vision in my right eye. It's why I couldn't join the army. I wanted to help people. I wanted to make a difference somewhere. So, instead, I'm making it here."

He looked at me with a conviction that belied his nineteen years and pointing his finger emphatically on the table declared: "Hey. I'm not an Indian. I'm a Native! The only way a person effects change in this world is by changing themselves first. I want to empower young Native kids. Tell them there's another way. They need to believe it's possible to be better than some people say you can be. Stephen Harper was wrong when he said the residential school is an ugly chapter in our history that is finally closed. No way! It's a generational disease! And it's my generation that will make a difference. Not the government, but us!"

He drained his coffee.

"Everybody should do what they can to make it better, right?"

With a nod of his head, the kid turns on his heel disappearing into a world he's dedicated to making a difference in.

Chapter Three

ADIDAS MEXICANA

Last time I saw my namesake before his stroke, I was seated at the kitchen table in that old house of his with no foundation. It sat at a precarious tilt, sinking into its lot on Steeles Hill, overlooking the once-booming coal town of Glace Bay, Cape Breton. Another stand-up tour of Atlantic Canada had brought me full circle to my birthplace for a gig at the Savoy Theatre, where, in a world when black-and-white television with one channel to watch was the only option, raucous gangs of children dropped twenty-five cents every Saturday afternoon to sit, mesmerized, watching matinees in garish Panavision.

The day after my show, I dropped by to see Uncle Ronald. Other than his niece, who kept house and cooked for him, the seventy-eight-year-old man lived alone. I sat with my back to a well-worn La-Z-Boy on the opposite side of the room where an almost-blind mutt called Mork lay sleeping.

"Don't sit dere, b'y, in case a'nudder rat comes up tru' da' floorboards.

I'll need a clear shot," he warned, patting the barrel of a pellet gun that rested beside his chair.

My cousin Diane reprimanded him.

"Ranal'! Ronnie might want you to say hello first. Jesus, eh? No friggin' manners," she said, looking at me and laughing, her red cheeks flush with life as she flipped the haddock in the frying pan. If they start handing out Orders of Canada for unsung saints who fly below the red-carpet radar, my cousin deserves one. She was the only one in the family who could spar with him. Her voice had the mischievous, rollicking cadence of an accent heard on the other side of the Canso Causeway, that harkened me back to a grandmother's kitchen where cousins smeared butter on gingerbread cookies as aunts chattered sparrow-fast over steaming-hot cups of King Cole Tea cut with canned Carnation milk. My gentle grandmother's Broughton-born sapphire eyes twinkled with goodness from a rocking chair, where she sang ancient songs in Gaelic to grandchildren whose faces have long since turned to age, their parents either gone or going.

"Ranal'! Ronnie doesn't want to hear about you shooting the rat. He's eating," my cousin declared.

Uncle wasted no time clarifying.

"Ronnie knows I knows he's here. He's right in front of me. But if I have to start shooting again, all's I'm sayin' is, he fuckin' well better duck!"

It's not every day you get a good rat story anymore, vermin having been eradicated from pretty well every kitchen I've had the pleasure to visit. But apparently, in Uncle's home, rats still crawled up on occasion from their cozy warren beneath the floorboards for a gander.

My cousin put plates of haddock with boiled carrots, potatoes and canned peas before us. Between forkfuls that Uncle kept lodged somewhere between his palate and esophagus (as was his wont when talking and eating at the same time), he told me about his duel with that rat. Did I mention he embraced profanity with the zeal a penitent would holy scripture?

"I heard Mork whinin', eh? I says, 'What's da matter, buddy?' And then I sees the little prick on the arm of the chair. A filthy fuckin' no-good goddamn-rat! Hissin' at me, too. Hissin'! In me own house! I says to Diane, 'Get me my pellet gun. I'se de last one he'll ever hiss at!'"

As she ladled more peas onto his heaping plate of food, my cousin interjected.

"I didn't know what he was gonna do with the pellet gun," she said, looking at me in disbelief. "He can barely hold a cup o' coffee without spilling half of it for shaking!"

Uncle held his hands out in front of me, oblivious to how badly they shook.

"Steady as a surgeon's, b'y."

He went back to the rat story.

"So's I cocked me pellet gun seven times. Raised da t'ing. Aimed. Squeezed da trigger . . . and, with a finger pointed between my eyes, said . . . 'Right dere!' I nailed it. And ho-leeee fuck! Out she squirted, b'y! Blood. Nutting but blood! Spraying like a Jesus garden hose. It was like da . . . da . . . da . . ."—searching for the right word, he exclaims—"da *CIS* show on TV."

Diane corrected him.

"*CSI*, Ranal'. *CSI*." She looked at me, laughing.

"Whatever it's called. Da t'ing staggers and falls off de arm of de chair to da floor. I puts two more pellets in da belly of the little fat bastard but . . . he's not dead yet!"

Uncle had his dinner stuffed in one cheek, and as he became more animated, bits of haddock and peas were falling out of his mouth.

"Den', holy ol' Jesus, doesn't he run into my bedroom and crawl up on da bedpost . . . sits right on top of 'er and starts hissing again . . . wit' da blood spraying everywhere." Much like his dinner was doing to me. I felt wet food hit my face.

"Then that rat—you'se got to give him points for being tough— didn't he rise up to his full rat height on that bedpost, like he was claiming it for his own? I says, 'That's the last time you'll raise your little rat arms at me, you son of a whore,' and *pow! pow! pow!* I puts t'ree more pellets into da little prick and he dropped. Dead."

He finally swallowed his food, and pointing at my face with his fork, said:

"You got peas stuck to your cheek, b'y."

Three years later, another tour brought me across the Causeway, but there'd be no visit to Steeles Hill. The stroke had hit fast one winter afternoon, ending his life in his own house and beginning what would be the last four years of it, at Cabot Lodge in Sydney. The home was a well-run, antiseptic and brightly lit gateway to the hereafter.

He lay prostrate on the bed, drilling me from the pillow with those defiant eyes of steel blue.

"How are you doing today, Uncle?" I said. He didn't answer, but his eyes did. Gauging. Judging. Evaluating.

"Holy fuck, b'y! Are you'se ever bole-legged!"

I roared laughing. He was his cantankerous self again, and a far cry from those first few days after his stroke, when he slipped in and out of consciousness in the hospital room.

"Good to see you, too! It's nice to know the stroke didn't kill your sarcasm."

"I wasn't being sarcastic. I was being honest. You're some bole-legged."

My Uncle Ronald. In an age where being politically correct, or even polite, is an expected social norm, he had clearly never received the memo. He never knew how *not* to say what was on his mind. There was no filter—ever. He was who he was, and you got what you got. In a world of posturing and pretense, his disposition was to tell it as he saw it, which made his moments of warmth all the more authentic.

Uncle was the only boy in a family of five sisters. They all lived in a simple house my grandfather built by himself with money made working in "the pit." The pit was a euphemism for the coal mine, which one relative once told me "was prison with wages." It's difficult to fathom the fortitude that made such a race of men who toiled, as the song says, "where the rain never falls, nor sun never shines." Crews piled into a metal cage that travelled gut-liftingly fast down a shaft drilled into the black belly of Earth, finally stopping a mile below the ocean floor. For eight to ten hours—day or night shift— miners pounded away under Dickensian conditions against a wall of coal with pick and shovel, in a rat-infested, dangerous, dark, claustrophobic world, for a feudal wage. I'm ready for a couple of cold beer after being onstage for two hours . . . and all I do is talk!

I swore the smell of that workingman's fuel was hanging in the air the day I visited Uncle. It was evocative of the steady employment the industrial heartland of Atlantic Canada could once lay claim to, back when coal was king and, as my eighty-nine-year-old mother recalls, "A person couldn't fit a dime between the shoulders on miners' payday for the size of the crowds shopping Saturday mornings on Commercial Street. No, they couldn't. Sure, you could try, but you couldn't. Mind you, I wouldn't want to try and fit a dime between a coal miner's shoulders. He'd puck your face off!"

Fifteen kilometres up the road at the Sydney steel plant, the best girders used to rebuild postwar Europe were made, and every smelter our wide country over used Cape Breton coal to fire the furnaces of their "satanic mills." I guess in a less environmentally enlightened day, one man's hell was another man's heaven, especially when there are mouths to feed. Take that, William Blake.

"He never really started drinking hard until he joined the army," they all said. Most letters home, from wherever Uncle was stationed, spoke of peeling potatoes on KP. Once he was discharged, he never held a job very long. Grade eight education doesn't bring you much at the best of times, but you could still land something steady back then if you wanted to.

When I was little, I never knew him not to be prisoner to the bottle—and not just pleasantly toasted, but hopelessly hammered, staggering three sheets to the wind up a quiet daytime street. Everyone worried. Phones rang between the sisters, wondering where he was or what he was getting up to.

"Is he driving again? He'll kill himself, if not somebody else first."

We sat watching TV in Uncle's room when a lost-looking man in a baseball cap stood staring vacantly through his open door. Looking at the man, then back to me, Uncle said:

"That's the son of a whore who stole my slippers."

"Does he have Alzheimer's?" I asked.

"I don't know, but he fuckin' well will if I gets a hold of him."

You gotta love that level of belly fire, especially in someone who's bedridden.

At this point, he'd been dry for forty-three years, with AA's *Big Book* beside his bed, which he read with diligence every morning. When I was little, he disappeared into the Big Smoke. Another Maritime refugee "gone down the road" looking for a better one, but finding a dead end instead. If full-blown alcoholism is the major leagues, then the fist-fighting coal town road of the early 1950s was the farm team. By the time you won your Stanley Cup in booze, you'd certainly earned it.

Perhaps a Christmas card would arrive for one of the sisters during his lost years. Or a cheque requested for a "bus back home" that was always cashed, but the ticket never bought. Still, despite all those haunted nights spent shivering in lonesome alleyways or flea-ravaged flophouses, he survived to wrestle his addiction to the mat. Once he did, his kindness knew no bounds and gift-giving came easily. Whether rent and groceries for a sister and her kids, Christmas and birthday gifts for a small army of nephews and nieces, or, in later years, a car to a grandnephew and graduation gifts for all of us. That was Uncle.

I remember that summer day he materialized as if from the ether in front of our house in Halifax. I remember it mostly because I was wearing a brand-spanking-new pair of Adidas Mexicanas I'd bought with my own money. When you're a shamelessly short twelve-year-old red-headed kid with a size four foot that only fits a two-stripe, bush-league, Canadian-made North Star but not the unattainable Adidas everyone in the hallowed ranks of the chosen was wearing, and you suddenly find yourself springing down the street sporting a brand new pair you bought yourself with hard-won lucre made delivering the Halifax *Mail-Star*, it was as good as life could ever get. No longer would you feel a kinship with the barefoot Amish farm boy taking his prize pig to market.

I saw a Casino taxi pull up in front of our house. That never happened. Nobody took cabs in the daytime, least of all to our place. A man slid from the back seat, double-fisting two-quart bottles in wrinkled paper bags, and staggered up the driveway, disappearing into the backyard.

This would be the "visit" that would see him institutionalized in the Dartmouth asylum, where he'd begin his long journey back to the light. That imposing brick matron sat (and still does) on a big green lawn on the opposite side of the harbour from Halifax. "Going across the bridge" was the local euphemism for being institutionalized. It's the way we talked back then, because no one knew or understood what it was like to be broken. No one cared to know what it was like not to be singing the song the rest of us knew all the words to.

We'd pick him up on Sundays for supper at the outpatient door. Wraith-white he stood, looking strangely incongruous in the morning sun, like some gothic apparition who'd forgotten to flee for the shadows at daybreak. He'd squeeze into the back seat of Dad's Plymouth between my younger sister and me, all pale and shaky, his hair matted, staring straight ahead.

"It's like deer were sleeping in it," I said to my sister later. She was a wide-eyed six-year-old who, although four years younger than me, was far more sensible . . . and still is.

"What do you mean?"

"Well, you know when deer sleep in a field of tall grass, and how in the morning, it's all matted down?"

"Kinda."

"Well, Uncle's hair is like that. Only with deer, you don't see white scalp and dandruff."

"If it snows, you do." (See what I mean?)

Mom always cried when Uncle appeared. He was her baby brother, and she saw his face forever pressed against the kitchen window in their childhood gone. He was all wide-eyed and sad, watching her and other neighbourhood kids play outside on a summer's day, but he was forbidden to join them because the house was quarantined for scarlet fever, and he had it.

Uncle hated for his food to touch. Carrots couldn't touch peas, nor peas potatoes, and he'd have to separate them on the plate. Well, when you're only a week into a thirty-day detox program, a steady hand is not one of your strong suits. His attempt to preserve a standard that anchored him to a world he was trying hard to return to was an effort worthy of Sisyphus. He'd ever-so-carefully raise his knife and fork from the table setting, the utensils threatening to slip from his fingers for the shaking. Then he'd lower that fork and knife to the plate, where the sound of them rattling on the porcelain was worthy of a Buddy Rich drum solo. Accompanied by our mother's gentle sobbing from the end of the table, he'd persevere, oblivious to the rest of us. Dad kept his head buried in his food, glancing up occasionally from the plate. My sister and I stared, marvelling at Uncle's defiant persistence in bringing those peas to his mouth. Despite their propensity to adhere to his fork with the consistency of mercury, he somehow managed to manipulate one lone survivor to his mouth. Once there, his cracked, chapped lips would wrap around that lone pea, to be savoured with the reverence a confessor would the Eucharist.

Our father made valiant attempts at small talk.

"So, plans for the week?"

"No." A rim shot rattled the plate as the knife pushed peas to the fork.

"Watching the Expos?"

"Yep." He raised the fork. All the peas would fall . . . except one. He'd get a bead on it. His eyes focused and his lips pursed with concentration. Then down went Sisyphus to the plate again, and another hard slog up his hill.

As mentioned, when I saw Uncle step from the cab, I was wearing a brand-new pair of rare and covetable Adidas Mexicanas. They had three shiny black stripes running down a body of burnt yellow-coloured suede. Put simply, they shouted, "Cool!" Today, you can buy any kind of running shoe in any size, anywhere, at any time. Not so in 1970. To see a pair—in size four, at that—sitting bright as a new dream in the front window of Phinney's Sporting Goods on Barrington Street was nothing short of miraculous. I imagined myself ripping up the track in the Olympics, where I'd stand on the podium, giving the Black Panther salute, even though I was a four-foot-ten, freckle-faced white kid who ran like the "bole-legged" man Uncle would one day in a far-off future bluntly declare I was. Never again would I wear the embarrassing two-stripe Canadian-made North Stars, whose paper-thin soles evaporated before the summer did.

(Phinney's, by the way, was a sporting goods store that also sold grand pianos. It wasn't uncommon to see one kid trying out new goalie pads while another tried out a Steinway. How's that for eclectic? "Will it be a Victoriaville hockey stick for the lad, ma'am, or the sheet music for Tchaikovsky's *1812 Overture* in E-flat major?")

The Adidas in Phinney's window were clearly an aberration. They must have been custom-made for a fleet-footed, diminuative Cuban sprinter whose daily steroid injections had caused a sudden growth spurt. I assumed he'd defected during a stopover in Gander, Newfoundland, while on his way to the Eastern Bloc for a Warsaw Pact track and field meet. Upon arriving in Halifax, he probably pawned the Adidas, box and all, at Phinney's, picking up a few extra bucks to start his new life. (How he got to Halifax from Gander remains a mystery I've yet to invent.)

I followed Uncle into the backyard, where he sat in a lawn chair, taking a long pull from one of the bottles.

"Hi, Uncle. How ya doin'?"

All bleary-eyed, wrung-out and wasted, he looked and said, "I hope you don't turn out like me, just 'cause you got my name b'y."

The thought struck me as absurd at the time, though now I wonder if I hadn't flirted with a drinking problem myself, having spent most weekends after the age of sixteen making a valiant effort to get there. The quest every Friday or Saturday night was to get someone to go into the Nova Scotia Liquor Commission for you. One pal could go all Lon Chaney Jr. on a whim and grow a full beard overnight. He'd stop shaving Wednesday, and by Friday evening, his look was so full-on Wolf Man, the only thing that could stop him from sauntering out of the "Commission" with a few pints of vodka was a silver bullet. The vodka would be poured into a skunky hockey water bottle and mixed with orange Tang, to be guzzled in the Camp Hill graveyard on bone-cold winter nights before high school dances. Sporting a bad case of "Tang lips," you stepped through the gymnasium doors with a courage primed by Smirnoff that propelled you into dance moves worthy of Soul Train—until the whirlies hit during a waltz to "Colour My World."

After a kid from a school in Dartmouth passed out drunk in the snow and almost froze to death, we started trying to get into taverns underage, and the seedier the waterfront watering hole, the better. One crusty refuge was home to Maltese stevedores and gangrenous whores who reeled round the floor in a liquor-pig ballet while sucking back skunky draft from rotgut kegs whose pipes hadn't been cleaned since Sir Charles Tupper caught his first case of Cumberland County clap. A two-ton Stygian vixen we called Enormous Doris sat beside the door to the men's room, furtively eyeing her prey. A young man was wise to give this nightmare a wide berth, for if one of her meaty tentacles should reach out and snatch you, up that skirt you'd go, never to be seen again! Having to use the toilet in that tavern, as opposed to just the urinal, tested the limits of courage. The seats danced with microbial spores carried from diseased ports of call from forgotten corners of the seven seas. They had not seen so much as a thimble's worth of disinfectant since the 1919 Spanish flu came through and killed the janitor.

There were no picture IDs then, and whether or not you were carded depended on the judgment of whoever was working the front door. This place had an ex-welterweight for a doorman called Winky McLeod, whose claim to fame was having fought a thirteen-round donnybrook against a ranked Russian middleweight during his days in the navy.

Winky was an imposing presence who sported a crewcut and a weathered face covered by half a dozen razor nicks. When you have to go out in public with more than five pieces of Kleenex stuck to your shaving cuts, I figure it's time to change the blade. The years he'd spent in the ring after that fight had left his noodle pummelled into such a state of punch-drunk grace, it was not uncommon to see

Winky swinging at shadows of former opponents while on duty, instead of watching for underage patrons.

You could always get into the Pirate's Quarters when Winky was bouncing, provided you walked in on his "bad side." That was the side where his eye, well, "winked" non-stop. The lid was covered in such lumpy folds of scar tissue, the doctor who stitched him up must have been convicted of crimes against humanity at Nuremberg.

But on that summer's day of then, with a *Mail-Star* bag slung over my shoulder, pockets heavy with quarters and springing down the street sporting brand new too-cool-for-school running shoes, Uncle's worry that I'd "turn out like him, just because I had his name," warranted only one response.

"There's no way that will happen, Uncle. Look what I'm wearing: a brand-new pair of Adidas Mexicanas I bought with my paper route money!"

I don't know how long or arduous Uncle's climb to sobriety was, but the man got there, finding hope, support and, most importantly, salvation in church basement meetings surrounded by an AA tribe of seekers all like him, just looking to find their road home.

Twelve years after I bought those Adidas, I also found myself in Toronto, only I was chasing an acting career and bartending at an Italian restaurant to pay the rent. The other bartender was also called Ron, and he was my senior by about, oh, five hundred and twenty-seven years. He was Nosferatu in a bartender's bowtie, with unsettlingly luminous raptor-length fingernails, and to this day, I swear the ectomorphic apparition cast no shadow. The owner of the restaurant carried herself with the haughty air of the Cosa Nostra doyenne she was. I recognized her husband from a documentary of the time about the mafia in Canada. He and three Tony Soprano prototypes always had lunch at the back of the restaurant. Their laughter was more a gurgle than a guffaw, and I imagined they were sharing stories of the body they had just dumped in Hamilton Harbour. Angelina called me "Stupid," because I had the same name as the other bartender and because I only knew three beers: Keith's, Oland's and Moosehead— none of which were available in Ontario. I really missed back home.

One quiet afternoon when I was wiping the counter for the umpteenth time, daydreaming about being cast opposite Al Pacino in Coppola's next cinematic masterpiece—even though the only thing I'd landed in a year's worth of auditioning was as a background extra in a CBC series lost to time—a customer walked in and introduced himself. A man in his late forties, his voice had that familiar accent— not as thick as if he still lived on the other side of the Causeway, but nonetheless, there it was.

"I'm your Uncle Ron's pal Danny, from Glace Bay, but I live in Mississauga now," he said. "We grew up together. He told me to give you this." He handed me an envelope with ten $20 bills inside and a note that said:

"Don't spend this on sneakers.
Uncle"

Chapter Four
THE LAND OF OPPORTUNITY

I owe Alberta a debt of gratitude, as do many Atlantic Canadians who once reaped big boons in the Land of Opportunity.

The Canadian West was sold that way from the very start. In the late nineteenth century, colourful posters of waving golden wheat under sunny prairie skies recruited the downtrodden, disenfranchised and oppressed from European backwaters, promising 160 acres of free land to those willing to take the bait. What those 160 acres turned out to be was gristle-hard prairie in a land so mean, it could eat you. I guess the government lied. Really? There's a first.

The immigrants' first homes were huts built of sod. You heard me—sod. There's a cozy crib for a first winter in the New World: a house built of dirt. Today, there's not enough profanity in the English language to get me through an afternoon trying to install a ceiling fan. But living in a house of sod? Life must have really sucked in the Old Country if that was considered winning the lottery!

They came all the same—legions of nineteenth-century serfs, driven by the hope of a fresh start in a country where you could be all that you wanted and not who you were. From Ukraine, Iceland, Moravia, Poland and Russia they came, leaving behind oppressive feudal backwaters where bad guys with big moustaches kicked you comatose just for looking happy. Hopping rusty steamships for a sea-sick ten-week bounce across the stormy Atlantic, they stepped ashore at Pier 21 in Halifax to be deloused by dockside authorities and stared at by local herring chokers selling skunky Ten Penny, then took a week-long train trip to the parcel of paradise that awaited them in the West.

And if you lasted in your new world of opportunity, the reward was to drive your body hard from dawn until dusk with no vacation ever, until you dropped dead in the field while pushing a plow at the ripe old age of fifty-seven. I'd like to see our self-help yoga-junkie generation suffer that torment.

The dream was the same for those of us born to lobster blood. When the oil boom hit, Alberta's clarion call to riches rang loud and clear, and the pilgrimage to the Promised Land was on. The East hadn't seen such an exodus of that magnitude since Charlton Heston parted the Red Sea! The only thing missing was a biblical soundtrack accompanied by images of fast-moving Israelites and slow-moving Egyptians.

From Gambo to Saint-Louis-du-Ha! Ha! and all points in between, the learned and the lost fixed their eyes to the horizon and made a beeline for where tomorrow was shining bright as a new dream. Some never made it as far as Alberta, though. I heard tell of one guy driving west who stopped for a leak on the road in Saskatchewan and just disappeared. He was last seen wandering the wheat, chasing a thought.

It was a time of plenty, with plenty of money to be made. Down payments on a home in the foothills, complete with a two-car garage, shortly followed by a new truck and Harley to fill it. Millionaires were everywhere, and the manifesto preached from the boardrooms to the bedrooms said it was absolutely possible for you to become one, too. Thanks to the gooey black gold called bitumen that drove a turbo-charged economic engine, Calgary shirked its dusty moniker of Cowtown, as skyscrapers rose overnight in testimony to its good fortune. Fort McMurray tripled its population in two years.

Fort Mac was the tough Athabaskan country Peter Pond travelled in 1795 with his Chipewyan guides, paddling their way upriver to a fur-bearing El Dorado that was now the gateway to a different one: the oil patch. Pond was, as his biographer Barry Gough writes in *The Elusive Mr. Pond*, "a hard man in a hard trade." Well, as much as things change, they stay the same.

Fort Mac was the kind of industry town where someone with a high school diploma could pull down 350 grand a year, working 24/7/365 for Syncrude, driving a truck the size of a duchy while sharing a two-bedroom apartment with six pals, all living on Kraft Dinner, canned wieners and crystal meth. Fort Mac, in its Wild West heyday, made an episode of *Deadwood* look like Sunday supper at the Waltons'.

One particular evening, I was headed to an infamous local pub called the Oil Can for a bite to eat. In the parking lot, draft-goggle patrons spilled from cabs into the street at the pub's front door, which opened to billows of second-hand smoke so Turkish-whorehouse thick, a person could lose three years off their life before they finished their first beer.

It made no nevermind, because the place was packed to the rafters with the singing, dancing, drinking proletariat, all doing their best to blunt the reality of doing hard time in this frozen outpost of the boreal forest.

Out the door tumbled a gang of rig workers on a two-week furlough. The leader of the posse was a ferociously tattooed, steroid-stoked, muscular bull of a man whose eyes bulged red from sockets shadowed by a proscenium brow on a shaved and leonine-sized skull. He looked closer to something King Minos might have kept in a cave on Crete than a human being. His entourage hopped and purred around him, punching the night air with fisted cigarettes and grunting laughter. I'm willing to wager that when rampaging Visigoths took their first dump in a fountain during the sacking of Rome, they looked like these guys.

The leader of this testosterone-fuelled freak show barked, "Let's hire a fuckin' cab and go to New York fuckin' City!"

This got the posse howling support, when suddenly from the bar doors burst half a dozen bleached blond sirens wearing dangerous-looking stilettoes and micro-miniskirts, their arms wrapped tightly round their vulnerable breasts in a futile attempt to protect them from the hyperborean level of cold. One of them downed the last of her fluorescent shooter and threw the glass into the street. Curses flew. People laughed. Another planted a big red kiss on the top of the leader's shaved head.

"We're going to New York fuckin' City!"

The leader spread a line of cocaine on his thumb, and a woman with chapped nostrils snorted it up. Others stood in line, waiting their turn, when someone said, "Watch out for the cops," and someone else said, "Fuck the cops!" Then, one of the women yelled, "I did!" The leader doubled over with laughter. The others were overcome with knee-slapping guffaws.

It was minus-30 (at least), and everyone was in T-shirts. Suddenly, like a flock of birds that for no apparent reason will suddenly veer from what seemed their intended course, the posse headed back inside. One of the women wondered aloud as she ran to catch up: "We're still going to New York City, right . . . right?"

I woke in my hotel room the following morning to an over-whelming smell of diesel fumes. Looking out the window, I saw an army of Dodge "Ram Tough" trucks idling in the parking lot—with nary a driver nor passenger in them. (It put me in mind of a short story Stephen King might write, where all the vehicles in a Maine coastal town inexplicably get possessed and kill their owners by swallowing them between the seat cushions, trash Main Street, then drive hell-bent into the sunset for a night of biblical reckoning.)

Whatever hole in the ozone was being punched open by the trucks' billowing exhaust was of little concern to the owners. When you're pulling down some serious scratch in "the patch," it's safe to assume one's personal impact on global warming does not weigh heavily on one's conscience. I felt the righteous anger of environmental concern rise in my chest and thought, "Hey, that's not right. I'm going to march right downstairs and tell them to turn those engines off"! But the feeling went away two seconds later when I realize they'd probably leave their carbon footprint on my face.

When oil was selling at $142 a barrel in 2006, every time a car blew up in Baghdad, two new trucks appeared in every Albertan's driveway! Everybody was making money.

Once, when playing the city of Kelowna, I met a retired couple from Cape Breton who were riding their bikes along the boardwalk. They owned the very first Subway franchise in Fort Mac.

"There were lineups round the block, Ronnie!" the man said. "We worked fourteen-hour days, seven days a week, for fifteen years. The town is filled with good people. It gets a bad rap, but it gave us everything." He pointed to a beautiful condominium overlooking Lake Okanagan. "That's ours," he said proudly. "Not bad for a guy with only grade eleven who made sandwiches for a living, eh?"

If you came with a willingness to work, the West gave back what you put into it.

That roaring Alberta economy built me a house in Toronto. We ran a tour every two years from 2004 until 2018. During the winter of 2006, we had non-stop encore dates across Alberta that kept us on the road from November to March, filling theatres from one end of the province to the next. We'd start our tour in Lethbridge, at the 475-seat Yates, head up to a sweet 700-seater in Medicine Hat, then over to the Memorial in Red Deer, where one year we sold out that 680-seat room just shy of half a dozen times. Add the 1,700-seat Jack Singer in Calgary, the state-of-the-art 2,000-seat Winspear in Edmonton, a 600-seater in Grande Prairie and several sold-out shows at Fort Mac's Keyano College, and we were living large. For once, I felt creatively *and* monetarily fulfilled.

Those of us who ply our trade in the feast-or-famine fields of the self-employed know a run like that is rare as a Stanley Cup parade on Bay Street. After all those years of beating the bushes for a gig worth celebrating, it had finally come to fruition. They were very good years . . . and they're over.

Dependence on the fossil fuel nipple made diversification a dirty word in Alberta, and the thought of saving money for a rainy day anathema to the ethos of the Promised Land. Suggesting a sales tax was sedition. Only a pessimist would think those days would ever end . . . but they did.

Time moves on, and industry, just like people, has to move with it. Marching backwards to the wrong side of history never got a person anywhere. The undeniable facts surrounding climate change altered the equation forever. Let the science deniers and conspiracy-addled true believers buy the first round at their next Sons of Odin run fundraiser. The earth is teetering on the precipice of climatic catastrophe. The polar ice caps are melting. A nuclear-level conflagration of forest fires annually rages across Australia and Western North America. Sea levels are rising at an astronomical rate. Biodiversity is imperiled and mass extinction of species a pending reality. I'm not willing to wait for the planet to rise another two degrees before we take our foot off the gas of runaway consumption. Jason Kenney and his United Conservative Party can victimize themselves into a self-delusional state of frenzy while they scapegoat the rest of us for their failure to adapt to changing reality, but I'll side with science, thank you . . . and that's coming from a guy who flunked the subject in high school!

"It's you!"

Her voice bounces across the restaurant of Calgary's Delta Hotel with that unmistakable, rollicking Celtic lilt of the Cape Breton highlands. I'm staring at a face, all rosy-cheeked and smiley-eyed, warm with welcome. I don't know this waitress who's greeted me, but I know where she's from. It's the unpretentious, informal greeting of a "Caper"—my mother's people, the other half of me.

"Didn't know you were in town. Some shows coming up?"

"Yes," I say, but I know her query is just an opening to start talking. They *all* talk. And can they talk! At eighty-nine and still going strong, my mother can do two hours without breaking a sweat talking about the colour beige!

"What part of Cape Breton are you from?" I ask.

"Inverness," she says. "I'm Lena McIntyre from Inverness."

Inverness sits on the western side of the Cabot Trail. Winters are long and mean and summers are short and stunning. A one-time working-class town of coal miners and fishermen who laboured either under or on the iron-hard Atlantic is now home to a world-class golf course and equally impressive hotel. (It can't be that good though, cause there's no royal theme room or suite with a stripper's pole. Just sayin' . . .)

My father knew Inverness in another day, when he and his union brothers at the Maritime Telegraph and Telephone Company bunked in boarding houses while installing dial tone systems for a people who had previously relied on party lines, back when the click of a neighbour's receiver guaranteed your business was now everyone else's.

I just sit there listening, as her life tumbles out. She says she's closer to seventy than sixty and has been out west since she read an article in *Maclean's* magazine back in 1976 about the "land of opportunity."

"I had to come west—and thank God it was here to come to," she says emphatically. "Because I had no choice. I was the oldest. Yes, I was, and left with all seven children to take care of after 'the accident.' There was nothing in Inverness for them to do back then. Nothing. No Girl Guides or Scouts, and with that many to feed, I couldn't afford hockey gear or skates. Nothing."

I put down my fork and decide it's best to let my eggs get cold this morning. I can have eggs anytime.

"Our parents were coming back from visiting my aunt and uncle on the other side of Kellys Mountain. That Sunday, the radio called for snow, and as the day wore on, it was coming down hard and getting worse. So Da decided to leave before dark, because he had to get back to Inverness for work at the pit in the morning. I was with them and remember heading to the door, about to put my coat on, but Ma stopped me. She had the oddest look on her face and said, 'No, you stay here, Lena. Two is enough from one family for Him to get tonight.'

"See, she knew. *She knew!* I'm still not sure why she got in that car, or even let Da pull it out of the driveway. Maybe she felt it was just their time. I don't know. I'll never know. Turns out they hit some hard driving not far from home, with the snow awful bad. That's when a truck came out of the blizzard on their side of the road. Da cut for the shoulder, lost control and hit the only tree standing in a farmer's field. Both were killed instantly. That's when my world changed. Changed forever, in fact. It was 1966. I had just turned seventeen. Was left with all the little ones to care for in that great, big house.

"You'd think the church would have helped more, what with all of us confirmed and never once missed Mass before the accident. Think again. The priest did the bare minimum. Bare minimum!" Her face gets fierce with determination now. "The Catholic church is great for making you afraid of hell and damnation, but hell will freeze good and solid if they'll ever see me put so much as a nickel in the collection plate again."

"It seems cruel for the church not to help you. I always thought small towns rallied round each other during times of tragedy," I say.

"Oh, don't get me wrong. Everyone did . . . at first. But after a while, people forget. They move on with their lives. Besides, they were scared around us, because we had ghosts."

Now, there's a word you don't hear every day over scrambled eggs and bacon at a Delta Hotel. I feel the goosebumps rise.

"Ghosts?"

"Yes," she says, so matter-of-factly that I'm the one who feels stupid for asking.

"It wasn't the ghosts of my parents, but ghosts that had always been on the property. I don't know who they were or why they were there, but two were nice, while one was mean. Mean as a March wind, it was! It would push you! Yes, it would! You'd be walking in the field and see these three balls of light coming at you, when suddenly, down you'd go with a shove."

Who was I to question her story's validity? Having heard of premonitions from my own people, I'd be the last one to doubt the woman. Dad said his Aunt Hilda, who lived next door to us in Halifax, had seen her husband, Albert, standing outside their house one afternoon. Nothing unusual about that, except he was across town in the veterans' wing of Camp Hill Hospital, dying of cancer—at the exact same time she saw him on the sidewalk, staring up at the house, dressed in his World War II navy blues.

I can still see that proud wraith, sitting on his porch while that rude disease chewed away at him. Wrapped in woollen blankets even during summer's hottest days, his racking cough could shiver me. Aunt Hilda was my grandmother's youngest sister, born at the turn of the century along Newfoundland's southwest coast, on Red Island. Once home to a thriving community and schooner fleet, whose people were indentured to St. John's cod merchants, it is now home to nothing but forgotten graveyards swallowed by the feral growth of forest.

Uncle Albert fought in the Battle of the Atlantic, as did all those Newfoundlanders from my father's side. Some were merchant marines, sailing on floating time bombs laden with petrol in convoys bound for Russia. Or they rode out gales through North Sea winters, protecting those very convoys in corvette navy ships, sometimes encased in so much ice, the extra weight threatened to sink them faster than the German U-boats hunting them. They were hard men of a harder world who carried the weight of the history they'd witnessed behind their eyes.

"Ronnie, my son," the crusty sea dog would bark, "go get me a pack of Zig-Zag tobacco at the store . . . and keep the change for yourself." Returning with the package, I'd sit and watch him gingerly sprinkle what was killing him into a rolling paper, which the nicotine-stained fingers of one hand would dexterously roll to tightly packed perfection.

Aunt Hilda told Dad that Uncle Albert was just standing on the sidewalk, looking up at the house. She opened the front door and called his name. He waved, turned and walked toward the corner, where McKay's Pharmacy used to be. By the time she made it out the door and down to the sidewalk, he had disappeared into the ether for ports unknown.

"His spirit had come to say goodbye," she told Dad, "because his body could not."

Maybe Dad knows where he went, because he's gone now, too. Born in 1932 on a pimple of Newfoundland granite called Vatcher's Island, to a Hobbesian world of toil, he'd tell how the old ones talked of premonitions. They put great stock in dreams, too. I think it's because they were tuned to life in a deeper key and not burdened by information overload. Their channels were cleaner.

"People stopped coming up to the house because it was the one with the ghosts. Like they were my fault!" Lena says. "I didn't know what they were doing there, either! So, I got on with the work of raising that family. I had two jobs, one sewing clothes and the other working at the IGA, while the two oldest boys got work on the boats or digging coal in the pit. Once they started getting big, they'd sit down at the table for dinner and shovel their food in, then be gone. I said, 'To hell with this.' That's when I got chopsticks.

"You bet I did! I gave them all chopsticks. Ever try to eat mashed potatoes and peas with chopsticks? That's how I got to know what went on in their day. They had to sit and answer my questions while they tried to eat dinner!" She roars with laughter, slaps me on the back and heads to another table.

Other diners come in. Lena seats them and returns. She's not done talking yet.

"I came here myself and got a job. It was a good job, doing secretarial work at an advertising agency. Flew those kids out, one or two at a time. Thirty years later, they've all done well, too. They're teachers, tradesmen, with a few up in the oil patch. Once they got out on their own, I went and married a fellow from California. Yes, I did. Real good-looking, too . . . like I was once," she says, winking while throwing an elbow into my arm.

"We lived in Santa Cruz. He wasn't a bad man, but he was all about image. His looks. He was a surfer. Loved nothing more than to be out on the water or looking at himself in the mirror. We had a son. He's a good kid who never seemed to click with his father, perhaps because he had too much of me in him—too much of the Caper. I'd take him back to Inverness for a few weeks during summer vacation. We stayed longer during the year his dad and I split up.

"One day, out of the blue—he's about seven years old, I guess—he says, 'I like it more here than California. Back there, people care about what's on the *outside*, but here, everyone cares what's on the *inside*. What you look like and what you've got, doesn't matter so much here."'

It's not lost on me that this is the same place where the priest was stingy with kindness after her loss, and I say as much.

"That was more than forty-five years ago. Places change. People change. That's why I'm going back to the family home and we're opening up a B&B. Time to do something for me."

I remember the ghosts and ask if she's worried they might scare away clients.

"Jesus, no! A few ghosts in the house will be great for business! It's eating potatoes with chopsticks they'll have to worry about!"

She drives that elbow into my ribs again, roars laughing and heads for the other table.

They live close to the weather out west. To say it's not for the meek is an understatement.

Before my meniscus tore and the wonky knees of mid-life hobbled my daily run, I made for the streets in whatever city I found myself for my daily six kilometres. Calgary was easily one of the best cities in the country for that. No hills! Just the great, flat pathway beside the Bow River. During a morning jog, if you caught a strong tailwind along with your endorphin buzz, you could be in Regina by dinnertime.

I pushed my luck running one minus-40 morning when sweat froze my eyelids shut in ten minutes. The brutal temperature did nothing to impede the city's hard-core cyclists, though. From out of a frigid dawn they came, a mounted cavalry of commuters astride their mountain bikes, all pumping, snorting, grunting and wheezing their way to work, looking every inch a devilish horde from some

Nordic hell arriving for a day of reckoning, each bedecked in neon-coloured, down-filled Gore-Tex parkas, toques, big, floppy mitts and beards of crusted ice home to foot-long snot Popsicles they no doubt sucked for sustenance.

These hardy westerners cycling through a frigid morn would have given Shackleton's suffering crew a run for their money in perseverance.

When I had a rare day off on tour, I always made for nature to look for quiet corners of country where I could slow it all down. Although the jewel in the crown of our national park system is considered to be the mountain town of Banff, I was always taken with the raptor-rich skies and sweeping vistas of southern Alberta. Standing small on one of those sun-smiley meadowlark mornings, watching the wind rule the rolling plains beneath a big belly of blue, even the most rabid of atheists couldn't help being moved to start singing hymns forgotten. Appropriately so, for that corner of the West is home to many communities of Hutterites and Mennonites, whose agrarian simplicities can rock an urbanite's reality. I held a door for a family at a hardware store in Lethbridge, and seven daughters walked out wearing bonnets and calico dresses, looking every inch like extras from *Little House on the Prairie*. Father strode out next, in bib overalls and straw hat, wearing the beaming pride of procreation worthy of an Old Testament patriarch.

He was yelling at his sons across the parking lot: "Zebediah! Aaron! Malachi! Slow down and wait for Mother!"

And then came Mother. Poor woman was pushing a stroller with a toddler in it and another in tow, dragging her tired limbs with that shell-shocked stare of overworked moms everywhere who've spent the last fifteen years in the diaper-wet trenches of baby raising, thanks to a love of Jesus, her husband's seed and a womb fertile as the green valleys of Canaan.

You've got to admire a people with the discipline to shirk the trappings of contemporary society. Sure, the gene pool might be shallow and home dentistry standard practice, but you're never going to wait for Bell customer service to pick up while you grow a bubble on your brain. Plus, no matter what political party is running the country, it's always 1857 in the barn!

Whenever I was headed south for a show in Lethbridge, I always made it a point to visit the UNESCO World Heritage Site of Head-Smashed-In Buffalo Jump. Of all the stops I've made criss-crossing the West, these four thousand hectares rising above a rolling plain cut by the serpentine path of Oldman River haunts like no other.

From 5800 BP until AD 1850, Indigenous people used natural barriers of hills, coulees and depressions to drive bison towards a cliff, where the herd barrelled over the edge and dropped to the ground ten metres below. The spirit of place is a tangible presence here, and the Blackfoot people, whose reserve it abuts, are the guardians and docents in charge.

During one visit, a guide walked me along the path and told me the river's name in Blackfoot. He pointed out a mountain way down south, too, that was used for vision quests. When a weasel, entirely white save for a black strip across its upper lip, popped its head up from behind a boulder to stare at us, the guide told me it was my spirit animal.

I said, "I'd always thought my spirit animal would be a monarch of the forest, like a grizzly bear."

"Hey," he said, "beggars can't be choosers."

We had a good laugh. Indigenous people have a whole different rhythm to their funny. An economy of words. They cut to the truth quicker that way. Way back in 1986, I went whale-watching off Tofino on Vancouver Island. The tour was run by a local Nuu-chah-nulth man and his young son. I stepped aboard their boat wearing my new 35-millimetre Minolta camera. He took one look at me and said, "What are you taking pictures for? Can't remember?"

As the sun started to slip behind the horizon, the guide blessed the day in a tongue that had been around, as the title of that book says, "since the world began." It was a privilege.

I got to thinking about those settlers who were given 160 acres of free land to farm. It wasn't really free. It was the home of the Blackfoot, Cree, Piegan and Shoshone and every other people of the plains who'd been displaced by the building of our national railway. The guarantees of Treaty 7, signed in good faith with the Crown, were ignored and the territory confiscated by pork-barrelling corporate fat cats aligned with imperialist Ottawa politicians who were fuelled by the prevailing Victorian myth of Darwinian determinism and its doctrine of racial superiority, a pretext for dominion over brown, red and black peoples cloaked in the economic policies of late-nineteenth-century colonial paternalism. Of course, I'm paraphrasing.

In Lethbridge, I found a funky coffee shop whose walls were lined with paintings by local artists that was run by gregarious, moon-faced millennials making muffins and cappuccinos. With Joni Mitchell on the speakers singing, "I could drink a case of you and still be on my feet," the tiny place held a Canadian morning in its hand.

Outside, the southern Alberta sky was a cobalt blue. I was feeling content with the response I'd received to the five new pages of content I'd broken in the night before. Breaking in new material in the clubs ended ten years earlier, when I stopped playing them, so anything new had to go from the page to the stage. I like the anticipatory belly hum that comes before the curtain rises, as I wonder which of the thoughts I've scribbled on a legal pad that afternoon might hit the bull's eye tonight.

That's the luxury of doing a two-hour show. It allows you room to roam. In the early years, I got bent out of shape so easily before dropping in new content. No more. And I have the road to thank for that. "Stage time, stage time, stage time," as George Carlin said. It's what you need to learn your trade. After all, the first hammer a carpenter picks up, he doesn't build a mansion. Show business feeds on that Jiminy Cricket, "When you wish upon a star, your dreams come true" malarkey. Well, here's a wake-up call, kids: not if you suck, they won't! There are no shortcuts.

Lesson learned: anything worth doing well always takes time.

I made the unfair assumption the man entering the café was experiencing homelessness, as his clothes had the dusty look of someone who's spent time on the streets. Then I noticed a self-assurance in his stride typical of those who are comfortable moving through the world at their own pace. Although I'd travelled plenty throughout southern Alberta, I'd forgotten how many people live much closer to the land down here, which proved I'd been in Toronto too long. His corduroy jacket, with its wool sheepskin lining, was well broken in, and a Royal Tyrrell Museum patch was emblazoned on the shoulder. Seeing as he was well over sixty, I figured he'd outgrown the fascination with T. rex a while ago and probably just worked there.

He sat beside me at the window counter and started buttering the scone he'd ordered. "That's some title for your book," he said.

I was reading *Death of the Liberal Class*, in which Chris Hedges postulates that America's Democratic Party sold its soul to big business long ago, making room for the rise of a virulent strain of aggressive right-wing Republicanism. The party FDR had once guided with a steady hand through the Great Depression and the Second World War had divested itself of its traditional role as champion of the workingman when it failed to address the corporate plunder and abuse that was driving a third of the United States into neo-feudal penury. Given President Biden's $1.9 trillion stimulus package, the correction is underway.

The gentleman did not sit to the right or left politically. He was a thinker who told me he graduated from university in the early 1960s with a degree in geography and lived in a yurt.

"There's something different about living in a circular house," he said.

"And what's that?" I asked.

"Don't know," he answered. "Haven't figured that out yet."

He started to talk.

"Those guys who taught me in the early '60s, who'd fought in the war? They had convictions. They saw and did things over there, and it *tempered* them. When they got home, they wanted to live a life of value. The government knew it, too. They *encouraged* it. In America, they called it the GI Bill. The government helped you get started again. It was their way of thanking you for your contribution to the war effort. For turning away the tide of fascism. Today, soldiers come back from Afghanistan and our government provides them with nothing. Politicians are great for waving the flag, but they provide nothing for the returning troops but crappy housing and an opioid habit. Counselling for their mental health problems, if they're lucky.

I'm not sure what we're fighting for anymore in Afghanistan. Neither is the rest of the world. I can live in a changing Lethbridge, yet the ironies of a world in collision are all around me. Fundamentalist Hutterites and fundamentalist Muslims living side by side.

"The other day, I saw a woman in a hijab do a double-take when eight Hutterite women walked past her, dressed as if they were headed for an outing in the 1860s. Both were wearing the uniform of their tribe. According to enlightened standards, they're oppressed, but by their standards, they are happy in their roles.

"Lethbridge is changing. In the early 1980s, it was still a ranch town. Cowboys who hadn't seen but a horse's head and a gopher's ass for months would come here to drink and whore. It worked! I was ranch-raised. Roping. Riding. I grew up outdoors. My folks loved me, but life was hard. It was *real*, though. Look at that daycare centre across the street in that federal building." He threw his head towards a generic government box across the street, void of any personality or charm. Its austere architecture would be right at home in a forgotten corner of the Soviet bloc.

"The poor little kids are dropped off in the morning and spend all day *indoors*! May as well be in a padded cell. Never see so much as a grasshopper or ant, even! Never have a cranky tomcat scratch you. Never seeing or smelling the world around you.

"You know what Thomas Hobbes said?"

I shook my head.

"'The first virtue is courage.'"

He drank his coffee. "Some things don't make sense to me. How and why is it the Mounties can kill a poor drunken cowboy, or take Neil Stonechild for a midnight death march outside Saskatoon, taser a delusional Polish man to death in a Vancouver airport, or blow a kid's brains out in Smithers just for getting lippy, yet—*yet*—a cocaine kingpin in Calgary can walk free 24/7 and nobody 'accidentally' puts a bullet in his brain?" He rose to get his coffee replenished.

I was just another dude in the coffee shop, having his morning java before he sat down. Someone at the counter mentioned I was on TV, though, and I saw both of them look over. When he returned, his tone had changed. He was tentative. Less relaxed. It's weird, the effect television has. I wanted to say, "Relax, it's Canada. All fame means here is I might score a round or two for free north of the treeline."

"So, you're Ron James? How about that. You stay put, and the world comes to you." He took a sip of coffee. "You're not gonna put anything I said in your show, are you?"

"No," I said, but I was thinking, *If I ever write a book, I will.*

It was 8:30 a.m. and the sun was nothing more than a feeble rumour, poking meekly through spirals of smoke rising from stacks of industry. A raven on the roof outside my window stood with a frozen Timbit in its beak. Or maybe it was an eyeball he'd scavenged from the head of a dead drifter somewhere in the hinterland? The morning was draped in a curtain of purgatorial half-light.

As for me, I couldn't ask for more perfect weather. This was the kind of Stygian gloom that gets patrons packing theatres with hopes of laughing their worries away. Otherwise, they could snap one morning and run naked through traffic, singing a Carpenters song.

The Starbucks sat in a big-box park across the street, and although I could see the logo from the hotel parking lot, the intersection I needed to cross to get there was murderous. All I could hear was the cacophonous roar of sixteen-wheelers bound for the oil patch. I should've turned back and taken my rental car. But with all the driving and flying I'd been doing for days on end, my legs were in desperate need of a stretch. They felt cramped and swollen with arterial thrombosis, and I worried that if I didn't begin to move them soon, they'd become lifeless appendages of bone and tissue.

The notion of waiting out eight hours until showtime in a claustrophobic, bone-dry hotel room is daunting. A comedian killing a day in a hotel can feel closer to a gangster who has ratted out the Mob and is now in the witness protection program, waiting for his disguise to arrive so he can walk the streets in anonymity, safe in the assurance that no hit man sent to exact revenge would ever suspect "that rat bastard" is the guy in an orange fright wig and a polka-dot clown suit, hopping up and down by the flower shop. Which, by the way, I witnessed from my Holiday Inn hotel window *every time* I played Peterborough, Ontario. The person in the clown suit must have been on bennies, or an aerobics teacher, or paying off a Faustian bargain with the Devil himself to put that much energy into a workday, that involved bouncing up and down—*outside . . . in the winter-time*—in a clown suit. I always wondered why the owners of the flower shop who employed the clown wouldn't have rented one of those whacky thirty-foot blow-up stick people instead, that you see in the parking lots of used car dealerships, flailing their arms about like a drowning person.

I watched that Peterborough clown for two hours one February afternoon when it was minus-27, and never once did they falter. Arctic vortex be damned. Snow Goose parkas were pulled tight around the heads of passersby. Not the clown. The person in that polka-dot jumpsuit just kept on givin' 'er! Nary a move was mailed in. Nary a breath taken for rest. If audiences ever enjoyed my shows in Peterborough, they have the clown to thank. No way was I ever *not* going to give it my all, when on the frozen sidewalks but five blocks south of the theatre, a clown was dancing in the cold with the commitment of someone hoping to save their soul from the fires of eternal damnation.)

The Grande Prairie intersection was not what you'd call "pedestrian friendly." There were no sidewalks. With sixty billion dollars a year in profit being pulled from the oil patch, pedestrians were not a priority here. I wondered if anyone had ever crossed this road on foot and lived to tell the tale. The walk signal appeared as a contemptible flicker . . . a tantalizing tease as if to say, "Go ahead, Ron. Try it. Now! Run across the street! Go! Now! Run!"

"Oh . . . SMUCK!! Too late, bro. You're dead."

There were no sidewalks to walk to either, just a ten-foot bank of razor-sharp crystallized snow. Industry's infrastructure whistled past on flatbeds moving full tilt through rough country, spewing a toxic soup of diesel and smoke. I clearly needed that Starbucks. Even though the hotel coffee was complimentary, after one sip I remember thinking, *If this coffee's a compliment, my wake-up call must be a kick in the nuts!*

Speaking of coffee, when I hit the road twenty years ago, Tim Hortons had already established itself as an iconic Canadian brand. It has since fallen far on the consumer scale of favourites, no doubt because others like myself took a sip of their 7,123rd cup one morning and thought, "Wait a second. This tastes like shit!" There was a day, however, when Holy Communion couldn't hold a candle to the religious reverence our nation held for the chain. A Canadian's need for donuts and a morning kick-start of java produced a level of worship heretofore reserved only for the Saviour's suffering.

When the reverence was at its dizzying peak, to disparage the chain from the stage was to denigrate the essence of what it meant to be Canadian. You could feel the barometric pressure drop and the audience pull out faster than a teenage Lothario in the back seat of his father's '72 Chevy. "It's only coffee and donuts!" I would rail from the stage. "Canadian soldiers didn't brew it on Vimy Ridge after they took that hill from the Hun!" And I'd hear crickets. But woe betide the cocky elitist who deigned to pass judgment on what is still affectionately called Timmies.

But how does love of country become righteously equated with enjoying a maple-glazed cruller and a double-double? The chain had no historic significance we could hang a hat on to warrant its anointed status—unlike, say, pemmican, which you can't find anywhere unless you've got an in with a Cree trapper and his wife somewhere north of The Pas.

The light turned, the walk signal blinked, and with only the ferric taste of adrenalin as company, I bolted hard for the other side, praying I'd make it to safety before being nailed so hard by a truck that the raven from the rooftop would be treated to another eyeball. My knees hadn't entirely gone to hell yet from all the years of running, and although I could hear cartilage flopping in my meniscus as I ran, I made it safely across just as a large garbage truck blared its horn. As I turned to flip the driver the bird, he began to wave. A huge smile crossed his face. The passenger window rolled down, and he yelled, "I'm coming to the show tonight, you funny little bole-legged bastard!" I wondered if he knew my uncle.

In twenty years on the road, I'd seen Grande Prairie go from a high-plains town of forever prairie to a sprawling suburban landscape of shopping malls and highways. A guy I knew from Halifax was making his living as a school principal in a small town two hours west, and regardless of what fury nature was throwing down, he and his wife along with another couple never missed a show of mine. I appreciated that a great deal. It reconnected me to the place I'd left several lifetimes ago, where in high school days Roman Catholics from St. Pat's and Protestants from Queen Elizabeth duked it out after Saturday night dances, hacked each other on the hockey rink or bruised each other good during Wanderers Grounds football games. We were now just Maritime exiles enjoying post-show pints in the Promised Land a love of comedy had brought together.

Their neighbour told me her immigrant story. She arrived from Poland in a mink coat and high-heeled shoes in the cab of her uncle's pickup truck after flying from Gdansk to Edmonton via Frankfurt. Her uncle was a hog farmer, and when this woman from fashion-conscious Europe opened her eyes after sleeping away the four-hour drive from the airport, she found herself parked outside the farmers' Co-Op on a bone-cold, muddy Monday morning in November 1981 in a desolate Grande Prairie that, no doubt, felt less welcoming than Poland after the blitzkrieg. Her uncle and his wife thought she'd like a cup of coffee, and this was the only place you could get one for 250 kilometres.

"I walked into the place," she said, "and there were no women, just men wearing bib overalls and rubber boots covered in muck. I cried every day for a year." And yet, twenty-five years later, she was still there. That was the West for you.

Having finally scaled the snowbank and made it across the street alive, I was safely tucked into the corner of that Grande Prairie Starbucks with my Moleskine notebook and a cup of coffee, when this giant of a kid loped towards me, covering the floor from end to end in three long and determined strides.

The young man was in his late twenties, and he had a ruddy complexion and wide smile. Callused hands the size of small tennis racquets poked from a weather-worn Carhartt jacket indicating a life of outdoor labour, that guaranteed should an issue arise where a physical solution was needed once all diplomatic channels had been exhausted, you'd want those gorilla-sized mitts fighting on your side.

"You're that funny guy from TV, but I don't know your name."

It's Canada. They never know your name. Even though this conversation occurred twelve years ago, it happens all the time. I told him I was Peter Keleghan, and he didn't know who he was, either.

(That is how it always happened. People would see me seated by myself at a coffee shop in some corner of the country, and they'd just start talking. Connections of this sort happened to my mother a lot, too. She'd be riding the bus in Halifax when an unknown lady would sit down beside her, and twenty minutes later, she'd know all about the polyp they found on the ovary of a Pekingese dog owned by her second cousin's daughter, who ran away to Boston and married a jazz musician her family wants nothing to do with.)

When he wasn't working in Fort McMurray on a drilling crew, the kid told me, he lived outside Grande Prairie on his parents' six-hundred-acre farm. But today, he was making a rare visit to town.

"It's too noisy here," he said. "I like our ranch. It's so quiet. You come to town and everything's moving. No one is still."

I told him I live in Toronto.

"Toronto? I can't imagine why anyone would ever want to live in a place like that. But I guess you have to, being in show business and all, eh? I mean, if you want to work in the oil business, you have to be here."

"I might live in Toronto," I said, "but the country's my home. I've got the best of both worlds. I get to make a living seeing Canada from coast to coast, and by living in Toronto, I can walk to the Air Canada Centre when the Leafs are playing."

"But the Leafs suck," he said, laughing.

(This conversation *did* take place before Auston Matthews, Mitch Marner, John Tavares and the rest of those multimillionaire wunderkinds showed up in hopes of revitalizing a franchise synonymous with fifty-seven years of losing. If entering a rink before the game dressed to the nines in tailored suits, looking every inch a gaggle of pimps on a catwalk, guarantees a team the Stanley Cup, Toronto should be seeing a parade very soon.)

"That may be the case, but I 'bleed blue,'" I assured him. "I've been hoping for my Buds for fifty years. You have to keep the faith. I just want to see them win the Stanley Cup . . . in colour!"

He laughed and said he'd gone to Edmonton once to see the Oilers play.

"Never again!"

"The game couldn't have been that bad," I said.

"The game was great, but the city was *way* too noisy! There was nothing but horns and sirens and banging everywhere. It was non-stop noise. All we hear on the farm are the cattle and the wind. I love the sound of wind. It just rolls over the prairie. It's so simple, and it doesn't cost a penny. Everywhere you go costs money, but that doesn't. I don't like leaving but I have to. Why?"

And he answered his own question: "Because you gotta make money. Work on the drilling crew, though? It's very dangerous. No one pays attention to safety. You're supposed to, but it's ignored.

That's the last thing on the list when you're looking to get your day in. Safety's the last thing on anyone's mind."

That point was made very clear to me a few years later in Brandon, Manitoba. I was at the hotel bar for a pint, when a couple of seriously liquored compadres looked at me, all wobbly eyed, and shouted, "We're coming to your show tomorrow!"

I said, "It was tonight. You missed it."

The guy in the Harley shirt and biker beard looked at his buddy and said, "Shit. How'd we miss that?" His spooky-eyed and very intense wingman yelled, "'Cause we're too busy making money!" And he downed a couple of beers in a gulp. (I hadn't seen drinking prowess of that calibre since Latta emptied a forty of Donini in one Herculean guzzle, back in '76 at the infamous Acadia Wine Bee.)

Even though it was an hour shy of last call, they demanded I have a drink with them. I respectfully took a pass, letting them know I had to be up at 7 a.m. for my two-hour drive to the Winnipeg airport to catch a flight back home to Toronto.

The guy in the Harley shirt said, "Toronto sucks." (It's something you hear an awful lot west of Mississauga.)

The intense one bored a hole in my head with his stare and said, "Buddy! I'm gettin' up at 4 a.m.! Running a safety course for seventy guys in my work crew."

I thought, *What kind of safety course can a guy who is shitfaced at 12:30 a.m. possibly run a few hours from now?*

"What is it you do?" I inquired, hoping it didn't involve explosives.

And I kid you not good reader, this teetering and sloshed-to-the-eyeballs hombre declared—with pride, I might add—"I'm in charge of pipeline welders for Enbridge."

"Money breeds crime," the kid in Starbucks said. "We went up to Fort Mac with a six-man crew, and three of them got mugged buying their smokes!"

He told me this in the glory days of the boom, long before the big fire came and turned thirty years of dreams to ashes, coming perilously close to claiming the entire town. I remember how the nation rallied round to help, donating everything from airplane flights back to Atlantic Canada to clothes and food. A big bin sat for two weeks in a storefront on King Street East, right around the corner from my downtown Toronto condo. It gradually filled up with clothes until it was shipped out for the needy of Fort Mac. For a country with the second-greatest national land mass on Earth, it's surprising how small-town Canada feels when tragedy strikes. But in 2006, when Fort Mac was seeing record numbers of newcomers every day and real estate prices had skyrocketed into the realm of the absurd, the province and the oil companies were fighting over whose fiscal responsibility it was to fix the four-foot potholes on Main Street, and to put chalk in schools and bandages in hospitals. Highway 63 from Edmonton was a two-lane killer with a gruesome attrition rate that neither government nor the oil companies made a move to fix for years. During the height of the Iraq War, the highway to the Baghdad airport was safer to drive!

The kid excused himself, and I went back to my journal.

Moments later, I looked up, and he was standing over me, holding a ceramic Starbucks cup.

"Here you go: a gift from me to you. A cup goes around the world. Let people know that just because we drill for oil, doesn't make us bad people. We're all just trying to make a living in this hard world."

Chapter Five

THE CANADIAN WINTER

I like to think of myself as a winter person. I'm sure the polyglot Celtic gene pool I'm descended from has something to do with it. Our blood is far more suited to soup-and-sweater weather than sweating in the tropics, getting semi-comatose on a margarita drip. In actuality, my genetic disposition is far more conducive to staring at a winter campfire, getting semi-comatose on a rum toddy drip.

Short of channelling our inner *ursus* and slipping into a cave for a winter's worth of blissful torpor until the crocuses come again, the only option when it comes to dealing with winter is to survive it. After all, the Inuit managed to eke out an existence from a pitch-black, frozen world of ice, rock and lichen five thousand years before Netflix, when the only light for eight months was a thin strip of blood-red sky stretching across an infinite horizon. (I bet staring at *that* got old in a hurry.)

In his book *Arctic Dreams*, Barry Lopez tells us the Inuit had a word for the time of year when forever night dropped the weight of life on their shoulders: *pereloneq*, which no doubt can be loosely translated as "One more day spent sitting in this igloo under total darkness listening to old Uncle Tulimak fart, and I'm running buck naked on the tundra." Too bad they never had the option of bolting for Florida like we do.

The pilgrimage of snowbirds for sunny Florida is easily several generations old. I've been envious on occasion when I see Facebook posts from retired friends enjoying a lunch of mahi-mahi tacos on a lanai in their exclusive gated community, especially when I'm suffering through a third polar vortex two weeks into February. It sounds lovely, but spending your golden years amongst pistol-packing, mammon-loving, science-denying Republicans does not stoke my northern mojo. I'd cross the line of expected social decorum by saying the right thing to the wrong person at the first neighbourhood barbecue and be shunned faster than a shoplifting Mennonite. That is far too steep a price to pay for a tan in February.

Sure, studies may say a prolonged respite from winter's hard haul adds an extra ten years to your life, but the notion of spending those precious years growing melanoma blisters on my pale leprechaun skin while sporting Bermuda shorts hiked up to a droopy set of "man cans" is a nightmare on par with an emergency root canal performed with a pointy stick.

When it comes to the sun, let alone a killer tropical one, I'm already doomed! Clinical studies say five serious sunburns in child-hood result in an 80 percent risk of getting skin cancer today. Then fit me for a wig and sign me up for a dozen bouts of chemotherapy now. *Five* sunburns? I've been covered in thermonuclear welts every summer since I was six!

That's why winter gets my vote. It's a season to be embraced, and many Canadians share my sentiments. Fingers turned black with frostbite after a gloveless day spent tobogganing on Mount Royal are standard badges of honour for those born in Montreal. I've seen entire families, *sans* hats or mitts, gleefully barrelling down that mountain face-first into the kind of wind chill that would have turned Frontenac back.

Those who like to ski live for winter. From Mont-Tremblant to Whistler, ski runs are ruled by fearless young snowboarders riding a piece of fibreglass at ninety-seven kilometres an hour down icy back bowls at an angle so sharp it would make Pythagoras puke!

Snowmobilers are rabid for the season as well. Soon as the first snowflake falls, they're pacing the living room floor with the enthusiasm of a Labrador retriever on the opening day of duck season.

Even ice fishing helps people get through the season. I'm not sure why it's called a sport, though. Sitting in a clapboard shack a Third World shepherd wouldn't shit in—that's heated to Amazonian jungle levels—while staring at six empty holes in the hope the perch will bite makes it seem a stretch to call it a sport. (Then again, professional darts matches are preferably played drunk, and that's called a sport, so they could have a point.)

It is said that smell is the most transformative of the five senses, and for the most part I agree, but with one exception: hearing your skates carve the ice of a frozen pond is a sound that sings a soul note in praise of the eternal. Simply put, it is transformative. Every time I do, I want to end the day in flannel pajamas, watching the Leafs play the Habs on a black and white TV while I eat a plate of homemade beans.

A couple of Januarys ago, while staying at my cottage in Nova Scotia, the mercury dropped to a perfect minus-20 for several windless nights in a row. Within three days, nature's magic had delivered such a bump-free, lump-free, frozen sheet of glass on the local pond, so smooth you'd swear it had been Zamboni-glazed to perfection by elves the night before. After breakfast, I hooked my Tacks over my hockey stick, stuck a puck in my pocket and headed down the road to commune with the timeless. I hit the ice with the confidence of that high school hockey god I never, *ever* was. House league pedigree be damned! I skated that day like I was born for the majors! Look at those Paul Coffey rinkwide strides! Had there been NHL scouts hiding in the cattails around the pond that day, I'd have most certainly had my call up to "the show."

All alone, and all day long, I pushed that circle of frozen rubber up and down the ice, oblivious to whatever woes bedevilled the world. With every stride I was fourteen years old again, playing shinny on frozen Chocolate Lake in the company of forever pals when those now gone were flesh and blood, moving immortal under a winter sun that cast our shadows long as life itself, back when all our gods were the same.

A lot of Canadian kids at one time or another have entertained the dream of making the NHL. Truth be told, I knew as early as peewee I would not be playing in the majors. It was after I got my first pair of skates. They were hand-me-downs from a cousin and came with buckles on them. *Buckles.* They looked as if some old fella had doctored up a pair of polio boots in his shed.

And my mother was selling me hard.

"Look at those skates your cousin gave you. They're practically brand new!" she exclaimed. "Those are really nice skates."

She saw the doubt behind my eyes—the abject refusal of an eleven-year-old son to buy her ludicrous spin.

"What? You don't like those skates? They're perfectly good skates. Yes. They. Are."

No, I thought, *they're a piece of shit.* I suppose the shaking of my head was as much a reaction to the clearly corrective footwear I was holding as to the audacity of her pitch.

She saw my head shake, and in turn, I caught her full fury as her voice began to rise in crescendo.

"You're lucky to even have skates! Your father never had skates when he was growing up in Newfoundland. Poor little fella, if he didn't wake up Christmas morning with a boner he never had a friggin' thing to play with!"

"I know, Ma. I know Dad had it tougher than me," I cried. "I know he moved from Newfoundland to Halifax when he was seven years old and had a paper route in the morning and one in the afternoon and even sold mackerel from a horse-drawn cart on Saturday mornings in the wintertime when he wanted to be playing shinny with his buddies on frozen Chocolate Lake, but he came home instead and gave the money to Nanny for rent, cause his dad was sick in bed with ALS and his older brothers were in the corvette navy, protecting convoys from the German U-boats prowling the North Atlantic. I know, I know . . . but there's fuckin' buckles on my skates! Leprechauns have buckles on their skates."

(Fifty years later, I can assure you I never had the guts to drop an f-bomb on Mom. I've added that for dramatic effect. Also, I am now very grateful I never had the Junior Tacks all the better players had. There's not a lot of laughs to be had, listening to somebody reminisce about how cool they once were.)

If you're wondering, I eventually did get what passed for a half-decent pair of hockey skates. Bauer Black Panthers. Strange that a style of skate would have been named after a black militant group who, besides distributing food to the poor of Oakland, California, also advocated armed overthrow of "the man." Purchased at Canadian Tire with money saved delivering newspapers, the thirty bucks I paid for them was literally a steal. *Someone* had conveniently changed the sticker price on the box. Life was simpler then.

When you're a kid, looking cool while playing sports was half the battle, especially if, like me, you weren't that good. Back in 1970, I tried to talk my father into buying me a Victoriaville hockey stick with a fibreglass blade that cost three dollars and twenty-one cents. This was beyond the realm of reason for a man whose toy at Christmas was, well . . . which explains his apoplectic reaction in Cleve's Sporting Goods. Although frightening at the time, I now understand it was perfectly reasonable for someone whose idea of a Saturday night treat in 1942 was splitting the head of a newly stewed rabbit with his brother Jack.

"Three dollars and twenty-one cents for a GD hockey stick? A hockey stick?! Lord Jesus, Ronnie! Bobby Hull doesn't have that slapshot because he's got a fancy hockey stick. He's got that shot because he built his wrists up milking cows on the farm!"

"Then get me a cow, Dad," I said, "cause I can't lift the friggin' puck!"

My protests were ignored, so I had to settle for the sixty-nine-cent Hespeler, the worst hockey stick on the market. I swear they were made of balsa wood. They were basically kindling with tape on them. After one shot, they shattered. The only thing they were good for was staking tomatoes in the garden come summer.

Not so today. Everything has got to be top of the line for kids playing the game, and half the time, it's their delusional parents setting that standard. Reality is so distorted for some hard-core hockey parents—the ones grooming their kids from birth to be the next Sidney Crosby. Soon as the umbilical cord is cut, the kids are practically thrown on a rink when they're still wet. Seal pups get less ice time! How about before you start mortgaging the house to keep little Bobby in gear, you do a reality check? He's eight! Let him be a kid first.

Of course, the vast majority play for the love of the game, and that's never more obvious than during hockey tournament weekends. Stay at any hotel when half a dozen teams have laid siege to it, and it becomes blatantly clear they're having a riot. Mongol hordes were easier on the furniture when they were sacking Constantinople! Back and forth from the games room to the pool; up and down the elevators barefoot, soaking wet and screaming; pillaging the candy, pop and ice machines all night long . . . and that's just the parents!

One afternoon I stepped into the hallway with my bags headed for my hotel room during a hockey tourney weekend and got corked in the cojones with a hard orange hockey ball shot by kids playing pickup hockey in the hallways—with their moms playing nets! That's the kind of quintessential Canadian tableau Krieghoff would have painted.

For a country known for saying "sorry" too much, we never apologize for loving this violent sport. A typical injury list during the playoffs reads like a casualty report from a Civil War hospital tent. But unlike wounded soldiers, they're expected to keep playing. It's why I have to laugh when professional baseball players are out for six weeks with a hangnail. When Sidney Crosby had his face reconstructed after getting hit by a seventy-five-mile-an-hour slapshot, he was back on the ice to win the Stanley Cup that same year.

I met an elderly gentleman over breakfast at the Delta Hotel in Saint John almost twenty-five years ago. People have always given me a

window on their world. They wanted to let me know there were
moments in their lives that mattered, and perhaps that in the sharing,
the moments would live on longer than they. He was easily in his late
seventies then, so I guess this story has. In a body bent over and hobbled by time, he had the gruff voice of those Canadian Legion lifers
who are permanently seated by the shuffleboard table with a draft in
hand. I'd not been on TV very much way back then, so when he
addressed me by name, I was taken aback. Sometimes I thought these
strangers were apparitions who materialized from the ether just long
enough to share their stories. I never knew where they came from or
where they were going. They just appeared, told their stories, and in
the blink of an eye were gone.

"How are ya, Ronnie? I used to be six-foot-four. Not anymore. Time,
Ronnie. Time. It's a son of a bitch!" the old man said. He continued . . .

"I used to play in the Wood Chopper's League back in '49 up by
Lake Huron. It's the seventh game of the playoffs, and we're playing
for the trophy. We're in the dressing room at the end of the second
period, and the game's all tied up, 2–2. Our star centre was buckled
over in tears. 'I can't go back out, Coach. I can't. It hurts too much.'

"Piles, Ronnie. He had a cluster of piles growing on the crack of
his arse you'd swear were a cluster of grapes." And then, with a hand
on my shoulder, he offered a conscientious courtesy: "I'm not both-
ering your breakfast, am I?"

"Of course not," I said, thinking, *It's not every day you get a great
hockey story involving festering piles anymore.*

He grew taller in the telling as his posture straightened.

"Our team doctor learned his trade on the battlefields of World
War II. He looked at Reggie, our centre, then back at us, and said,
'Pin his arms to the table, boys,' which we did . . . much like in the

hazing, but I don't have time to get into that now. Then that doctor dropped Reggie's hockey pants and sliced those piles off with a straight razor! No freezing! He whipped a handful of ice and a bread poultice dipped in mercurochrome on the crack of his ass! Thirty minutes later, we were skating round the ice with that trophy."

"How did he do it?" I asked.

"Who?" he grunted.

"The guy with the piles," I said. "How did he get the winning goal?"

"Christ, Ronnie, *I* got the goal. Poor Reggie sat on the bench crying, and barely walked again." Then he roared a great, gravelly laugh, punched me in the arm with a bony fist and said, "Put that in a book someday."

So, I did.

Unless you live in the frigid West, the days of backyard rinks and frozen ponds are disappearing. No one can depend on a consistent run of cold weather anymore.

Lake Ontario acts as a bulwark to cold and snow in Toronto, so instead of an enjoyable white winter, the mild temperature drapes a funereal grey curtain over the city for weeks on end. That's when seasonal affective disorder kicks in. Lethargy rules. Moods darken. The weight is real. *Pereloneq!*

No amount of time spent on the elliptical, releasing endorphins at the gym, can chase the blues from your system. Your body is in dire need of a dose of vitamin D, well beyond the thousand milligrams you're getting from that bottle of Lakota every morning. You need to feel some *real* sun on your face, and the best place for that is far closer to the equator than Toronto, so to the tropics you go. (Of course, those lacking the necessary scratch for a Caribbean vacation can opt for a trip to the local tanning salon instead, where they'll receive a generous dose of ultraviolet light to chase the SAD from their system. Mind you, too-frequent visits could turn testicles to raisins or a uterus to dust, so it's your call.)

No matter how intense your love of the season, everyone hits a winter tipping point. Mine was at the tail end of a gruelling twenty-five-date tour of Ontario, on a blistering-cold March afternoon in Pembroke. As I pulled my suitcase from the 4Runner in a Best Western parking lot, I failed to realize I had not zipped it shut, and the entire contents spilled to the ground. While a profanity-laced diatribe danced from my cake hole, I watched the wind carry my clothes far across the parking lot in a dozen different directions. (You just know this kind of stuff doesn't happen to comedians playing Vegas.)

Just as I was about to go chasing my Stanfield's into the bush, a group of snowmobilers miraculously materialized from the forest adjacent to the hotel and began picking up, then returning, my clothes. I thanked these apostles of winter whose faces were covered in reflective visors and their bodies in thermal suits made for rocketing across snowy fields and through woodlands at eighty kilometres an hour . . . drunk. Feeling like a lost member from a party of polar explorers who'd been saved by the Inuit, I watched as my benefactors headed back to the forest from whence they'd come, leaving me with enough to survive the elements until I found sanctuary—or, in my case, the reception desk.

And that's when I decided to take my family to an all-inclusive resort on Mexico's Riviera Maya. We would join legions of pale, sleep-deprived Canadians at the airport at 3 a.m. for the 6 a.m.

flight, so psyched to be putting the snow and cold behind us, we'd have duct-taped ourselves to the wheel wells to escape.

We took a charter flight on Air Transat. I'll wager conditions were more humane on a POW troopship. At five-foot-three no one has ever accused me of being tall, but some legroom wouldn't have hurt. It's not like I was a seven-foot first-round draft pick for the Toronto Raptors, but Jesus H. Christ, a ventriloquist's suitcase would've had more room! Arterial thrombosis was swelling my joints and we hadn't even left the ground yet. A person needed to be a ninth-level yoga master just to get the cup to their lips for a sip of the brake fluid they were passing off as coffee.

The plane was packed with 498 punchy, sun-hungry travellers drawn from the vast and sprawling armies of the middle class, bound for the Yucatán sunbelt. Everyone still wore their pale winter skin, too, so after ten minutes in the tropics, those not smeared in 60-plus sunblock would very soon be starting to bubble.

On landing, we were processed by a listless, couldn't-give-a-shit-if-you-were-bringing-in-yellowcake-uranium Mexican customs official, then herded onto shuttle buses for the resort and driven for an hour past bone-crushing, corrugated-tin-hut, spooky-eyed poverty, where scrawny village dogs sporting pendulous nipples suckled their rabid broods beneath diseased palm trees. I got really indignant.

This is a crime, I thought. *We've got to help those people.*

Suddenly, our opulent hotel appeared through the jungle mists like some magical kingdom in the clouds, and the feeling went away.

"Well, those people are probably happy in their own way," I thought, as a hotel waiter put a Mai Tai in my hand.

The hotel's massive buffet had the kind of spread you'd see rolled out for a Third World dictator, while outside his stately palace, his people are eating old shoes and dog shit. The North American masses were wobbling up and down the aisle in all their gluttonous glory, heaping their plates with gravy-drenched meats and heart-seizing sweets, one cream puff away from having a five-alarm coronary in the surf.

You do get to engage with Americans on these trips, and it's always an eye-opener to meet some of the neighbours we share a continent with, whose government can spend sixty billion dollars a year on intelligence yet have half their country be comprised of the geographically clueless.

I overheard a conversation at the buffet table between a couple from Georgia and a woman from Saskatchewan. With her exceedingly polite Southern drawl, the Georgia peach inquired as to where the Canadian woman was from.

"Saskatoon, Saskatchewan," I heard her reply.

"Where did she say she was from, dear?" asked the husband.

"Damned if I know," was the reply. "She was speaking another language."

That's rich, because the entire week I had been listening to a cacophony of Appalachian accents the likes of which had not been heard since callbacks for *Hee Haw*'s road show.

Canada is not immune to garish patriotism. If you've ever believed there's no such thing as the "ugly Canadian," drop by Señor Frog's in Cancún during happy hour and the myth of our peaceable kingdom and her genteel citizens will be forever debunked. You'll see gangs of muscle-bound, party-hearty bros and their bleached-blond Gold's Gym sirens, all sporting NHL team's jerseys happily face-first in tequila Slurpies, singing Stompin' Tom's "The Hockey Song." And that's just the first night. By midweek, those cyborgs will be sitting in the shade at poolside, wrapped tip to tail in gauze, suffering such severe sunburn that as soon as they get home, they'll be losing half their asses to skin grafts.

Mexico spooks me. If you get murdered in Mexico, they will never find who did it. *Never.* Mexican cops are so hopeless, they couldn't catch a killer during a game of Clue! If you're murdered on the Riviera Maya, there are always two versions: the Mexican version and the truth. You can just imagine the conversation between you and the detective.

"It is clear the victim jumped from the balcony of his hotel room."

To which you would counter, "But he's been shot in the head."

Whereupon the detective, with a dismissive shrug would say, "Then he must have pulled the trigger on the way down."

Case closed.

The dogs are reading the vibe in Mexico, too. I have never seen a dog wag its tail there. Last time I was in Tulum, I was petting one for an hour at an outdoor café before I realized it was dead.

Returning home can be a different story. Here's a tip: remember your parking spot. Today, of course, we can use our phones to take photos of the spot. However, back in the Stone Age—say, ten years ago—a person had to write their parking spot down. Imagine! To forget was to flirt with death. I recall seeing a family, still sporting flip-flops, shorts and tank tops and carrying a Sherpa's weight in duty-free swag, wandering the parking lot at Toronto's Pearson Airport on a frigid February night, looking for their car because they'd forgotten their spot. I bet by the time they finally found it, half of them were suffering hypothermic shock. Mom probably showed up at work the next morning still sporting cornrows, a nice tan and both thumbs black with frostbite. Had she stayed home in Canada, a good pair of mitts would have prevented that.

Chapter Six

OUT WHERE MY MOJO LIVES

A stage with only a microphone is freedom made manifest. There you answer to no one but the audience, who provide a comedian with the luxury to line up the planets and make sense of the chaos we're all walking through—in the language of laughs. The audience is the great litmus test of what works and what doesn't—unlike network television, where gaggles of censorious lawyers skilled in arcane semantics vet your satire, and network apparatchiks who've drunk the corporate Kool Aid enact executive dictates. On the other hand, a non-televised run of live consecutive dates in packed theatres is not held hostage to institutionalized standards. On the road, the inmate runs their own asylum.

I once believed a television series was the grail at the end of the trail and the summit of creative achievement. Granted, playing to sold-out theatres on my own and shooting a well-received one-hour comedy special each year in a different Canadian city was a hell of a lot better than working for beer tickets before a room of sarcastic

Toronto comedy snobs at the Rivoli, but still, it wasn't enough. I had to land the coveted television series, but when that happened, I soon discovered that feeding a medium with an insatiable appetite for *content*, placed far greater demands on *creative* than the one-hour specials ever did.

For one thing, those first five one-hour television specials had a wealth of material whose laughs had been honed diamond-hard touring the regions I'd eventually feature. The bits with the strongest legs would act as adhesive to the overall narrative of the seventy-five-page script I'd write, memorize and shoot. It was a great system that had worked for seven years: hit the road, write new content—some thematic to the region I was touring and some not—keep what works, lose what doesn't, return to Toronto, lock myself away in my office come summer to bang it out on the computer, then shoot the special in the fall before a paying theatre audience, edit it down from the one hundred minutes we'd shot, to the forty-five it had to be and then deliver it to network.

Although I wrote the first five one-hour specials myself, the final four were co-written with the erudite Windsor, Ontario–born Paul Pogue, and the Winnipeg, Manitoba–raised scholar Scott Montgomery, whose collective comedic intelligence, soul and work ethic not only made me a better comedian but a more enlightened person as well. When I missed three weeks because of my father's passing in August 2017, a consummate stand-up and son of the Canadian Shield, Wawa-born Pete Zedlacher, stepped into the room to cover for me on that final special until my return. Executive producer Lynn Harvey brought a thirty-five-year television pedigree to the table and set an unimpeachable standard of production value from our very first collaboration. Everyone from lighting, set decoration, direction and editing was instrumental to the success of those specials as a New Year's Eve viewing tradition seen by millions of Canadians in our coveted 9 p.m. time slot—not just the guy with the microphone. Lesson learned: success is always a team effort.

Although the last place I ever wanted to find myself at fifty-two was fronting a TV series with sketches, *The Ron James Show*, which ran for five years, found me performing them before a live CBC studio audience who sometimes weren't very *alive* at all. Watching a neon applause sign light up in corners of the studio, as if it were tazering the comatose awake, was anathema to everything I believed. Still, you address the mandate of the ones cutting the cheque, put your shoulder to the mule and plow.

The writing room for the series was headed by multi-award winning Garry Campbell, who besides an affable and accommodating nature brought to the table thirty years' experience as a comedy writer in both Canada and LA. Along with me, Gary led a platoon of hard-working foot soldiers whose gregarious *esprit de corps* delivered twenty pages of original stand-up each week for thirteen weeks, as well as four new sketches and an animated cartoon that eventually had to be drawn, cast, voiced and edited. It was more than a blast working with the best sketch actors in Toronto (of whom 95 percent had earned their comedy chops in the Second City) but in order for the public to watch a show, a network had to promote it. Oh, well. Our series wasn't the first and certainly won't be the last to lose that battle. Looking back on several episodes in those earlier seasons and the time spent addressing an executive's vision besides searching for our own creative path, CBC's shunning could easily be construed as a blessing in disguise.

Why they never publicized the show after greenlighting it is a mystery on par with the riddle of the Sphinx. We were bounced around the dial and given seven different time slots for reasons known only to God and whatever inaccessible network mandarin at the top of the food chain was then calling the shots.

Compare that to the warm welcome received at every theatre stretched across Canada (all of them, as I write, rendered hauntingly quiet by COVID-19's curse). Some are shiny new two-thousand-seaters like the brilliant Winspear in Edmonton; there's the thousand-seat Centrepointe in Nepean and the haunted eight-hundred-seat Grand in London. There's a sweet seven-hundred-seater in Belleville, called the Empire, whose renovation by local Royal LePage–owning guitar maestro Mark Rashotte eighteen years ago also had the tertiary impact of revitalizing the downtown core. Although we shot our *West Coast Wild* special at the impressive two-thousand-seat Royal in Victoria, British Columbia, we play the funky thousand-seat McPherson in Chinatown when on tour with Shantero whose audience always turns up with their laughing pants on, just as they do on the other side of the country, in the Confederation Centre in Charlottetown. There's a city that loves laughing! Only 150,000 in the entire province, yet they fill that theatre half a dozen times a year in support of stand-up comedy.

Several turn-of-the-century houses, like the Burton Cummings (formerly the Walker) in Winnipeg, the Capitol in Moncton or the Avon in Stratford, Ontario, carry the spirit of those who once toiled on an unforgiving vaudeville circuit, when luxury was a hotel room without bed bugs. (Apologies to those theatres not mentioned. My editors at Penguin Random House suggested listing them all would sound too "inside baseball" and I'd like to get another book out of them.)

By the time this book hits the stands, you will have seen me in the twenty-fifth anniversary of the Ha! Festival, shot in Halifax in

October 2020, when the largest city in the Atlantic Bubble was proudly COVID-free. So confident were the producers their zone was virus-free, audience members weren't required to wear masks and they were seated onstage at tables just an arm's length away from the performers. I didn't discover that until I stepped onstage. Not going to lie: it came as a shock. I remember thinking, *If there's a hidden carrier in the pack who suddenly starts sneezing, this room will be intubating in bulk!* I'd been assured all necessary precautions had been taken, and I had no reason to doubt them. Knowing the CBC's aversion to bad press, I doubted they'd relish being held responsible for pollinating a room full of people with the plague. It wouldn't have made for a great opening story on *The National*.

Besides, after the loss of more than a year's income, and worse, the ability to actualize my calling, once I heard the first laughs from that room, Ebola-carrying rats and flying Zika monkeys could not have moved me from the mike. This is what I'd so desperately been missing the past seven months: the sight and sounds of people sitting shoulder to shoulder, laughing together.

Though we only got the bare minimum of publicity to let viewers know when the television series was actually *on*, I did get invited to participate in CBC "Culture Days."

The mandate of Culture Days was to sell the CBC to the country and let the people know we were there for them, because I guess no one knew—or something. After serving time in a cold tent with an inadequate heater, meeting people on the lookout for something free to do on a rainy Tuesday afternoon in April, you attended a party where regional executives spent a great deal of time telling a room packed with other executives, headset-wearing publicity people, television actors, newscasters and radio personalities all drinking wine and snorting up a cracker-load of finger food, how great a job they were doing. When we were interviewed on camera, it was our job to sell the season's lineup to whatever members of the public were couch-surfing in the hinterlands and wishing they had HBO.

At one of these functions, I was seated beside an actor with a couple of movies under his belt in the States who was now starring in his own CBC television series. I tried to make small talk, which, given his obvious lack of interest, proved a challenge.

"Congratulations on the series," I said.

What a liar. I didn't watch it. Okay, I did catch it . . . *once*. A scene where a polar bear had wandered into a kitchen. It was the world's only trained polar bear, a species of *ursus* notoriously averse to taking orders, buckets of free seal meat or not. Wild animals change the dynamic of a set because, well, they're *wild*.

Indulge me a tangent here. Years ago, while living in LA, I shot a corporate training film (I know—here he goes again with more stories about the glamour of Hollywood) where we had chimpanzees on set. The use of chimpanzees is, thankfully, not permitted in the Canadian film industry, because our more enlightened nation knows that a chimp is but one chromosome away from being proficient at calculus. We were shooting in some nondescript warehouse in the San Fernando Valley, which, given the post-coital reek of our fetid dressing rooms, had clearly doubled quite recently as a pornographic film set. There was an odoriferous barnyard hum in the air and the floors hadn't been cleaned, to quote the homemade vernacular of my late father, "Since the Year of the White Mice." (When that infamous year actually occurred and the impact it had on civilization are unknown. But rest assured, good reader, scholarly discussions on par with Socratic debate occupied many hours—seated round canoe-trip campfires with pals during times gone, all pleasantly baked on Gaspereau homegrown—trying to figure that one out.)

Howie Mandel's OCD would have been off the charts had he been shining his black light into those crusty corners of our dressing rooms. But Howie would have never been shooting a corporate gig with a baby chimp in a diaper. Why? Well, because Howie had a legitimate career, that's why! And he had a career not only because of his stellar and unimpeachable gift for hosting game shows, talent contests and pulling a surgical glove over his head for his closer but because he had a great agent, and I did not. My agent was a cranky, barrel-bellied little dude called Ernie Dole, whose sad, bare office was a second-floor walk-up on Ventura Boulevard, squeezed between a karate studio and a beauty parlour. Anytime I dropped in for a meeting, I always heard kicks and grunts coming through the walls. I was never sure whether someone was getting their hair done or the shit kicked out of them. Or better yet, getting their hair done *while* getting the shit kicked out of them. (I bet people pay for that in Amsterdam.)

Ernie's dyed-blond perm was complemented by a volcanically red face, while his daily ensemble from tip to tail was always black pants, red shirt, red suit jacket and black tie to match his shiny, pointy, black, zippered dress boots. It wasn't hard to imagine him as a lesser satanic minion, running the Tilt-a-Whirl in a forgotten corner of hell's midway, which, given his office and the status of my acting career, he probably was.

Ernie's star clients were a couple of little people, Billy and Eric. They were actors, but primarily wrestlers; in the waning days of what went by the now politically incorrect moniker, "midget wrestling," where entertaining rednecks who hadn't received this memo still provided them plenty of work on the county fair circuit. Their current claim to fame, however, was having come off a good run as "special business extras" in the Val Kilmer movie *Willow*. (I know, I'm going back. By the way, special business extras are one step above background extras, meaning they get fed and you're not allowed to hit them.)

Billy and Eric carried themselves with a regal indifference to the rest of the world. They entered the room with a three-foot-seven swagger that said, "Get out of my way, or I'll flip you faster than a drugged calf at a dime-store rodeo." As a five-foot-four man who's been the recipient of more than his fair share of short jokes his entire life, I couldn't help but admire their defiant king-of-the-hill confidence. Oh well, at least I was working. Granted, it was with a chimpanzee, but that never hurt Ronald Reagan.

The animal wrangler had a doozy of a claw mark running from under his collar up to a horribly mauled eye socket. Apparently, a surly chimp in his menagerie had taken umbrage with its direction and made a point of protesting by using its six-inch fangs and gnarly jungle strength, which could snap the femur of a forest roaming dik-dik in half without blinking. Little-known fact: a simian's first line of attack is to—wait for it—chew your face off! That's right . . . *chew*! So next time you're thinking about picking up an orangutan for the family because everyone's tired of owning a cat who does nothing but eat, sleep, shit and sit at the window, licking itself comatose all day long, best to stock up on goalie masks first. Just saying.

So, to get back to where I started, a polar bear is a very difficult animal to train, as it's the only bear that will deliberately stalk and kill a human being. Therefore, taking down an extra who's standing beside the craft-services table, staring mindlessly at their own reflection in the whistling aluminum kettle, too self-absorbed by their daily fantasy of one day getting a speaking role to actually hear the bear coming, would be a breeze.

I watched the show for ten minutes, and when nothing happened other than actors screaming and running around in circles (much like they do at award shows), I changed the channel and found a nature show, where biologists happened to have drugged a female (non-thespian) polar bear for radio collaring.

By the way, I bet those scientists have some great blooper reels, like when the bear suddenly jolts awake because they never gave it enough dope, and even though it's sitting glassy-eyed and wobbly in its semi-comatose state as poor ol' Elvis on the toilet, it manages to muster enough energy to grab one of the eggheads by the leg. While he's screaming like a man being eaten alive (which he is), one of the other scientists acts quickly and shoots another loaded dart into the polar bear's ass. Thankfully, the bear is out cold before it can make a meal of his colleague's appendage, which is now being pulled, horribly mangled and bleeding, from the drooling jaws of Nanuk.

If I had been the scientist who was bitten, you can guarantee I'd be getting mileage out of *that* close call for, oh . . . the rest of my life! It would be the moment at one of those boring dinner parties you shouldn't have gone to in the first place, where you hit your tipping point discussing bourgeois inanities and accidentally spill the third Scotch you should never have poured in the first place. That's when "the attack" would be mentioned.

The other guests would cast knowing glances at each other with an eye-roll. Someone would excuse themselves and bolt for the loo.

A whispered "Oh please, not again" would be heard, but I wouldn't notice, because I'd be back on the sea ice of Lancaster Sound with my leg in the mouth of *Ursus maritimus*. In an instant, I'd roll my pant leg up and plop it on the dinner table. The other guests would squirm in their chairs, but I'd be too self-absorbed to notice as I regaled them with the damage left by the creature's seven-inch fangs, when my leg was pulled from its hungry jaws and the meat scraped clean to the tune of 357 stitches, whose hideous purple scar was now shining bright as the silverware no one was using anymore because I had wrecked dinner . . . *again*.

It would be the only topic of conversation on the way home in the car too.

"No one gives a shit that a bear had your leg in its mouth," she'd say. "No one! It's not like you were hunting it, wounded it and it back-tracked the sea ice to stalk you. The poor thing was drugged. It didn't even know it was your leg. The bear was so high, it could have been licking its own balls and wouldn't know it! You bring it up all the time—'Look where the polar bear almost chewed my leg off! Look!' Nobody cares! Why does everything always have to be about *you*?!"

And that's when I would mumble, "It couldn't lick its own balls. It was a feeee-male." Then I'd shut up and drift back to that day on the ice floes of Lancaster Sound when I'd never felt more alive.

Anyway, back to the original gist of the story.

"Thank you," the lead actor said, as sincerely as someone who fakes emotion for a living can. I could tell by his stone-cold stare that he was already bored shitless with me.

"You sure are getting lots of publicity. They are really behind your show," I said, hoping he'd say my show was great.

"Yes, they are treating us like gold. I couldn't ask for more."

I could ask for way *more,* I thought. Like a solid time-slot, for Christ's sake. Secretly, I was more jealous that buddy got to work with a man-eating polar bear. I worked with a baby chimp wearing a diaper. Comedians get different perks.

So, as I've done my entire life, I made a joke.

"Actually, CBC publicity is investing more time in our promotional campaign by organizing a Girl Guide cookie drive on our behalf, and we get to keep the money they make selling the chocolate ones."

Not a great joke, but a joke, nonetheless. It was delivered *as* a joke, with a cynical tone honed over forty years spent doing just that but it did not find purchase. It hit the brick wall behind his eyes and died instantly as he stared at me with the doleful expression of a child who's seen his first dandelion seeds fly to the wind.

"The Girl Guides are donating money earned selling cookies to your show? That's wonderful! Just wonderful!"

How do you respond to that? You don't. You shut up, because you know you've fallen into a valley of the comedically clueless.

Someone walked by our table and asked if I was doing another comedy special and I replied, "No. I have a series now" but they made a face like I was joking and kept going. With interest piqued, the star said he and his Hollywood pals wanted to start doing some stand-up. "You know," he said offhandedly with that carefree nonchalance of the uninitiated, "just working some stuff out at the clubs. Any suggestions?"

For a fleeting second, I thought about enlightening the actor, giving him exactly the "suggestions" he was looking for—insights that might help him in the new-found "hobby" that he and his posse of confident young LA actor bros would soon be dabbling in. After all, they were just looking to "work some stuff out." The inference was clear. It's always the same. A familiar, patronizing curiosity. Everyone thinks it's easy. They always do. After all, how hard can it be? You just walk onstage, stand in front of a microphone and start saying the same stuff that made your friends laugh. The only difference is, you're *onstage* . . . in front of an audience. But that *is* the difference! *The* difference, in fact. Stand-up is an exponential leap from real life to the high wire. It's why everyone *doesn't* do it. Stand-up comedy is the kind of job that 99 percent of the world would run from faster than the undead at daybreak.

Only those of us who have been bloodied in battle know. We remember all too well that baptism of fire called "amateur night." The step you took from behind the curtain to the stage might as well have been into the void of empty space, with you untethered from the mother ship. You have never, *ever* felt more alone. Your heart is trying to escape from your chest and bolt for home. Why did you ever come here?! Rivers of perspiration flood the palms of your hands as your mouth opens to speak. Your tongue conspires. It will not work. You have no spit. Your tongue is stuck to the roof of your mouth with the adherence of a tenacious mollusc to a government pier. *Open your mouth, open your mouth*, your brain says, knowing full well survival depends on it. It opens, but your mind goes blank. You can't remember your act! You had it memorized and everything! You see nothing but black beyond that terrible solo spot that's drilling a hole in your forehead while the coiled contempt of the audience for the comedian you have the audacity to believe you are expresses itself as a deafening silence. Your joke lands dead-sloth flat at your feet as your soul slides off the stage into the cigarette-butt-strewn street, while the quiet of the room screams, *"Get off!"*

Then, the next amateur night, bruised but not beaten, you try again—but they laugh this time. And that's enough to keep you coming back, until you have an act that's good enough to warrant a pauper's payday that will hopefully get you farther on up the road.

Instead, I told the movie star it's best to stick with what works. And I went to get some finger food.

Chapter Seven
PIT STOPS

On *The Ron James Show*, there was a regular two-minute travelogue called "Road Odes," where we tried to capture a quirky sense of the personalities of towns and cities across the country, much as my earlier specials did. It didn't work. CBC's *Still Standing* succeeds far better in this regard, where a comedian travels to rural corners of Canada, interviewing small-town locals in the first half of the show while gleaning material about their town for the stand-up comedy set he'll later perform for an appreciative audience in town.

Something happens when you're about to put non-professionals on camera. Soon as they hear the word *action*, things get weird. The gregarious old gentleman who, moments before had been full of charming anecdotes about the history of the town in which you're shooting, suddenly goes stone-cold quiet while others practically turn into the singing frog from the *Merrie Melodies* cartoons, but unlike that frog, they never shut up. When the crew and cameras were gone, I found people were far less intimidated. People felt safe to be themselves and some shared stories of substance that, from my experiences, I've come to believe are better served by the written word.

We were on a shoot in St. Andrews, New Brunswick for a couple of days when I took a walk around town. Sitting on a peninsula jutting into Passamaquoddy Bay, St. Andrews-by-the-Sea is one of those charming Maritime towns so close to America, you can practically reach out and grab a mittful off their money tree—which, by the looks of the stately nineteenth-century mansions round town, many wealthy families once did. Founded in 1783 by affluent United Empire Loyalists who were exiled after siding with Britain in the Revolutionary War, St. Andrew's well-preserved historic architecture is so evocative of another era, you can almost hear the ghosts of Irish cholera victims coughing up a lung in the local coffee shops.

Sitting on a hill, dominating the town, is the very majestic and supposedly haunted Algonquin Hotel. It's rumoured that after spending summer vacations here as a kid, Stephen King used this imposing old matron as his inspiration for the Overlook Hotel when he wrote *The Shining*. In its turn-of-the-century heyday, the hotel catered to filthy-rich industrialists like railroad magnate William Cornelius Van Horne, who summered in this playground of the privileged when he wasn't in the Rockies, barking demands at Chinese labourers forced to hang half-naked from a cliff face in straw baskets filled with dynamite. St. Andrews catered to the anointed of the Gilded Age, where wealthy white fat cats like Cornelius would take in the salt air, play croquet, eat lobsters, get drunk and wife-swap.

That's a lie. I think Cornelius was allergic to lobster.

A funky gallery sits at the end of the main drag, where genteel shops reeking of lavender potpourri and all selling the same thing are packed with swag-happy tourists looking for something more to bring home from their Bay of Fundy trip than the chunk of lobster meat stuck in their annoying molar's food trap, that nothing short of being shot in the mouth with a water cannon will remove.

The gallery is different than those craft shops. For one thing, it doesn't look like an anal-retentive Martha Stewart SWAT team had hit it overnight, surgically cramming placemats, scented candles, lighthouses and bottles of jam in every spare corner. This place is a riot of disorganization, bursting at the seams with authentic relics of Canadiana: exquisitely hand-carved wooden boats, Mi'kmaq-made snowshoes from the 1870s, walking sticks, wooden carvings of forest animals, and at every turn are paintings: kaleidoscopically coloured folk art canvases of owls, caribou, raven, deer, moose and bear, travelling the myth-rich dreamscape world of shape-shifters.

"Just putting these images on canvas is how I make sense of the world," the proprietor says. His name is Brian, and he's a David Crosby look-alike who's been running the gallery for ten years or more.

I tell him I feel the same way about stand-up. In a world that's increasingly fractured and polarized, getting a thousand people from different walks of life on the same page for two hours lets me know we're not so different from each other after all.

The place is authentic, and I say as much, adding, "What's here is exactly what *isn't* sitting in the stores on Main Street. That's the kind of stuff you'd give a grandmother."

"Much appreciated. I try to keep it real here," he says. "A world traveller came into my shop a few years back and asked what the hell is going on in the stores uptown. 'I want to buy something made in St. Andrews,' he said. 'I don't want to go home with a tiger lamp made in Indonesia!'"

Brian is clearly obsessed with bears, because their likenesses are everywhere in his shop. Carved Indigenous bear masks of West Coast origin, carved local figurines and unique fetishes from Bavaria. Those figurines are synonymous with German folklore, where a frequent running theme involves a bear dropping by a woodsman's humble abode in human disguise on a snowy night in search of shelter and a feed of strudel. If refused, he eats the woodsman, trashes the cabin then poops in the fireplace. (It's not my joke. German folklore is notoriously scatological.) "Bears won't suffer a lack of hospitality" is the moral there, I guess.

"Mom told me that as a little kid, I dreamt of bears all the time," he confesses, "and woke yelling about them. Thing is, since I started painting, I don't dream of them anymore. Bears were my messengers and they helped release my inner voice.

"The inner voice," he emphasizes, "is what it's all about. It's about trusting yourself. It doesn't come from your head, either, but your heart."

Strangely enough, I'd just finished listening to George Carlin's autobiography on CD, posthumously read by his brother. Carlin talked about finding his authentic voice, and how once he did, he stopped worrying what people thought about what he said, and he just said what he thought. He also stopped worrying about getting laughs, apparently, because when I saw him onstage in Vegas in front of 2,500 people six years before he died, he never got a single one during a ninety-minute set and never really cared to. Seriously, not one laugh. That takes guts. If I didn't hear belly laughs every thirty seconds from the audience, I'd commit hara-kiri as a closer.

"Dad was a peacekeeper who wore the blue helmet. Proudly, too. It's why I keep it on my desk. Good energy. Good karma." Although it seems incongruous among the other historic relics and paintings on display, its presence is soothing, reminding me of Canada's valued contribution to the world before America's imperial march to forever war after 9/11 altered the equation, and the preservation of peace took a back seat to the perpetuation of conflict.

He continued: "We were stationed in Lahr, Germany, not far from the Black Forest, and we'd vacation there. Every little inn has its own bear effigy at the front desk. The Germans revere bears."

Knowing full well I'm invoking Godwin's Law, which postulates that online conversations reach their nadir as soon as someone mentions Hitler, I go for it all the same.

"Too bad the Germans switched their reverence from bears to buddy with the odd little moustache back in the 1930s," I say. "It could have saved them and the rest of the planet a world of hurt."

"Funny you'd bring up Hitler," he says.

"If you knew me, not so much," I say, laughing. "My daughters used to rib me mercilessly about my choice in reading material. 'Hey Dad, we see you've bought a new book, and it's not about the Battle of Stalingrad. Is everything okay?'"

"Do you believe that energy travels in things?"

I guarantee you this is not a conversation being had in the craft stores up the road.

"I suppose . . ."

"There's a friend of mine in town who had a terrible year. Her husband passed away suddenly, and soon after that she got in a very bad car accident. Nothing was working out, so I told her to get rid of a painting she had. Her father had been at the Nuremberg Trials in 1946. I'm not sure what he did there, but he came back with one of Hitler's paintings. She kept it in a drawer. I saw it once, but I wouldn't touch the thing. It was of a factory: dark, mean, cold and depressing. What stayed with me were the belching smokestacks."

"It gave off a terrible vibe," says Brian. "Anyway, her daughter came home one day and mentioned I'd remarked about the painting. 'Mom. I think about that thing you've got in the drawer and how it should be sent away or destroyed.' So, that's what she did. She sent it off to the Canadian War Museum. As far as I know, it's buried in the vaults, where it belongs. Life has gotten better for her ever since."

Despite the claustrophobic heat of his small gallery, grape-sized goosebumps rise on my arms. Lesson learned: never buy any sketch at a lawn sale that might have been drawn by Hitler.

You have to feel bad for the Germans, though. Picking two world wars like that, and even though it's been seventy-five years since the end of the second one, and despite their enlightened environmental ways that set an example for the rest of the world, they still take serious flak for the egregious sins of their grandfathers. Maybe that's why they have an inordinate predisposition to saunter nude on every beach in the tropics? Not to stereotype an entire nation as unapologetic nudists, but you can always count on seeing more than a few on any tropical beach, splayed on the sand like drying codfish in the sun as if to declare, "We no longer have anything to hide!"

Some like the fog, too, and swear by its healing properties. In fact, there's a white elephant of an abandoned hotel on the Aspotogan Peninsula, along the South Shore of Nova Scotia, that was built specifically to attract those German tourists who believe in the benefits of walking naked in the fog. The place went bankrupt, though, because the fog was so thick, they couldn't find it. (By the way, while vacationing in Nova Scotia, if you should chance to see somebody walking naked toward you through the fog . . . don't say hello in German . . . run!)

We speak of bears again, and their haunting presence in the imagination of man. I tell of the first grizzly I saw walking a Yukon side road at dusk. Watching that monarch of the wild move with self-assurance into the enveloping night lent a predatory power to its measured stride that made me really glad I was in a truck.

I'd been up in Whitehorse for a couple of shows and got the invite from local businessman Craig Hougen to join him and a couple of pilot pals for a day of fishing in Dry Bay, Alaska. Two hours before dawn, we drove from Whitehorse headed for the small air strip in Kluane National Park, where we'd follow the Tatshenshini glacier down to the sea. Once in Alaska, I spent a day of uncontested bliss at the foot of the St. Elias Range, standing waist-deep in waders under a sky of cobalt blue pulling twenty-pound chinook from the Pacific Ocean on ten-pound test. It was the best day of fishing I'd ever had in my life. With the sun sinking behind us at the close of the day, our small plane taxied off a frugal strip of grass that laughably passed as a runway and lifted us above the alluvial plain of delta for the flight back to Kluane.

As we climbed the crest of a rolling green hill, my eye caught an object out the window. I remember thinking, *That's a weird place for somebody to sit and watch the sun go down.* It wasn't a somebody though, but a monstrous bear reclining comfortably on the hill with arms crossed—pardon me . . . *paws* crossed—looking every inch a man on the porch of his cottage.

"That sight never left me," I tell Brian. "The only thing missing was a pipe in its mouth and a cold brew in its paw. The bear just looked *so* human."

"That's because they practically *are*," says Brian. "The Natives knew it, too. In fact, the Tlingit tribe of the Yukon thought bears were *half* human. It's why they never ate them."

"I used to dream of bears all the time before I started stand-up," I tell him. "I'd be taking a walk in the forest along a gentle path, when this bear would suddenly show up, blocking my way. It chased me up a tree, but as I continued to climb, it climbed, too, pushing me ever farther out on the limb. Soon as I started stand-up, the dreams stopped."

"Because you found your inner voice," he says.

"But now I dream I'm standing naked onstage in front of an empty room, delivering lines that don't make sense into a microphone that doesn't work."

"You might want to ask a professional about that," he said. "I'm just a painter."

Leaving with paintings of an owl, a caribou and a carved reclining bear holding a metal bowl on its belly that may or may not have sat on the mantle at Berchtesgaden, I hope I'm carrying good karma into the world. I'm sure whoever bought the tiger lamp made in Indonesia at the Main Street store has never had that thought cross their mind.

Easily six-foot-four, almost toothless, with white sideburns, a goatee, an affable charm and an accent closer to Maine than the Maritimes, the man townsfolk called Ol' Ben was seventy-four years old then and a keeper of memories. Seated on a bench in front of the town hall, he beamed when I said hello, and it wasn't long before the sage started talking.

Pointing at a busy boardwalk, Ol' Ben says, "We'd play on that beach right there all day long when we was kids—dig periwinkles, clams and have a boil. Now all the kids are doing is gettin' in shit! Smoke in their mouth, pint in their pocket and a head full of wacky tabacky. We were too busy to get in trouble.

"During the war, the boats would come in. All those navy ships. One day, I must've been about eight years old, the corvette *St. Stephen* towed in a captured German U-boat! The captain gave my buddies and me a tour." He points, eyes shining. "Yis, sir. Right down the'ah where all dem to'rists is. Yis. I'll nevva forgit it.

"People tells me my memory is good. I say I can't remembah what happened yistaday, but I sure can tell ya what this town was like sixty-five years ago!

"I used to work at the lobstah plant. All kinds of fish was in the hahba back then. Flounda. Halibut sometimes, too, would be there, and always lots of herring, but all the herring's gone now. Caught in weirs by all those monstah ships. Only mackerel come in now.

"I'll tell you a story, God's honest truth. Fellah used to sit ova' the'ah by the post office when two people from Nebraska showed up. Nevah seen the ocean befowa. Want to bring some home in a glass jar. Ol' Jim tells 'em, "Well, if you is, you best be only filling yo' jar halfway full o' water, 'cause when the tide rises, that water's gonna rise up and ovaflow de top of 'er!" And as true as I'm sittin' here, those people from Nebraska believed him!

"God knows how long that half-full jar with Bay of Fundy water sat on their kitchen shelf with them waiting for it to ovaflow. God knows."

If predictions are on target, our planet's turbocharged run to climatic oblivion will soon make a February morning in Canada humid as high noon in the Jurassic period. Therefore, it could be argued that winter no longer defines our national character as it once did. I beg to differ. Why? Because there's Winnipeg. Winter *owns* that city! This is the place where *thoughts* freeze. It's a teeth-splitting, will-killing cold that comes flying with a fury across the treeless flatlands, straight from the lair of a Norse demon there weren't enough virgins in the Viking village to satisfy. Winter is not just a noun in Winnipeg, it's a station of the Cross, where wind-worn survivors suffer the elements with a masochist's conviction.

And they built a city there! What were they thinking? Six immigrants bound for Calgary got off the train for a smoke, lost three fingers in five minutes to frostbite, and said, "If it's colder than this farther west, to hell with that. I'm staying!"

Then there was God's second curse: spring! What were the early settlers thinking when they set up shop smack dab in the middle of a Red River flood plain? If the river wasn't spilling biblical levels of water over its banks, its perfect breeding grounds were launching airborne armadas of blood-sucking mosquitoes who, to this *day*, hold 'Peggers hostage for weeks on end every single summer. And after finally getting warm, the locals start praying for the winter cold to come again and kill the bugs, before the malathion that the city sprays on the bugs kills *them*!

The popular vernacular used to describe the spraying is "fogging." Sounds less carcinogenic, I guess. In the Maritimes, "foggy" means you can't see the beach. In Winnipeg, it means "Keep the kids indoors!"

Some people don't mind the malathion, but the positive outlook of the 'Pegger I was talking to was very disconcerting.

"Sure, I may have lost all body hair and there's a tumour on my spleen the size of an eggplant," he seemed to brag, "but it's the first night I've been able to sit outside on the porch since May."

Then, more power to you, brother!

Winnipeg exists for those of us who never caught lightning in a bottle or won a prize in a Cracker Jack box. Winnipeg is the big-boned girl who was always the bridesmaid but never the bride.

Ultimately, Winnipeg is the same as most of us: forced to do the best you could, when you could, with what you were given. Forced to fix your eyes to the horizon, grit your teeth in the face of the gale, put one foot in front of the other and just . . . keep . . . going. Because when you're this far down the road, it takes more effort to look back than move forward. (Besides, the blizzard has probably covered your tracks and the wolves'll get you anyway!)

Don't be thinking you'll be getting home from Manitoba frostbite-free either, just because you dropped top dollar for that double-fleece-lined Patagonia ski toque. You'd best be sporting a lid peeled from the back of a fur-bearing creature of the boreal forest. Fur is what you want on your noggin there. Sure, that fox hat with the legs and tail still on it might get some radical anti-vivisectionist chucking a bucket of pig's blood in your face on the streets of Manhattan, but it will keep Jack Frost from wearing your ears as trophies in the 'Peg. (And you won't have a pair of weird-looking, mummified black prunes sticking out of your head as topics of conversation. Just sayin'.)

Life has always been hard there, let alone getting there. Canada never had legions of prairie schooners crossing the western frontier, because they couldn't get through the curtain of spruce forest round Lake Superior. In fact, way back in 1860, they tried to build a wagon road from Thunder Bay to Winnipeg, but only got forty kilometres built in eleven years. Anyone who has ever braved that section of the TCH knows they're still working on it!

In the days I played Rumor's Comedy Club, they'd put us up at the Fort Garry Hotel, just up the street from the Forks, a beautiful park of pathways where the historic Red and Assiniboine Rivers meet smack dab in the continent's middle. One typically bright and sunny prairie winter afternoon, with the temperature sitting at a cozy minus-a-million, I saw an old lady feeding the squirrels and asked, "Do you feed them every day, madam?" To which she replied, "No. Only when it's warm."

Besides Toronto's Laugh Resort, Rumor's at the time was the best-run independent comedy club in the country. In fact, it was the *only* other one. For years, the management had been notorious for favouring American comedians, but when most of them got famous and too expensive to book, the club started hiring us. A paid flight out, paid hotel room, cab to and from the club, and once you were there, all the free burgers, fries and chicken wings your arteries could handle. Life in the fast lane.

Winnipeg Comedy Festival founder Lara Rae regularly headlined the club, whose vision of thematically structured stand-up performances, first televised in 2002, has mushroomed into CBC's highest-rated comedy festival series. Another stalwart player in the Winnipeg comedy scene is Big Daddy Tazz (the Bi-Polar Buddha), whose annual gala benefit performance at the iconic Pantages Theatre and year-round, non-stop dedication to the cause has raised thousands of dollars for mental health. There's a generosity of spirit that permeates the comedy community in that town, where getting paid will always take a back seat to supporting those in need.

Unlike Toronto and Vancouver, whose attentions are forever focused southward when it comes to entertainment, the media in the 'Peg really support their own. The *Winnipeg Free Press* entertainment editor, Brad Oswald, has diligently covered club, theatre and festival appearances for the past twenty-five years, while Geoff Currier at CJOB, and broadcasters at other private stations and at local CBC radio, don't shy away from vigorous promotion, either. The welcome mat Winnipeg rolls out makes it a pit stop in a place that always lets you know you're wanted.

As I pulled my luggage through a three-foot snowdrift to get backstage in Cornwall, Ontario, my mind drifted back to Los Angeles and its world of endless summer another lifetime ago. We lived there in a townhouse community at 6146 Coral Pink Circle. *Coral Pink Circle.* Sounds like something you'd catch swimming in the shallow end of a public pool that hadn't been treated with chlorine. The community sat on a hillside that used to be an orange grove, but was no longer because developers tore it down to make room for people like us. When I found that out, the convenient environmentalist in me got all stirred up—"That's not right! We ought to do something about that!" But then we went shopping at Target, bought three T-shirts and a pair of pants for seven bucks, and the feeling went away.

In California, the consumer was king. I used to buy forty ounces of Captain Morgan dark rum for $9.95 at a place called the Liquor Barn. *The Liquor Barn.* A theme park to booze . . . and a temple of homage for any Maritimer.

"What're you doing today, Ron?"

"Nothing at all. Just perpetuating a regional stereotype and dancing on down to the Liquor Barn is all! 'Oh, the Liquor Barn. The Liquor Barn. We're all going to the Liquor, Liquor Barn!'"

There were deals to be had around every corner, and the intoxicating lure of the Golden State's bounty was never more apparent than when Maritimers came to visit. I lost my dad for days on end in the tool department at Sears. Every time he went to the mall, he brought home a new wrench.

"Have a gander at that, Ronnie b'y. Two feet of tungsten-steel, chrome-wrapped wrench. A buck ninety-five. Steel, b'y. *Steel!* You don't get that at Canadian Tire."

"No, Dad, you don't. But you *do* get fake money that's good for trips to the Third World."

(I gained first-hand knowledge of the versatility of the now-defunct Canadian Tire "money" when, during a 1974 high school trip to Spain, our group crossed the Straits of Gibraltar for a day trip to Morocco. At a leather store in the ancient casbah, where one-eyed Arabs stood looking medieval with falcons on their shoulders and street urchins tried to sell our teachers hash, several of us bought leather jackets with that "currency." I know . . . that's just wrong. Karma had the last laugh, though, because back in Spain, forty-eight hours later, those smooth leather jackets began to . . . grow hair. That's correct, hair. To this day, somewhere in my eighty-eight-year-old mother's basement, there's a plastic-wrapped, orange-coloured leather coat with a simian-like strip of fur running down its back. Apparently, the tanning process for soaking leather in North Africa involves camel urine, whose odoriferous properties love to secrete in the rain. I did mention I'm from Halifax. It can be very wet there, so wearing a semi-hairy leather jacket that smelled of camel whiz to a high school dance worked wonders in guaranteeing you'd be sitting out the last waltz.)

And even when you're doing what you love, what you know you were *born* to do, the road still gets old. A nomad's calling, this. Forever on the move. A life built one gig at a time. Nothing comes for free. The road takes no prisoners, and comedy doesn't suffer fools. When I was getting standing ovations, my wife was getting loads of laundry alone at home. Not a lot of laughs at her end. Plays and dance recitals missed. Birthday wishes sent long distance. Arguments left hanging when there were planes to catch. Not what she signed up for.

The road lingers long after you've pulled into your driveway, too. It takes a week to decompress. You're nocturnal. Fidgety. Still on your own time with your system still in perpetual motion, racing from gig to gig; still tuned to the driving pulse and pace of the tour. This is a perfect calling for those who can't sit still. (The fact I got this book finished is a miracle in itself!) Shows line up like dominoes, one after another. On the night of a performance, new bits written that day slide shotgun shell–smooth into the chamber and hit the mark. Laughs explode like clay pigeons picked out of the air. The adrenalin rush of it all . . . you can finally do something right! You've finally found something you don't suck at! Is it a blessing or a curse?

The time I went fishing after the Whitehorse gig was the first of several visits to that magical corner of Canada that has called me back half a dozen times since. People up there tell of the Yukon's supernatural pull. "If you come here once, you'll come here again."

A few winters back, I hung out for a couple days in a cabin at Tagish Lake. A woman who ran a store in town named Nancy Huston offered it to me. She'd seen the show the night before and it was her way of saying thanks. People are like that up there.

It had been unseasonably mild that January, but the day I went for a walk in the woods was after a flash freeze had hit and turned the slush to stone. Following wolf tracks in a light dusting of snow up a mountainside, communing with nothing but my breath and heart-beat, a few hours in, I noticed grizzly bear tracks—frozen now, but made in the slush but a day before. Perhaps it had felt a rumbling in its tummy and risen from winter slumber with the warmer weather in search of a snack? Omnivore or not, should we cross paths its Snickers bar most certainly would be me!

I turned on my heel and made a beeline for the road. Remembering I'd been forgetting to make noise so the animals will hear you—because if they don't, and you surprise the wrong ones, they *will* eat you—I broke into a song. A rousing rendition of "Battle Hymn of the Republic" at the top of my lungs, actually. (And because I'm Canadian, I knew all twenty-seven verses.) Racing to my car, out of breath and giddy with relief to be alive and not dragged semi-conscious and bleeding to a bruin's cave, I drove back to the cabin, slept, and woke ready for my drive to Whitehorse, where I'd catch my plane back home.

It was one of those winter mornings you only get in Canada's North. The constellation of Orion was sitting so clear on the horizon, his sword looked sharp enough to cut me. Outside the town of Carcross, I saw a lone figure standing beside the road with a thumb out . . . hitchhiking. It was 6:30 a.m. during a minus-35 Yukon dawn.

Soon as I passed, I stopped the car and thought, *If it's a serial killer, it's going to take them an hour and a half to get the butcher knife out from beneath the layers of Gore-Tex.* So, I backed up and opened the passenger-side door. A weathered face belonging to an elder Indigenous woman poked its way into my car. She pulled her hood back and smiled, saying, "Whoa. Good vibes in here, eh?"

She told me her name was Helen and she was on her way to Sunday church service at the Salvation Army in Whitehorse. I pulled away and we started talking.

"What are you doing way up here?" she asked.

"I was working in Whitehorse but had a few days off, so I hung out at a cabin in Tagish Lake and went hiking in the woods."

She sat straight up in her seat and looked at me in disbelief.

"By yourself?"

"Sure."

"Whoa," she warned. "God was watching out for you."

"Why?"

"The mild weather has the bears confused," she explained. "They're coming out of hibernation early and they're hungry. One of them is eating the dogs down by the lake and taking everything but the head."

Remembering the story from Tlingit folklore of a shape-shifting she-bear who kills and then eats her suitor, I found myself thinking, *I hope my passenger isn't one of those; otherwise, she's going to really trash this rental car.*

I said, "Oh, no worries. I was singing 'Battle Hymn of the Republic' really loud, and my voice is so out of tune, every wolf or bear within 120 kilometres would have had their paws over their ears."

Her hands went up in the air, and she howled with laughter.

"Oh, my goodness," she said, smiling. "You should be a comedian."

Chapter Eight
MAGNETIC NORTH

Watching the Yellowknife airport empty of passengers as we waited for the ride from our outfitter that never came, I found myself second-guessing the decision to take my fifteen-year-old daughter kayaking to the Northwest Territories. I remember thinking, *If this tour operator has forgotten to pick us up here in a truck, what's to stop him from forgetting to pick us up in a bush plane on the tundra when the trip is over?* Once the Chef Boyardee ravioli ran out, I'd be trying to feed us by recalling the rabbit-snaring skills my father saw as elemental to survival.

During his high-school days in the early 1950s, he'd snare them in the winter on the outskirts of Halifax, then sell them by the pair for a buck fifty to a barber in the city. Why a barber bought them I haven't a clue, but every time I heard that story I visualized a satisfied customer, sporting a new trim, sauntering out the door swinging a pair of dead rabbits by the feet.

"Jesus, that was big money back then, Ronnie!" he'd say. He went on to advise me, "If you know how to snare a rabbit, you'll never go hungry."

Thankfully, once I moved to Toronto in 1980, I got all the food I ever needed from the same place most people do: the grocery store. Besides, once I landed an agent in '82, expertise in rabbit snaring was not a necessity in my line of work. An actor would need skills appropriate for . . . well . . . *acting*, and since I came from a Second City background, where we learned to think on our feet, deliver a punchline and take direction, that skill set more often than not involved auditioning for television commercials. Booking one of those kept the bills at bay for at least awhile, because as everyone in the legions of the self-employed knows, just because the pot is laden with lard today, don't get too cocky, because you could be licking it tomorrow.

Still, work was work. Plus, it garnered peculiar stares of recognition from strangers trying to figure out where they knew you from, so you kind of *felt* like you were in show business. In truth, doing commercials put you one step away from being an organ grinder's monkey.

The audition process involved sitting in a casting room with a dozen other hungry actors, trying to pump life into thirty seconds' worth of inane script some coked-out copywriter from Ogilvy and Mather had written during a molar-grinding 3 a.m. pique of creative genius. When the casting agent called your name, you entered a bare room and stood thirty feet away from several uninterested-looking people seated at a long table covered in fruit plates, half-eaten croissants and Styrofoam coffee cups.

One was a producer from the production house charged with budgeting the commercial. Another was somebody behind a video camera hired to film you, so they could review the auditions afterwards. Another was the director. Also sitting amongst them was the person who had the final say, the client: a pinched and buttoned-down corporate suit, looking about as comfortable as a duck on skates. They were fawned over by a shamelessly sycophantic advertising executive, who hung on their every comment with the kind of desperate attention one would give an oncologist's biopsy report.

Every now and then, you'd get a director who empathized with the pressure an actor was under in trying to pump life into five lines about toothpaste at 9 a.m. while standing before a row of stone-cold expressions that said, "I'd rather be home, waxing my Mercedes."

Several commercial directors took a different tack. Matthew Vibert was one of them. He'd honed his chops as a first assistant director on the five-continent cinematic adventure *Quest for Fire*, as well as dozens of other feature films before he started directing commercials. It may seem insignificant to the uninitiated, but simply by getting up from his chair, crossing the floor, shaking your hand and discussing in non-condescending, professionally relatable terms what kind of performance the clients were looking for, the man instinctively equalized the status levels in the room. Making that extra effort—which many of his profession did not—let you know you mattered. By that one simple move, suddenly those strangers staring at you from behind the table weren't so intimidating anymore. It made a process that, for many just looking to make rent, was an exercise in desperation seem not so bad at all. Every actor in the waiting room afterwards said as much, too. Even if they knew they weren't going to book that ad in a million years, at least they left feeling less of a monkey than when they walked in.

Given that this was the audience an actor had to win over to land the "spot," it was all the more remarkable when you did. If it weren't for booking commercials when I was starting out, there's a good chance I would have been roaming Toronto's urban greenbelt, snaring rabbits for supper as Dad had suggested.

The owner of the eco-lodge that was a three-hour bush plane flight north of Yellowknife went by the name of Tundra Tom. That moniker should have been a dead giveaway that weird energy was afoot, but who was I to question a handle like that? His name had a reassuring alliterative ring that clearly validated him as a stalwart true son of the North. Tundra Tom. That's a cartoon I would have been glued to the tube watching in grade six! Each episode would find Tundra having daring adventures all over the North, accompanied by his trusty Inuit sidekick, Ulu (also deadly with one), who always showed up in the nick of time to save Tundra from certain death at the hands of Colombian drug cartel hit men. (Okay, the last part needs work. Perhaps a B story involving Wanda! The Seal with a Human Brain. No? Anyone?)

Websites were still in their infancy when I booked the trip, and Tundra Tom's was very impressive. Besides having endorsements from every major nature photographer in the business, there was a photo of Tundra himself. It showed a middle-aged man whose wide, welcoming smile and ruddy complexion exuded character carved by the elements, while atop his leonine skull sat a weathered and very well broken-in Tilley hat. The thing looked as if it had once passed through the digestive tract of a barren ground grizzly and then been chewed for sustenance by subterranean voles in nocturnal warrens all winter long. Casually leaning on the wing of a bush plane, Tundra Tom looked, if nothing else, authentic.

As for the term *eco-lodge*, I now realize the name had been used with a flippant disregard for accuracy. I'm not sure what standards an outfitter's lodge had to meet in order to warrant the label *eco*, but if it meant running a rudimentary rat nest of plastic pipes around the property from the lake for water, a scattering of empty oil drums and discarded plane parts, Quonset huts sinking sideways into the melting permafrost, a menu whose major food group was canned peas, and a staff of semi-feral wanderers Tundra Tom had found panhandling on the streets in Yellowknife dressed in shirts held together by safety pins that weren't already sticking out of their face, then I guess *eco-lodge* was spot on.

The most appealing aspect of Tundra Tom's website was this: the lodge sat on the migratory route of what was then the 325,000-strong Beverly caribou herd. And where there are caribou, there are wolves . . . and wolves are cool.

The symbiotic dance of survival between *Canis lupus* and its prey had held my imagination since Farley Mowat's classic *Never Cry Wolf* was required reading in public school. Farley was, and still is (for my money, at least) the author who, more than any other, sired my generation's imagination of Canada's North. When my tours took me to the storybook village of Port Hope, nestled along the Ganaraska River in southern Ontario, I would visit with him and his wife, Claire. Their cozy cottage was straight out of Hobbiton and filled with memorabilia from a life fully realized. I was thrilled when Farley—eighty-eight years of age at the time of my visit, with nothing but a frugal collection of wispy hair now left of his once trademark bushy beard—lived up to his reputation as that cantankerous raconteur of legend, and cracked a bottle of London Dock well before noon. I remember thinking, *Farley's what Yoda would be like if he enjoyed a drink of rum!*

After lunch with this bona fide veteran of the bloody Battle of Ortona and survivor of a character assassination at the hands of *Saturday Night* magazine in the 1980s, we stood in his living room, musing.

"Well, there it is," he said, nodding. "A lifetime." We were looking at a wall of shelves running from floor to ceiling, containing the forty-eight books he'd written, all with matching copies in what appeared to be every language except the dialect of the Kalahari Bushmen. Clearly, Farley's love of the North had resonated with readers the wide world over. That he never let the truth get in the way of a good story, as Farley was fond of saying, didn't seem to cripple his popularity.

We'd not be standing with our knapsacks in the Yellowknife airport, looking forlorn and stunned, had we taken an easier vacation and gone to say, Disneyland. When we lived in Los Angeles, the very child I was now taking kayaking happened to be addicted to the Disney Channel. Trust me, the living room can feel like a small world after all when that song plays constantly. It was her religion. I'd later joke that if you wanted your child to believe in Jesus, all you had to do was slap a set of mouse ears on the Saviour's head. Then I'd launch into the *Mickey Mouse Club* theme song, only with different lyrics:

"*Who's the Son of God who was born in Galilee?*
J-E-S U-S-C H-R-I-S-T.
Jesus Christ! Jesus Christ! He cured a leper rotting on the road!"

It's clear I don't share the reverence for the Disney fantasy that the truly devoted do—those who gain fulfilment watching their children's eyes sparkle with unmitigated joy as legions of minimum-wage employees perpetuate the myth of the "Happiest Place on Earth" by toiling in the trenches of Mousewitz eight hours a day, dressed as Donald, Mickey, Goofy, Minnie or Fuckface Magoo. (I stand corrected. There is no such character as Fuckface Magoo, although if there were, he'd be my favourite.)

Speaking of Disneyland, I was once seated in a Jasper, Alberta, café, killing a free day on tour listening to a local hiking guide tell bear stories. If you want wild, it's not Banff you go to, with its tour-bus traffic jams, kitty-corner Starbucks and strip of stores selling everything from skis to thirty-million-year-old fossilized crocodile coprolites (which I bought); it's the Rocky Mountain town of Jasper, a four-hour drive north from Edmonton.

The guide was telling me how he took a family of four from Anaheim, California, on a hike behind the impressive Jasper Park Lodge one beautiful spring morning in June. They were forty-five minutes into their stroll along a forest path that opened to a meadow where a herd of elk and their newborn calves were grazing, birds singing and bees buzzing. Disney animators could not have sketched a more bucolic tableau had they placed a knock-kneed Bambi in that meadow, chatting to Thumper himself.

Instead of a cartoon, though, these visitors who lived but a stone's throw from the Magic Kingdom got a far closer look at the natural world than they'd bargained for. As they continued quietly along the path that skirted the meadow, minding not to spook the herd, the parents remarked to their ten- and twelve-year-olds how this was the real thing and not some animatronic creation of Disney "Imagineers." In fact, some calves had just slipped fresh from their mammalian yolk sac to solid ground but minutes before, and, still funky with goo, had begun taking their first wobbly steps in the big wide world.

Unbeknownst to them and their mothers, not thirty yards away there stalked a primal reality hardwired to break the blissful reverie of this California family's idyllic morn.

When the natural balance is about to be radically altered, the birds always seem to sense it first, and on this particular morning everything with a beak ceased its happy chirping. A foreboding silence fell. Even the gentle breeze stilled. The elk raised their heads and with the fury of a runaway train there burst from the forest six hundred and fifty kilos in a blur of fur and fangs. In a nanosecond, a grizzly bear was in the middle of the scattering herd all running pell-mell for safety, save for a lone calf who'd been staring at butterflies. With one calibrated swipe from the bear's paw, it was conveniently sliced in two. Struck dumb with fear, the family saw the grizzly bury its face in a pink stew of the still-wiggling ungulate and flagrantly embrace the circle of life. There's a scene that would require very different lyrics from Sir Elton's song.

"The parents wanted to sue me!" he said. "They held me responsible for their children being traumatized for life. Mom was crying, the children were crying and Dad wanted to punch me in the face. I told them, 'I don't control nature. I am not God. Blame God, not me!'"

He looked at me and said, "They lived next door to Disneyland. If *that's* not cause for trauma, I don't know what is."

Which is why, I suppose, we were visiting Yellowknife in August, about to experience ten days of mosquito-biting onslaught, paddling sub-arctic finger lakes and following wolf tracks atop sandy eskers way up north in the Land of the Little Sticks. Because you don't get *that* at Disneyland. You also don't get a narcoleptic, chain-smoking drunk as a tour operator, so it all balances out, I guess.

When a shuttle van pulled up from our hotel, discharging passengers for a later flight, we hopped in.

"What brings you to Yellowknife?" the driver asked.

"My dad and I are going kayaking for a week," my daughter piped up cheerfully, "with some dude called Tundra Tom."

At the mention of the man's name, the driver's eyes went saucer-wide with alarm as he looked at me in the rear-view mirror.

"Not *the* Tundra Tom," he said in a voice dripping in portent.

"You mean there's more than one?" I said half-jokingly, knowing full well that the man who had failed to arrive at the promised time was the same one whose name had made the blood drain from our driver's face.

"Good luck," he whispered, and gripping the steering wheel tightly, stared straight ahead, never mentioning the name again, as if doing so would curse those who heard it.

The gentleman at the hotel's reception desk was a dead ringer for Christopher Lee, who played Dracula with regal malevolence in those Hammer horror movies in the 1950s and '60s. Tall, gaunt, pale and imperious, sporting a set of incisors and cowl worthy of the Count himself, the only thing compromising the illusion was his Newfoundland accent. It's not every day you get to chat at a hotel's reception desk with a vampire who sounds as if he's from Fogo Island.

"You'se is in room seven-o-hate, m'son."

I swear that Newfoundlanders are the lost Tribe of Levi. Perpetual wanderers they are, driven by necessity to step beyond the economic limitations of home in search of a better run at a new day. The definitive accent is heard anywhere there's employment. Your plane could go down in the thickest jungles of the Congo, and dollars to donuts, within twenty-four hours, a Newfoundlander would be knocking on the broken window. You'd still be strapped in your seat, semi-conscious and bleeding while he'd let you know in an accent thick as a pot of fish 'n' brewis that "I was busy trapping monkeys for the Chinese circus, me son, when I seen de plane go down las' night. So, I machetes me way t'ru de jungle to see if der' was anybody from 'ome on it."

It must be hard to leave a place so rich in personality, where the people stir the spirit as much as the land does. Where women punctuate the end of their sentences with "Yes, my love," "Yes, my little darlin'," "Yes, my honey . . ." A waitress told me that management asked them to stop talking like that to tourists because "The come-from-aways thought we was coming on to them and their wives was getting pissed off." This was the same waitress who, when I was wrestling with whether or not to have my second plate of cod tongues fried in pork scraps because I was worried about my high cholesterol, said, "That's no problem, my love. Have a'nudder glass of red wine and it'll balance 'er right out."

On another occasion, I stepped from my room in a Grand Falls hotel early one morning and said to housekeeping, "I'm heading out for a run and will be back in an hour. You can make up my room now if you'd like."

"No way! You just woke up. It's still right stinky in der'!"

St. John's is one of the the best cities in the country to work off a feed of fish and chips, and on one windy autumn day electric with character, I headed out for a stroll to Signal Hill, a national historic site where a noonday gun still barks religiously from that rocky promontory rising 167 metres out of the great big sea it commands a view of. Besides falling to England during the last battle of the Seven Years' War in 1763, it's also where Italian geek Guglielmo Marconi, who, like those über-geeks Steve Jobs and Bill Gates a hundred years later, would change world communication by inventing the internet of his day when he succeeded in receiving the first transatlantic wireless communication from 2,100 miles across the sea. When his turn-of-the-twentieth-century geek buddies in Poldhu, England, tapped out a Morse code message asking how he was doing, local St. John's lore swears that Marconi replied, "If I spend one more night getting hammered on George Street till 4 a.m., I'm putting myself in rehab."

The national park path that traverses the Battery to get up the hill literally crosses the front steps of a person's house. You'd get the cops called on you for doing that in every other Canadian city and shot for it in the States. But not in a city with streets named Merrymeeting Road and Hill o' Chips. Go farther inland and there's Tickle Cove Pond, Joe Batt's Arm, Dildo and Itchy Balls Corner. (I made that last one up.) The elderly owner was sitting on his front porch, smiling into the sun, the day I walked past. He saw me coming, and as ol' timers will do, he threw a non-sequitur in my direction just to see if I was on my toes.

"How much is a case o' beer now, b'y?"

I was quick on the draw, though.

"I don't know, my buddy. Haven't paid much attention to anything since I got back from the war."

My riposte was acknowledged with a twitch of his head, as is the wont of every male over forty living there, and a "What odds, me son? What odds?" (I don't know exactly what the phrase means, but I think it's got something to do with being helpless in the hands of fate, and anyone who's waited two days for a flight out of St. John's thanks to a demonic brew of weather roiling in off the Atlantic has an idea. Plus, it's way better than "Whatever.")

Waving goodbye, I went up and over Signal Hill profuse with blueberries, huckleberries, asters and tiny wildflowers clinging tenaciously to that big lump of Precambrian granite overlooking a humbling body of water.

Newfoundland always had a way of wrapping me in a blanket of belonging to something bigger than the gig that brought me there. It always felt like I was going home to a Halifax lost. Going home to days when Uncle Percy called up tunes from that squeezebox of his on those humid August nights in my mother's kitchen, that was damn near close to bursting at the seams with all that Burgeo-born Foote, Vatcher and James blood as we watched our father tap-dance himself over the hardwood into a state of near transcendence, feet pumping with the ferocity of that runaway train he was imitating, accompanied by a chorus of rum-fuelled, rosy-cheeked laughter and shouts of support from all those Newfoundlanders in exile.

After an October night in old St. John's spent among faces flush with pints aplenty at the Ship's Inn, all singing along with Ron Hynes playing his haunting ode to their hometown harbour, I woke bleary-eyed but happy the following morning for a six-hour drive west to the pulp-mill town of Corner Brook, "The City That Grew from the Forest."

Crossing the Avalon that day, the needles of turning tamarack trees had wrapped the peninsula in an autumn halo gold as a ruler's crown. My father's country was rolling out a welcome mat for me over more than a billion years' worth of bedrock doorstep, that was already old as God in some long-gone Beothuk dawn. Two cars passed me headed east, each carrying either end of a moose on its roof. From the head, its two-foot pink tongue flapped in the breeze at 100 kilometres an hour. *There's* a picture that won't make the tourist brochure! Moose are everywhere in Newfoundland—or, as a hunting guide in Gander confirmed to me, "Lard Jesus, m'son, the woods is maggoty with them."

On that trip I saw a man in his truck beside the road with two dead partridges and three dead rabbits on the hood. I parked, got out, walked over and asked, "Are those dead animals on your hood for sale?" He turned towards me sporting that saucy, sarcastic twinkle behind the eyes they all get before setting you straight, and said, "Well, they're not there for decoration, are they, skipper?" It's that easy for them. I don't know why anyone pays to see a comedian in that province, because most people living there are ten times funnier than half the ones in my profession!

I was headed there years ago on a flight from Toronto when an elderly grandmother going back home to Deer Lake from Mississauga, where she'd been to visit her grandchildren, told me of her life. She was a small, wrinkled matriarch whose weeping family I watched her wave goodbye at Pearson Airport as we passed though security. Soon as we started taxiing up the runway, the grandmother started talking. I put down the book I was reading, knowing there was no sense in cracking the spine for this flight.

She told me the grandson I saw at the airport was one of fourteen, along with two great-grandchildren from five sons and daughters, born to her and her husband, now gone two years.

"I took care of him at 'ome," she said, "'cause he wanted to go looking out the front window at the brook and trees. He got his wish. Cancer is what took him. Leukemia in the lymph nodes was all t'ru him. Before he died, he hadn't had a drink in over seventeen years. I remember the day he stopped, too. I come back from my son's place, taking care of the little ones, and he'd been home by himself, into the bottle all day. Not eating, just drinking and shaking something fierce.

"He says, 'Call the doctor. I'se dying.'

"I says, 'No.'

"He says, 'But I'se dyin'.'

"I says, 'Then if you'se dyin',' stretch out on the couch and die, 'cause I'se tired and going upstairs for a nap. If I wakes up and you'se dead, I'se 'll call the funeral home.'

"When I woke up, there were two men from AA sitting in the kitchen. He never took another drop.

"So now I'se all alone," she said, with quiet resignation. "Got enough potatoes for the winter, lots of corn, turnips and a fridge full of pork. Gets me a piglet in spring. Lets him get to be 110 pounds, then slaughters him. Bacon's right lean. No fat to speak of. I'se got a woodstove. In fact, I'se burning wood me 'usband split two years ago. Every day he was out there, knowing someday soon he wouldn't be. Swinging the axe until he couldn't. A great big pile of wood he chopped me, lined up right nice and neat beside the back door. Now, every time I gets me a load to put on the fire, soon as the heat starts warming the kitchen it's like his arms is wrapped around me giving me a big hug."

"That's poetry," I told her.

"It's not poetry. It's true."

She stared out the window, pensive, then suddenly perked up. "So now I gets to go and see my kids on their flying points they gets from flying back and forth from Fort McMurray!"

"My father went blind at thirty-five from a disease what ran in the family," she continued. "I can still remember the severance pay he got from the pulp mill in Corner Brook: five thousand dollars. No workers' comp. No pension. No nutting. He always said, 'Don't complain, 'cause some has it lots worse.' He couldn't read or write, so Mom signed the cheques for him. After his setback, he bought land and built houses."

I thought, *"Setback"? There's an understatement. The man went blind!*

"Hold on," I said, trying to fathom what resources this man called on to turn his life around, long before motivational memes and self-help books were here to heal our First World problems. "He went *blind* and then built *houses*?"

"Yes, b'y."

I asked whom he built the houses with.

She looked at me like I'd missed the point.

"By himself."

"Like, alone? No help?"

"Yes, b'y."

"Christ," I said, "I can *see* and I'm lucky to get away with all my fingers just sawing the top off a hockey stick!"

"He had no use for a level neither," she assured me.

"No level? Every carpenter needs a level," I said.

She stared right through me, as if I'd entirely missed the point.

"Not if you can't see the bubble you don't."

Not if you can't see the bubble, you don't.

See, it's that easy for them there.

Although the runaway hit musical *Come from Away* beautifully captured the generosity of Newfoundlanders as true ambassadors of the human heart, they *can* be blunt. When my father turned seventy-five, I took him salmon fishing to Haida Gwaii, in British Columbia. We had family friends from Halifax living there and one night were invited to a party with nothing but Newfoundlanders.

So eager was Dad to embrace his tribe, the man practically did a tuck and roll out the passenger-side door onto the road before the car came to a stop. The kitchen was filled with drywall craftsmen, roofers and carpenters whose contracts had expired with whatever they'd been building and who would soon be bound elsewhere, looking for work. Their wives sat together in the living room, smoking cigarettes and laughing, while the men were corralled in the kitchen, making a serious dent in several bottles of rum. Working-class nomads the lot of them, from a birthplace my father had left at the age of six, but to which he was still anchored with a pride bred in the bone.

Entering the house as if it were his own, he ruled the place with the skill of a seasoned road comic, regaling that kitchen with bawdy jokes in his typical machine-gun delivery and bug-eyed animation. His face took on that familiar glow born of a good buzz, as our hosts poured rum after rum for this elfin trickster, whom I'm sure they thought had left a hidden forest kingdom for the night to work his magic amongst mere mortals.

He tap-danced along to buddy whaling away on a squeezebox, got moist and all teary-eyed maudlin when they sang "Let Me Fish Off Cape St. Mary's," and, in his telling of crossing the Cabot Strait at the age of six on the ill-fated *Caribou*, torpedoed by German U-boats during the Battle of the St. Lawrence in 1942, he practically put himself in a lifeboat with survivors, even though he made the crossing three years before it was struck. Never let the truth get in the way of a good story.

I wasn't quite in the kitchen, but standing off to the side, when the wife of one of those men came up, looked me square in the face and said, "I heard you'se a comedian, b'y. Tell us a joke."

That request is the number-one method for getting any comedian I know clamming up faster than a tongueless mute. I tried to be polite and explain the difference between "telling jokes," which my father in his prime could do effortlessly by rote, and my own work as a professional comedian. What I came up with was, hands down, the most pretentious explanation ever to escape this writer's cakehole.

"I don't tell jokes so much as describe the regional idiosyncrasies of Canada, hoping at the end of the day to elevate the virtues of people and place by unifying an audience through laughter."

I watched her nose wrinkle in disdain and her eyes narrow suspiciously, like someone trying to locate the source of rotting food in the fridge.

"You'se not funny at all, b'y." And, pointing to my father, who at this point was holding up a dishtowel he'd turned into what looked exactly like a skinned rabbit, said, "But him? Now *he's* funny!" Then she pushed me hard in the chest and walked away.

Like I said . . . blunt.

Once settled in the room, I sat down to phone Tundra Tom himself. It was still early, so I naturally assumed either he or one of his assistants would be there to take my call and allay any fears I had of the trip going completely south. I phoned five times and let it ring. No answer. *They must be out*, I thought. Four hours later, at almost 7 p.m., I was still phoning and getting no answer.

The following morning, I tried again. The voice that answered was what you'd hear after waking a mountain ogre from a winter's nap: a voice thick with phlegm from a three-pack habit and an attitude so far removed from courteous, it belonged behind the customer complaints counter at a communist department store in a forgotten corner of the Soviet bloc. He growled into the receiver.

"What do you want?!"

Praying to whatever angels watch over lapsed Anglicans, I hoped this wasn't *him*. Hoped this would not be the man I was entrusting with our lives for ten days in the wilderness.

"I'm calling for Tundra Tom."

"You're talkin' to him."

From his esophageal recess, he rolled up a hefty ball of mucus that, when he spat, I heard it hit his wastebasket with the weight of a stone.

Mustering my courage, I soldiered on.

"It's Ron James. You didn't show up at the airport yesterday as promised."

"I fell asleep and forgot."

No apology. No sorry. No "Did you get to the hotel okay?" Nor was there an attempt to cover his tracks with a well-crafted lie, or even a charming fib. I'd even have welcomed flagrant bullshit, because God knows, running an outfitting enterprise in an area as vast as Canada's North certainly lends itself to an imaginative tall tale.

"I couldn't pick you up at the airport because I had flown bear-tagging biologists to some denning sites, but one of them got eaten alive."

I'd have believed that.

"There's a lot of spooky stuff happens up here. We followed a black-ops chopper with no markings until we ran out of gas."

I would have endorsed that explanation, while swearing myself to a lifetime of secrecy.

"I found a perfectly preserved woolly mammoth when I was digging for diamonds, so then I took some skin grafts to a lab—and they're going to clone it and I'm gonna raise it!"

I'd have been on board. I read *National Geographic* and know that because of global warming, creatures from the Ice Age are poking their desiccated snouts out of the permafrost with regularity. Who wouldn't want to raise a cloned woolly mammoth, provided they had the space in their backyard?

But no. Turns out Tundra Tom *just forgot*. Whatever he was, he certainly was not a liar.

"You fell asleep and *forgot*," I repeated with incredulity. "My kid and I are about to go kayaking for a week in the wilderness. That doesn't make me feel very secure."

Although personally motivated to salvage the trip, and out of a greater fear of antagonizing this ogre any further, my last words were conciliatory and understanding. "Well, everyone makes mistakes," I said. "We're all human."

And that's when the inner Vesuvius ruling his lizard brain exploded with such an f-bomb-laced diatribe, it would have made the darkest devils in hell weep.

Let me be clear. I am no stranger to spontaneous, purple-faced rage. The James patriarch was once formidable in this regard and could deliver a door-slamming, foot-stomping blind fury as his Burgeo-born blood hit the boiling point igniting a litany of alliterative profanity that would make Wordsworth himself envious. Oddly enough, Dad's explosive rants at baseboards he'd cut too short, plumbing he didn't understand, spilled paint, the Toronto Maple Leafs blowing a two-goal lead in the third, and a temperamental furnace, were entirely devoid of any f-bombs.

Tundra Tom, on the other hand, opened with that heavy artillery right off the top.

"Then fuck off and go home!" he barked. "Just fuck off! Fuck. Right. Off! The trip is cancelled! Cancelled! I've got forty people strung across three hundred kilometres of territory, and here's some guy from *To*-ronto telling me how to run my fuckin' business?! Look, buddy. I'm a bush pilot! I save *lives* for a living!"

A sensible person would have hung up, filed a complaint with the Yellowknife Chamber of Commerce, taken the loss of the deposit and gone home. Instead, I said, with my voice cracking, "But we came all this way to see wolves and caribou and stuff. Does this mean we won't see them?"

"How am I supposed to know if you'll see them? They're animals! It's not Disneyland up here!" (That's when I wished we'd gone there instead. We could be on Mr. Toad's Wild Ride right now getting motion sickness.) He uttered a war-weary sigh. Tundra was clearly a man overwhelmed by circumstance.

"Look," he said. "I've got everyone from geologists to German filmmakers dropped all over the tundra. Picking you up at the airport didn't seem like such a priority. But since you're here, be in the hotel lobby in two hours, packed and ready to go."

My daughter had heard the entire conversation and, closing her journal, matter-of-factly offered, "I guess he didn't like it when you called him human."

We sat in the hotel restaurant, enjoying a breakfast of thirteen-dollar bagels. Food all across the North is off-the-charts expensive, and nothing is ever fresh—unless, of course, you're a grunt moiling for diamonds in the Diavik mine.

I had a gig once at their mother ship of an outpost, 225 kilometres south of the Arctic Circle. Employing a thousand people with an airport big enough to accommodate a Boeing 737, the company had a cafeteria at this sprawling complex whose counters were bursting with enough fresh fruit and vegetables to supply a Loblaws store in any southern Canadian city. That's not the case for most people living up north. About the only green you'll see in the grocery stores of Canada's Arctic communities from October to June is on a Gore-Tex jacket. Don't get me wrong: a person can *find le*ttuce . . . they just can't afford it.

No wonder people living in our northern communities think Canada's Food Guide, with its emphasis on maintaining a diet of fresh fruit, vegetables and water, is utterly contemptuous of their daily reality. It's all well and good if you're part of the 87 percent of our population strung along the American border, but by the time produce gets to the North in wintertime, it's practically compost. I bought a banana in Inuvik once that was so bruised and beaten, it looked like Chiquita had kicked it there from Brazil!

People who live in the North sometimes tell you things about living up there that rattle your southern perspective. I once flew with a couple of teachers from Fort Simpson who were headed to Florida for a honeymoon, and they told me about Wild Dog Day. The outskirts of towns and reserves across the North are overrun with neglected and abandoned domestic dogs gone feral. "You'd be better off seeing a pack of wolves than wild dogs," they told me, "because wolves still have a fear of man, but a collie who used to sleep at the foot of your bed, not so much."

I imagined fighting for my life in some snowy wood, surrounded by a pack of chihuahuas and pugs, half-crazed with hunger, attacking my Achilles tendon. Getting eaten by wild dogs is a tragedy, but getting eaten alive by pugs and chihuahuas, that's just embarrassing.

"It's true," they insisted. "We have Wild Dog Day. The local butcher dumps a wheelbarrow of meat in the middle of the street just on the outskirts of town. Townspeople wait a couple hundred yards away with their rifles, and when the dogs come for it, they shoot them."

"That's got to rile the SPCA," I said.

"Rile the SPCA? They organize it!"

My daughter's pupils widened as I heard that unmistakable voice from the phone talking at the reception desk.

"I'm here for Ron James."

"That's him," my daughter gasped.

I turned to see a man who easily tipped the scales at three hundred pounds stride into the restaurant. He was of a Cyclopean stature and wearing a filthy sweatsuit so crusty with last week's breakfast, I'm sure it must have doubled as a tablecloth, while on his feet were—wait for it—slippers.

That's right. Slippers. I had no idea something I'd wear around the house on a lazy, rainy Sunday was the preferred footwear of the fabled northern bush pilot. You learn something new every day.

The man's bedhead was an extraordinary arrangement of hair that hadn't seen a shower, I'll wager, since it was patted down by his mother's spit in church on his confirmation day. In one ham hock–sized fist, he clutched three large packs of Player's Light, while in the other were squeezed a mittful of pepperoni sticks. As he stood over our table, I got the unmistakable sour whiff of yesterday's whisky bender.

"I'm Tundra Tom. Let's go."

With a foolish disregard for our own safety, we obediently rose from our chairs and followed the hungover, slipper-wearing ogre.

My daughter, always one with the quick quip, mumbled under her breath, "Just because an outfitter has a great website, Dad, doesn't mean he didn't learn to build it in prison."

People still ask me why I went way up there, let alone take one of my daughters. Well, my youngest was at camp, my wife didn't like to tent and my eldest thought it would be cool to see caribou. Besides, it would be the last August she'd have free before summer jobs and friends monopolized her time, so why not spend it paddling face-first into a thirty-knot headwind on Arctic finger lakes in a tandem kayak with her ol' man, as waves crashed over the bow while he sings "We're Gonna Hang Out the Washing on the Siegfried Line" and other World War II marching songs no fifteen-year-old wants to hear. Scratch that—*anyone* under the age of ninety-three wants to hear.

The other reason I went is because I don't golf. Chasing a little white ball around from dawn to dusk on a beautiful weekend, hoping to blend your short game with your long game in one elusive moment of bourgeois perfection before a five-alarm coronary drops you face-first to the floor of the nineteenth hole, doesn't stoke my mojo.

Let me be clear: I'm not judging those who golf—but as most golfers will agree, it is one of those sports that takes a modicum of proficiency to enjoy. Years ago, I invested a summer's worth of leisure time in the sport and discovered that wrapping a 9-iron round a tree after my twenty-third slice of the day didn't work wonders for my stress level. If I'm going to be humbled, I'd prefer the learning curve be shorter than an entire lifetime.

Tom shuttled us to a loading dock on the shores of Great Slave Lake, where a bush plane sat. It definitely wasn't a new one. I'm sure it was the pride of the North in its day, but this being 2004, I found that flying in a single-prop Beaver that came off the assembly line Rosie the Riveter worked on was reason for worry. It was banged-up and dented from a lifetime of tackling the Arctic and it was made for carrying cargo, not people. Obviously, it could never have taken ground fire from enemy troops but judging by the holes in the fuselage below my seat, it sure looked like it had.

A mechanic in grease-smeared overalls lifted his head from beneath the opened engine bonnet and, holding what looked like a set of distributor caps, turned to Tom and said, "That's why it was stalling on you." Stalling. Hmmm. The thought of stalling in a bush plane with a narcoleptic Tundra nodding off at the controls did not inspire confidence.

Back in 1972, a bush pilot called Marten Hartwell, flying from Cambridge Bay to Yellowknife with a pregnant Inuk woman, an Inuk boy with appendicitis and a nurse on board, crashed in a snowstorm in the uncharted wilderness of Great Bear Lake. The nurse and Inuk woman died on impact. With two broken ankles, Marten survived for thirty-one days, thanks in large part to help from the boy—and the dead nurse, whom he ate. That's correct. *Ate*. Which reinforces a rule of thumb: when flying any distance in a bush plane, always pack a substantial lunch and more Mars bars than you think you'll need, because should you crash and not be found for a while, things could turn ugly as soon as the pilot's jujubes start running low.

Given Tom's impressive girth, his appetite was probably formidable. *Summertime or not*, I thought, *if this plane goes down, that fat bastard will be drooling over us as soon as his pepperoni sticks are gone.*

If you ever have the need to feel small, take a bush plane flight over this corner of the country. The vast glaciated topography of the barren grounds running west from Hudson Bay clear to the Arctic Ocean is twice the size of Alberta. It's an uncompromising hyperborean world of dwarf willow, stunted spruce, birch and alder that cling tenaciously atop eskers of Caribbean-fine sand, formed by the till of subterranean rivers that once ran beneath seven kilometres of ice. During their retreat, these glaciers scraped the Earth's surface clear to its mantle, leaving behind a blanket of moss and lichen where a people beyond our knowing once pulled a living from this primal plain, hunting antlered armies on the hoof with nothing but bone, stone and sinew, a million moons before Romulus and Remus suckled on the She Wolf's nipple. Playing golf just doesn't provide me that level of buzz.

However, when camping in Canada, the mosquitoes will give you far more buzz than you bargained for. Don't hold back when it comes to bug spray, either. Go nuclear and settle for nothing less than Muskol. That is *not* your average fly dope. It's closer to basement bucket slop from the cooling towers of Chernobyl. No need for a Coleman lantern to light your way round camp at night when you're sporting a cloak of radioactive isotopes. Sure, your hair might fall out in a couple weeks, but if you're like me, you at least won't mind losing it off your back.

You need to be smeared in serious levels of DEET when you're on the radar of the *Culicidae* family. There are eighty-seven types of mosquitoes in Canada, but only five that bite: no-see-ums; gnats; blackflies; horseflies; and big bastards I don't know the name of that come humming round your ears, sounding like B-17s on a bombing run over war-torn Berlin. Baptize yourself from head to toe in Muskol, or you'll bleed out before the bacon is done.

Mosquitoes will abate, however, when the wind picks up. And in a place where a six-foot tree can be considered old growth, there's nothing to stop its relentless blitzkrieg. Did you know it's tricky taking number two on the tundra in a windstorm? If you ever have to, here's a tip: don't take your drawers off when you do, because when Mother Nature calls the shots, she connects you to the fundamentally elemental, and nothing knocks the urban cocky from you faster than having to run bare-ass naked, clutching your shrunken junk, while chasing your pants as they're blown across a primal stretch of real estate.

Millions of geese and waterfowl visit to breed during the fleeting summer, and the sky is filled with loons, jaegers and dive-bombing Arctic terns who do not suffer trespassers. Their hatchlings sit in such brilliantly camouflaged nests on the ground, a person could easily step on one and not know it until they felt that sickening, soft squish under their boot. The parents defend their nests from above by diving for your face with a bone-chilling shriek worthy of a Stuka strafing the beaches of Dunkirk. Best to give these winged velociraptors a wide berth. I figure if you're genetically hard-wired to fly from pole to pole from spring to fall every year, *just to sit on an egg*, you deserve respect.

When we headed out kayaking, it wasn't Tom who took us but one of his guides. The kid was a thirty-year-old West Coast Earth cookie who could start a campfire with nothing more than incantations and a handful of dried ptarmigan turds he kept in a bag attached to his belt. One night, he told me to start the fire, so I squirted half a quart of kerosene on the wood, threw a match in and it erupted with a *woof* worthy of Little Boy. Despite the loss of my eyebrows, I highly endorse this method.

We camped on and explored these eskers, home to gyrfalcon, caribou, wolf and fox. Although we never spotted the true landlord of these parts, the barren ground grizzly, it does wonders for the imagination to stumble on their tracks in the sand, knowing full well one could lumber into your campsite unannounced and radically alter the equation.

One evening at sunset, clearly bored with our company and itching for some alone time, our guide disappeared over the hill. He was gone until well after dark, no doubt enjoying a toke while shape-shifting with the Caribou People. Minus any rifle or bear spray for protection, we sat in a dinner tent covered in mosquito netting that Tom had flown in a few days before. The smells of the Hamburger Helper we'd had for dinner must have been tickling the olfactory of whatever member of *Ursus arctos* was within sniffing distance. And knowing how acute a bear's sense of smell is, I imagined a surly gang of bruins making a hungry beeline across the tundra for our camp. In fact, a bear had passed by recently; its scat sat in a pile not far from our tent. When the guide returned two hours or more after leaving, I admonished the high-as-a-kite, squinty-eyed simp for his negligence.

"You left us alone with no gun or bear spray, and there's a pile of bear scat outside the tent!"

"Relax, dude," he said with that condescending confidence we'd grown to hate the past six days. "You've got a better chance of being hit by a car than attacked by a grizzly."

Stretching my arms wide in emphasis, I implored, "Do you see any cars up here?"

What we did see plenty of were caribou, back when a herd of 325,000 moved in mind-boggling migratory numbers across the tundra as it had for millennia. But that was seventeen years ago. From the Torngat Mountains of Labrador to the Rocky Mountains of British Columbia and all across the Canadian north populations of this iconic ungulate are nosediving. A lethal combination of resource development and global warming has reduced the once-thriving herds to dire levels, with neither Conservative nor Liberal governments doing squat to stem the collapse. The feds pass the buck to the provinces and territories, which in turn sweep the issue under the carpet in the name of progress. If the caribou disappear, wolves and bears won't be far behind, nor will the lives of the First Peoples across the North who, since time immemorial, have depended on caribou for sustenance.

By the time we returned to camp, word had gotten out about what I did for a living, and the change in Tundra Tom was unsettling. He'd gone from an apoplectic, piss-and-vinegar-filled, profanity-spitting ogre to an ingratiatingly accommodating host. I missed the former.

"Why didn't you tell me you were on TV?" he said with arms stretched wide in welcome. Now that he realized I was "someone" and not just a run-of-the-mill worrisome client whose head he'd bitten off in a telephone tirade, he was obviously worried I'd use whatever superpower you get from being on television to destroy his reputation. Clearly, he'd never seen my work, or he would have known it amounted to a handful of commercials, a special that aired on CTV's Comedy Network and an ill-fated television series whose handful of viewers were comprised of grade seven history teachers, twelve-year-old boys, War of 1812 re-enactors and shut-ins. I was hardly a player of influence. Still, my fame brought dividends that night when we weren't served canned peas again.

One day, a Dene elder called Joe, whom Tom had flown in from Fort Resolution, came looking to hunt caribou for his people. A middle-aged Indigenous co-owner of the camp named Charlie was guiding him, so I asked to tag along. Leaving my daughter at the camp, who was content to hang out in our Quonset hut, probably writing in her journal about what lapse in judgment made her join her Dad up north in the first place. With a wary nod they agreed, and in the chill of a late-August morning, we headed across the lake for wilder country beyond camp. Pulling the craft ashore, we ascended the hill, careful to keep the wind in our face so that our smell wouldn't give us away. Caribou are peculiar creatures that, provided they don't get a whiff of you, will actually walk towards you with a stunned stare of bovine curiosity . . . and that's when you shoot them.

Cresting the hill, I saw a pair of ravens flying overhead and remembered, as a kid, reading in Farley Mowat's book *Two Against the North* that these birds and wolves actually hunt together, with the raven providing the ears and eyes for the wolf, while the wolf provides the kill. It's even been proven that they communicate with each other—and given the raven's love of language, if you've ever heard them shooting the breeze on telephone wires, a person wouldn't need to be David Attenborough to believe it.

While following those birds in flight, I caught a blur of marshmallow-pure white moving hard across the land. "Wolves," I said, pointing at a pair of them. These were tundra wolves, looking almost spectral in the dawn of a new day whose clouds were broken by sunbeams that bathed their coats of fur in angelic light. I had never seen wolves in the wild before, nor have I since, but watching them move across the land as they have for millennia was as close to a vision of Creation as a fellow can get.

It was a good sign. Where there's wolves, there's caribou.

We dropped our packs and settled behind an erratic dropped twelve thousand years ago by retreating glaciers. (Or, depending on your literal reading of biblical scripture, dropped *six* thousand years ago by Noah from the ark because the pair of elephants in the bow who wouldn't stop mating threw the ballast off. I'm not even going to ask how he fit a pair of blue whales aboard, but I guess that's what they mean when they say, "God works in mysterious ways.")

Sitting with our backs to the boulder, we broke out bologna-and-mustard sandwiches on white bread, washed down with steaming-hot cups of tea, watching weather from one extreme to the next play its way across the firmament—delivering rain and sleet one minute, a Phoenix-in-July level of heat the next. It's not an exaggeration to say a person could get sunburnt on one side of their face and frostbitten on the other. (Okay, it *is* an exaggeration, but an innocent one.)

Charlie was forty-nine—seventeen years ago and a residential school survivor. We sat waiting for the caribou to come. He was smoking a Player's Light and passing one to Joe. Sharing smokes is one thing I miss about the habit. (Not so much the getting of cancer.)

When lunch was finished and the tenth cigarette smoked, Charlie poked his head slightly above the boulder to glass the land. So far in the distance that it was barely visible to the naked eye sat a growth of trees. "All we've got is the moment," said Charlie. "I bring people up here to photograph wolves. You've got to be patient. Don't matter how much high-end gear you've got, unless you can sit and wait, you're not getting nothing."

He took a drag and looked at me.

"So, television, eh?"

"Well, I mostly work live. I'm on the road. A stand-up. Started in the clubs but made the move to theatres a few years back."

"How many years have you been at it?"

"Twenty-three in 'the business,' but just ten in stand-up," I said.

He looked at me hard. Not to see if I'd say something funny, but to see if I was telling the truth.

"I guess that's long enough to know what you're doing."

"I suppose. It's still a mystery, though. As soon as you think you've got it figured out, you're back to point A again."

Charlie agreed with a nod and turned to glass the hillside. Then his story rolled out.

"I studied to be a cinematographer," he said. "Twenty-five years ago, I left my rez north of Sioux Lookout. For two years, I went to Vancouver Film School. Graduated, too. There wasn't a lot of call for an Indian cinematographer back then, so I started driving cab in the Downtown Eastside. Graveyard shift. Nothing but junkies, pimps, killers and whores. That was my clientele. I found them to be more upfront than most people in showbiz. Saw all the great bands. Go down to Seattle. Always bought great seats. It cost peanuts in 1980. We'd get right up front.

"I started using heroin. Been clean for ten years. I blame the residential school. A Jesuit killed me, and a Jesuit resurrected me. Talk about coming full circle, eh? Like you say, it's a mystery.

"I met a great woman," he continued. "She's Cree. She teaches yoga. We moved back to my reserve, three hours north of Kenora, to take care of my parents. Just buried them last year. They died six weeks from each other. Dad was Scottish. A trapper. Mom was an Ojibwa from Fort Frances. They lived to be ninety-one and ninety-three. That's what living off the land does for you.

"We help the kids up there now. There are lots of suicides. It's epidemic. We lost twenty-three kids last year. Twenty-three. If twenty-three kids hung themselves in Toronto, it would be front-page news. They send social workers up from Toronto with all kinds of letters after their names. Some don't last a week. One guy was there less than a month and went home. Came highly recommended. Best in his field, they said. Two kids hung themselves when he was there. We found the first one in the barn. He said, 'I'm not trained for this.' I said, 'I don't care what you're trained for, help me cut this kid down.' He threw up instead.

"I don't blame him. Reality is hard to face. Life is fleeting. All we've got is the moment. Right now. Right here. You've got to make the moments matter, otherwise you're nowhere."

I sat between these men from another world for a good hour or more. Neither spoke. They just sat there, staring across a forever belly of tundra as if willing their quarry into being. Now, I come from people who talk . . . a lot. The Celtic tribe is clinically uncomfortable with silence. Many of us never shut up until we're dead, and even then, we're haunting castles and inns with a ghostly howling only an exorcist can silence.

Sit I did, though, and never said a word. A record for me! The last time I sat still that long without talking was during a grade nine detention at Chebucto School . . . that I *got* for talking!

Charlie turned and raised his binoculars. "Hey, Joe," he said. "You want a moose?"

Joe said, "No, too much meat to carry."

Wondering what moose he was referring to, I raised my binoculars, pointing them towards the very distant patch of spruce, and saw absolutely nothing.

"He's right there," Charlie said without turning around.

I glassed the same trees until my eyes watered, and still I saw absolutely nothing. Twenty minutes later, the sun broke through those bible-picture clouds as that elusive moose rose from a lone thicket a day's walk away—a solitary speck on a vast canvas of tabula rasa. It stood stoic, and then nonchalantly ambled away, one stride at a time, living moment to moment.

"How in the hell did you see that?" I asked.

Charlie looked at me and, pointing to his face with a grin, said, "Indian eyes."

I laughed and said, "You guys have a whole different rhythm to your funny."

"You got that right."

It occurred to me right then, had I turned tail and gone home after my phone call with Tom, this moment of connection would never have been. Sure, the condescending kayaking guide, with his ludicrous self-assurance in bear country, could have ended badly had a bruin got a whiff of the Hamburger Helper leftovers and come scrounging, but sitting against a boulder as old as the world in timeless communion with Charlie was worth the chance I took.

Suddenly, Joe tapped him on the shoulder and the spell was broken. Pointing across the ridge, they saw half a dozen antlers sticking up from shapes on the ground. As if hit by an electric shock, a once-sedentary Joe and Charlie slung their rifles over their shoulders and were up and running full tilt, back to the boat. We followed the lake and beached the boat at the foot of where the reclining caribou would be.

"We want to shoot them sitting down," Charlie told me.

"Why?" I asked.

"Good eatin'," explained Joe.

We scrambled from the boats and up the hill. I was waved back by Charlie, when suddenly five caribou crested the hill from where they'd been lying. The wind was in our favour. I figured Joe would drop one with a bullet between the eyes and kill the other before it even knew his buddy was dead. Joe let loose a fusillade of shots from his semi-automatic Winchester . . . and missed them all!

They turned and bolted, never to be seen again. As Charlie walked past me, he said to Joe, "You can't be shooting like that when the white guy's here."

On the way back to the boat, several more caribou walked in front of us, and without missing a beat, Joe raised his gun and dropped one.

"Perfect," he said. "Right by the boat."

They had it gutted, skinned and quartered in under forty-five minutes, leaving the offal for the ravens and wolves.

Motoring back to camp, we discussed Tundra Tom. I mentioned his meltdown on the phone and his forgetting to pick us up.

"We've barely got eight weeks of summer to make it happen up here in tourism, and he's full-on 24/7. He works too hard, drinks too much, smokes too much, and then he just passes out, falls asleep and forgets where he's supposed to be. Anywhere but here, he'd be out of a job, but the North lets a lot of stuff go. You have to. It's the North."

Chapter Nine

ACROSS THE GREAT DIVIDE

Steve Earle singing "Another Town" carries me over the Rockies to that enchanted land on the other side, where the hand of time is held at bay and everything east of Golden is suspect. Beautiful British Columbia, where "starting over" is the mantra for those laden with the weight of another world, all hoping to score what they're looking for on the other side of the Great Divide.

In 2007, the real estate gold rush for a piece of paradise was on. Every hillside from Selkirks to Courtenay-Comox had an active-lifestyle baby boomer retirement community on it. Talk about great timing! Baby boomers scored all that inheritance money left them by hard-working Depression-era parents who wouldn't know a day spa from a can of Spam. Now their pampered sons and daughters will be dropping dead in a gated retirement community at a sun-punished age of 107 during a loofah-seaweed body scrub, with a Cabernet in one hand and a life coach in the other. Life coach. There's a scam: some New Age knob charging you money for something you should get from a friend for free: advice. "Quit drinking so much. You're an asshole!"

And active? You'd better believe it. In the high, dry desert climate of Osoyoos, people are regularly living well past a hundred. A pair of sun-weathered, mummified elders rode past me on a tandem-bicycle and I thought, *Shouldn't you be under hermetically sealed glass at the museum?*

Everything is extreme in BC. I went for a run in a mountainside conservation area, and just when I thought I was doing all right, keeping the Reaper at bay, some über-woman with cannonball calves blasted past me on the forest path, carrying a deer on her back! (An exaggeration, yes, but not by much.)

Caribou crossing endless miles of tundra for springtime calving grounds have nothing on the migration of Canadian retirees bound for the idyllic, sea-kissed climate of Vancouver Island. Despite the 350 years of built-up seismic energy that's pushing against the Pacific plates, which, when released, will most certainly move the stately homes of Oak Bay, Victoria to a driveway in Honolulu, they keep coming. Prairie people particularly love it out there. Can you blame them? If you were at the mercy of nosediving mercury for seven months of the year, you too would be counting the days till you could bolt for Shangri-La. After all, how many February nights can you spend at the curling rink in Regina before you want to drop the rock on your own head?

Everything exacts a price, and there's not a person I've met who doesn't feel held hostage to the BC ferry service. As a visitor, I find a ferry ride represents the most egalitarian of Canadian virtues, because everyone is literally in the same boat. You've got a Mercedes sedan–driving West Vancouver venture capitalist headed for their multimillion-dollar cedar retreat on Hornby Island, parked beside a '97 Subaru with more holes in the muffler than a JFK assassination conspiracy theory, being driven by a couple of semi-feral hard-core Earth cookies from the forest, who've been living so long off the grid, their ass cracks are turning to compost.

After the hellacious white-knuckler of a drive three winters prior, suffering primal blizzards on avalanche-prone mountain passes, this crossing is a breeze. Spring has arrived and is shirking winter's yoke in a seasonal tsunami of meltwater. Hope rules defiant once more, as slabs of ice slide from cliff faces like body armour dropped after the battle has been won. In the distance, sunbeams catch the prisms hidden in sheer curtains of rain and stretch across the sky in a rainbow so spectacular it would get Noah and Pride parade marshals alike doing cartwheels down Main Street. Snowbanks crumble and dissolve into rushing streams flowing down to the Columbia River in the shadow of the Kootenays. Scruffy bighorn sheep, sporting scraggy winter coats even the homeless would leave on a rack at the Sally Ann, pick at frugal strips of new grass along the Trans-Canada. Yes, indeed, it is *very* different than last time . . .

British Columbia is a province of geographic and climatic extremes. I've been humbled quiet standing small before dwindling old-growth giants in her coastal rainforests, where shadows and sun build pillars of light beneath a canopied cathedral of green. I've caught a fine Cabernet buzz more than once in the fruit-bellied farmlands of the Okanagan, where bourgeois wine snobs live in pseudo–Santa Barbara bliss in their California climate, all but a four-hour drive from the swine-rich Fraser Valley lowlands, where God-fearing Chilliwack and Abbotsford abut Vancouver sprawl.

But woe betide the careless traveller, lulled into complacency while sitting beneath blossoming cherry trees on a Victoria February afternoon, who assumes the weather in the town they're headed to tomorrow will be similar to what they're enjoying today. Because I did, driving a rental car with tires baby ass bald and windshield washer fluid made for far more temperate climes than the subarctic lumber country of Prince George, where I was bound.

The coulees were dusted with snow during the drive into Kamloops, as red-tails and sharp-shinned hawks floated thermals on a blue-sky day, hoping to snatch a groundhog supper for their hungry hatchlings, eagerly waiting in the nest for a mouthful of their mother's regurgitations. (Every time I get to wishing I was a hawk I remember that fact—and the feeling goes away.) I like this high, dry country of rolling grasslands, trout-happy lakes and sweet-smelling sage overlooking the Thompson River.

It's named for David Thompson, hands down the greatest geographer in Canadian history, who mapped ninety *thousand* kilometres of Canada for the HBC—kilometres he'd either canoed or hiked. There's a dude who walked the talk! What's even more impressive, he managed this Herculean feat of wilderness travel without ever once visiting Mountain Equipment Co-Op. (Now, *there's* a gang of hippie capitalists who have redefined the meaning of fleece. You can't help but be overcome by a compulsion to spend money in one of their stores. All you're looking to buy are a couple of propane canisters for your weekend camping trip, but *seven hours later*, you've maxed out the Visa and are loading up the truck with enough water-resistant, sweat-wicking, state-of-the-art down-filled adventure gear to circumnavigate the polar ice cap on foot.)

Unfortunately, I had no time to linger and enjoy the view. There were 476 kilometres left to drive if I was to make Prince George that night and be ready for the radio interview at 6 a.m. the next morning.

That winter of 2003 was my first tour across BC, and I had to sell the show. Doing radio morning shows was a coup my producer worked hard to procure. Going live with Type A DJs who've been mainlining caffeine since rising at 4 a.m. is a serious jolt to the system. You've got to have your game face on. Keep the jokes coming fast and furious. They've no patience for long set-ups. They want laughs *now, funny man!*

The experience of a high-octane early morning radio interview is like sitting in the cockpit with a couple of pilots trying to land a 787 Dreamliner in a thunderstorm while Zeus rattles lightning bolts off the nose cone. Those DJs are remarkably skilled at multi-tasking; flipping buttons, reading charts, delivering their riffs while listening to your answers and trying not to fake-laugh. CBC radio interviewers, on the other hand, have a very different energy. They are just as skilled, but far less effusive. Their radio interviews are so earnest, once they're over, you feel like you've just had a nice chat with a United Church deacon about wallpaper and sourdough.

The sun was going down as I left Kamloops and headed for the Gold Rush Trail. It's one of those historic travel routes families in Winnebagos drive in summer, looking to relive the journey miners took in 1897 on their way to the Klondike with nothing but a mule, forty pounds of flour and a shovel. I, conversely, was travelling it during the winter of 2003, looking for comedy gold instead, wishing

I had a mule instead of a car with Kleenex for tires, which I'd rented in a very rainy and mild Vancouver.

Darkness fell fast as I passed through Cache Creek, where listless packs of ferret-faced townies loped like shadows from a fever dream, stopping occasionally to kick at desiccated roadkill as they watched my car pass by with furtive stares. I'm sure they're a jovial bunch up there come summer, but whenever I mention that town's name onstage one hour south in Kamloops, the entire audience lets out an audible gasp and makes the sign of the cross.

Not salt, but sand is the preferred method of combatting ice on British Columbia's highways, and it's not uncommon for eighteen-wheelers blowing past at an unholy clip to kick up chunks of gravel that whistle into your windshield with the deadly *ting* of 75-millimetre artillery shells hitting a D-Day landing craft from the heights above Normandy. Pushing on, I stopped for gas in 100 Mile House, wrestling with whether or not I should bunk there for the night. Ten minutes outside town, I wished I had.

The snow fell fast, heavy and wet, smothering the windshield in a dough-thick blanket of white. My high beams only exacerbated the blizzard, so I turned the headlights to low and could barely see at all. I slowed from a confident eighty klicks to a ten-kilometre-an-hour crawl. One of those miner's mules would have been faster than me.

I hit the wiper fluid. It wouldn't squirt. It was frozen block-solid as the forehead of Frankenstein's monster. The wipers suddenly stopped, too. They were too burdened by the weight of the wet snow and wouldn't budge. I couldn't see my hands in front of my face—and I was *in* the car.

Easing over to the shoulder, I felt my tires sink with a sickening give, and fearing the vehicle was seconds from sliding over the embankment, I cut the wheel hard to the left, which got me back to solid ground. As I did, the car was filled with a retina-blinding light worthy of a nuclear flash at ground zero, seen seconds before your silhouette is burned into a brick wall. It was a double-trailered twenty-two-wheeler bearing down full throttle with nothing but malignant contempt for whatever unfortunate had the temerity to impede its passage. The big bastard was hell-bent on flattening me into oblivion with the same commitment a Panzer tank would a wounded Russian on the road to Moscow.

Its driver lay hard on the horn, ripping the night open with an eardrum-bursting blare that I will bet good money was a decibel level higher than the opening artillery barrage at the Battle of the Somme. To this day, I'm still impressed my bowels did not liquify.

A scream filled my vehicle with a surround-sound wail, coming from somewhere between my soul and scrotiliac (I made that word up too). The rear end of this rented piece-of-shit Chevy with paper-thin tires slid back and forth on the road with the fluidity of a gelatinous-assed bingo-playing duchess on a church basement chair.

At the last possible second before collision, the driver roared past with all the malevolence of the Great White Whale buffeting Ahab's dory. Once past, its backdraft threw a glutinous wave of slush into my windshield.

I can't see! I cannot fucking well see!

The car was in the middle of the highway at a dead stop. In fact, I wondered if I might already *be* dead. Maybe that truck dinged me into some Nordic Valhalla, and this snowy netherworld was its purgatory? My only route of escape from eternal imprisonment would be a hero's quest through their underworld. If my recall of Nordic myth is correct, that would involve engaging in feats of strength with magical dwarves, fighting a giant sturgeon and *not* succumbing to temptations of sex with a Valkyrie seductress at the crossroads who transforms into a three-headed witch with snakes for pigtails, before ultimately facing a rune-reading dragon full of tricky riddles, seated before the Golden Throne of Asgard. Or something like that.

I didn't dare get out of the truck to clean the windshield for fear I couldn't find my way back to the driver's seat. So, I leaned my head out the window and wiped the snow off with my left hand while I steered with my right. That's when another set of trucker's lights roared out of the night behind me . . .

Compounding this flirtation with death was disappointment at the recent cancellation of my first television series, *Blackfly*. Two years before, I'd sold a premise to Global Television that sought to "satirize current social and political trends in the context of the eighteenth-century fur trade." The cast of characters I'd created were archetypes plucked from the pages of Canadian history. With plenty creative liberties taken, I threw them together in a stockade fort somewhere on the shores of Lake Superior in 1783 and hoped for the best.

Stepping into the fray of my first television series proved a Herculean task—the equivalent of juggling a million moving pieces while strapped to a rocket . . . *blindfolded*. Despite an original premise and great cast (Colin Mochrie, Shauna Black, Cheri Maracle, Lorne Cardinal, Richard Donat and James Kee), the series never got the chance to fulfil its true potential. Global Television's idea of humour was broad-based, hokey-jokey corny slapstick and not the satiric tone I'd envisioned, as exemplified by *Blackadder* and the Monty

Python films, which used historic context to maximum comedic effect. I'm sure they had their own share of battles with the powers that be, but finding yourself contractually bound to follow inane network notes, coupled with the benign neglect of the production company, Salter Street Films, led critics to compare us to the goofy *F Troop* television show from the 1960s. Not the comparison I was hoping for.

When it comes to comedy, having editorial control of your own vision is crucial. I did not have that. Michael Donovan, the regally aloof owner of Salter Street, insisted a laugh track be added to the show, which I fought against but eventually acquiesced to, based on the inordinate number of industry awards lining the walls of his office.

Who was I to argue with a visionary who'd given the country *This Hour Has 22 Minutes* and financed the brilliant award-winning television industry satire *Made in Canada*, and would go on to share an Oscar with Michael Moore for *Bowling for Columbine*?

Judging by the first episode of *Blackfly*, though, it was blatantly clear that whatever skills the man had producing television sure as shooting did *not* apply to laugh tracks. It wasn't "laughter," either, but *cackling*. A wild and unhinged cackling of the kind heard only in asylums for the criminally insane during a total lunar eclipse, rather than the kind of laughter a "regular" audience would make while enjoying a lighthearted comedy set in a fort . . . in the forest.

The experience proved a Faustian bargain. You are forced to answer to powerful people who don't trust your funny, even though they've hired you to *be* funny. The paradox is that the "you" they want you to be . . . isn't you! So, instead of channelling the affably subversive tone of my stand-up act, in *Blackfly* I acquiesced to network demands, accepted a patronizing production company's indifference and became an eighteenth-century Gilligan in a tri-corner hat.

Lesson learned: just because someone has the power, it doesn't make them right.

The silver lining in *Blackfly* was seeing a frontier fort rise from the forest along Nova Scotia's South Shore, where a myriad number of trades such as drivers, carpenters, caterers, editors, writers, directors, cast and crew made a good living for two summers in a row. That an idea whose gestation period had rolled round the amniotic fluid of my brainpan for several years was finally made manifest proved a validation of the imagination. Given the unholy amount of money spent on Spielberg's Hollywood blockbusters, the man must have had daily nerdgasms on the set of *Jurassic Park*!

During twelve-hour days spent on my feet shooting (which, half the time, meant falling down), or in the writing room either breaking story, writing scripts or fixing ones we'd commissioned (that came in either three days late or fifteen pages too long), I'd remember those lean years of struggle in Los Angeles. Just to stay sane in that paradise of non-stop unemployment and ever-mounting personal debt, I threw my name in the hat with thirty other unknowns at local cof-fee-house amateur nights for the privilege of performing a five-min-ute set. The acts were an eclectic collection of poets, comedians, singers and what I swore were the guitar-playing, grown-up illegiti-mate spawn of the Manson clan who wandered in from their sage-brush warrens somewhere north of Chatsworth, looking for the love that Charlie never gave. Remembering those nights reminded me the production demands I experienced were good problems to have, compared to following someone who said they'd been abducted by aliens . . . and had the scars to prove it.

Having a television series is constant creation, negotiation and compromise as you stick-handle your way through production deadlines and network demands 24/7. The fight for your vision gets tiring. You win some and lose some. But you stay the course because the only way you'll ever win is by never ever giving up.

Besides, last I heard, the banks don't accept pride as a mortgage payment.

That's why I love the road. It's just you, a microphone and an audience, all there for the same thing: laughs. On the road, your creative integrity is not at the mercy of powerful network mandarins, but rather a fickle, omnipotent God whose price for allowing you to follow your bliss is to stick you in a primal blizzard straight from the Pleistocene on the way to Prince George!

My car rocked again, but I had an idea: follow his tail lights! Follow them! Follow them to sanctuary!

And I did just that. With my head out the driver's-side window and steering with my right hand, I tailgated that leviathan for twenty-six klicks into Williams Lake. The hotel I was booked into appeared in the distance. Thoughts of the loss of *Blackfly* had fled. After all, nothing lasts forever. And besides, I was alive and no longer stuck in a Nordic purgatory about to wrestle magical dwarves.

The hotel's entranceway illuminated an iron silhouette of a heavily knapsacked voyageur with a musket in his hand, head bent into the wind, making his way to some far point of frontier. The irony was not lost on me.

My phone rang, waking me at 7 a.m. It was the DJ Prince George, sounding half-a-dozen-Red-Bulls-into-the-morning way-too-chipper.

"Heard you were having some trouble on the highway last night. What? No winter storms where you come from? This is how we roll up here! Hope you've got something funny to say about that . . . and we're on!"

After that drive in 2003, I wrote this in my journal: "I know one thing. I'm not going to be out here at sixty, looking for laughs at the far points of frontier, dodging death on killer roads." *Bahahahahaha!* Think again, pilgrim!

I did exactly that not long ago in December 2019. On the way to Fort St. John, the non-winter tires on my Avis rental (because in all provinces but Quebec companies are not legally bound to provide winter tires) flagrantly rebuked my driving skills on a two-lane road glazed with a death-smooth coat of freezing rain. Those tires were forbidden purchase on the icy wet surface, and just as before, my fate was placed in the hands of a fickle Almighty, who thankfully wasn't sleeping on the job that day.

When the temperature rose and began to thaw the ice rink I'd been driving on, fifty-ton goliaths with nuclear waste warning plaques on their grilles blew past in the opposite direction, throwing great tsunamis of a bitumen-rich soup up all over my windshield. Lessons still being learned: life is all about the long haul.

I'm headed for the BC Interior first and make the turn at Revelstoke, where a museum to the infamous Canadian Pacific Railway sits. A mere forty-five kilometres west, in Craigellachie, you can see where, in 1885, after ten daunting years of sweat, death and engineering genius (not to mention graft, kickbacks and an audacious level of political corruption), the actual last spike of the CPR was hammered, linking the new nation of Canada from east to west. It also made a lot of white dudes with the right political connections filthy rich. I guess as much as things change, they stay the same.

Under a sky of cobalt blue, menthol-cool breezes dance down from marshmallow-white mountaintops, tickling the nape of my neck with the softness of a lover's kiss. It is 2007, and spring has returned to the Slocan Valley of Kootenay country in a mighty scream of green. Aspens leaf. Blossoms burst. Trout lilies sprout sentinel-tall from wetlands where beavers, those obsessive-compulsives of the animal kingdom, push the limits of logic with feats of engineering. It's not hard to imagine the domestic chatter in the lodge:

"I've got to build another wall, honey."

To which she responds, "Can we have just one Saturday where you're not doing anything? Just one?"

In aeries high above, eagles are hatching; bears in caves are scratching awake; and sasquatch mothers, perhaps, are suckling their young in secret groves of old-growth forest. On the backs of several cars and trucks, I see bumper decals depicting the shadow of a sasquatch above the statement "I believe." (By the way, if sasquatches are real, why do we never see footage of baby ones? In most simian subgroups, babies are the most curious and least fearful of humans. It's always the babies coming out of the jungle that steal your binoculars, play with your foot or break into the camp's medicine chest. Just sayin'.)

There's always been the myth of magical mountain valley Shangri-Las hidden from the wider world, home to those who live a life of blissful reverie mere mortals like ourselves can never hope to know . . . unless you live in Nelson town, that is. It's wonderfully, warmly welcoming here, with a live-and-let-live vibe, home to fresh-faced, heart-warm neo-hippies, semi-feral vagabonds looking like they've been on the road since Neil Young was in a garage band, and trust-fund ski-bum nomads, come to carve orgasmic Kootenay powder.

This mountain town of heritage buildings is flush with restaurants, cafés, art galleries, indie-hipster coffee shops and sports stores filled with the kind of adventure gear you'd need for that weekend you're looking to spend in a snow cave. There's a sidewalk food truck called Bite that serves salmon burgers named after David Suzuki and lactose-conscious poutine in cups to friendly, smiling people strolling down Baker Street.

For those who enjoy a toke, the town is flush with head shops. For some reason, authorities turned a blind eye to the marijuana trade in Nelson for years, and as a result, the enterprise was well ahead of the curve before legalization, playing a pivotal role in setting a standard look for an industry whose future had yet to arrive.

Every head shop was operating-room antiseptic in a smooth, Zen-clean setting, with engaging staff in starched white lab coats coming across more like professional pharmacists than the tie-dyed Jerry Garcia look-alikes traditionally associated with the selling of dope.

You remember those proprietor stoners of youth? They were always running their illicit businesses from a secret hole in the wall where you needed to know a password to enter. I stopped smoking up years ago because I found the pot grown today far more potent than the innocent, munchie-inducing homegrown ganja of yore. After one toke of the turbocharged weed they were pulling out of hydroponic warrens prior to legalization, you went cross-eyed, had no spit, and in ten minutes were squirrelled away beneath the sink, talking to Jesus.

The pioneers of the Kootenay region's marijuana industry were American draft dodgers who crossed our undefended border in Volkswagen vans during the Vietnam War with fifty bucks in their pockets and Bob Dylan on the eight-track. With close access to a porous border, Nelson became the illicit trade's epicentre, as tons of the wacky-tabacky headed south for a generation.

Twenty years prior to legalization, organized crime had knocked a lot of mom-and-pop operations to the curb, but now that the bud is legal, they've begun to proliferate once again. In fact, several years ago, Mounties raided a grower's operation in the backcountry and discovered the operation was "guarded" by half a dozen docile, non-threatening black bears lounging round the property. (It's been rumoured two were playing backgammon and another was shooting hoops, but this can't be confirmed.) Turns out the bruins were all royally fried. The owner had been feeding them marijuana cookies. You don't hear stories like that in Toronto.

I was enjoying lunch beside the Bite truck, overlooking Kootenay Lake, when a tired woman whose arms were laden with grocery bags sat to rest. She said she was a massage therapist whose husband had moved her to Canada from Germany, where they'd met.

"He took me to Edmonton. It was dark, cold and had no culture. After Europe, can you imagine? I hated it." I remembered those raucous nights playing to two thousand people at a sold-out Winspear Centre and thought she must be talking of a different place.

"Did you know Nelson's built on a crystal mountain that sits below the lake? People find crystals there all the time. The Indians came to fish, hunt and bury their dead, but wouldn't live here. The energy's too intense. The town is criss-crossed by vortex lines, like they have in Sedona."

When I hear stories about vortex lines and energy belts, I start to check out. In fact, I camped in Sedona, Arizona, when driving back to Toronto from LA in '93. High-end spas and too many shops selling everything from T-shirts to dream catchers hadn't turned the town into a cornucopia of New Age commercialism yet. It was still a natural wonder of red rock canyons and pinyon pine with no bumper-to-bumper traffic jams choking the main drag, provoking irate townsfolk in their cars to swear at visitors in *their* cars who'd come to get their chakras cleansed. I set up my tent in a private campground beside a brook—and a couple with clinically desert-dry, cracked skin that I assumed they'd earned from too many days spent staring up at the sun while wandering the canyons high on peyote. These drifters in love told me there were 137 different vortex lines in Sedona, but "the strongest was up behind the Dairy Queen."

The woman continued: "After standing there and buzzing on the energy for an afternoon, we couldn't sleep for a week." I told them they'd most likely been kept awake by the Mr. Mistys they'd been drinking. "That DQ treat is so cold, it freezes the temporal lobes that house the seat of reason in the brain," I said, "making people who believe in the power of a vortex to cure everything from a stutter to a brain tumour even more susceptible to bullshit." I bade them good night and prayed they wouldn't murder me in my sleep.

Vortex lines are supposedly swirling fields of energy emanating from the Earth's surface that are conducive to spiritual healing . . . and other stuff. So, that explains things! Nelson is the *only* place in my twenty years spent criss-crossing Canada where I've seen a six-foot-seven man in a white beard the length of Gandalf's wander through town with a walking staff, telling anyone who'll listen that there's an extraterrestrial landing base north of town . . . and not be considered crazy.

In fact, Gandalf's double could be on to something, because not far from Nelson, the artist's enclave of Kaslo has the most UFO sightings in Canada. Then again, given the potency of the BC bud I bought, you don't need a mother ship to get to another planet. (When I said I no longer smoke up, what I meant was *a lot*. I don't smoke up *a lot*.)

Now a new breed of nomad is showing up: wanderers with money. They arrive with fat portfolios, driving a Lexus, while they listen to Bruce Springsteen on their playlist sing songs about the working man. In a region where gold and silver were once pulled from the Earth in a mad turn-of-the-century scramble for riches, real estate has replaced mining as the predominant industry.

It's the only thing I hear from everyone everywhere. I once stopped for breakfast at the Main Street Diner and struck up a conversation with the manager. I commented on the number of luxury cars I saw in town.

"Now that the land around Fernie's been all bought up," she said, "they're coming here with their oil-patch millions, driving land values through the roof. Pretty soon, none of us will be able to afford to live here." (Mind you, this was thirteen years ago, before oil prices tanked, Alberta's economy took a nosedive and racist yellow-vest rednecks took to looking for scapegoats.)

"There's ghost towns above the Slocan Valley where miners lived before the gold got played out back in the 1900s," she continued. "Been empty for generations, but now people have returned to claim their birthright to that real estate, bequeathed to families long before anybody ever thought it would matter as much as it does today."

Farther south of Nelson and tucked into the rugged East Kootenay country between the Rocky and Purcell Mountain ranges is Cranbrook. It's more Alberta than BC, with an authentically rugged working-class soul. It's far rougher round the edges than the gated communities farther west, where Cabernet-soaked Boomers golf away their golden years. Cranbrook is where Mom and the kids pile into a ram-tough Dodge truck to pick up the groceries at IGA, as opposed to West Vancouver, where a nanny in a Range Rover visits Whole Foods with the children of the mother she's working for, hoping to snag the last half dozen ten-dollar Peruvian mangoes.

Cranbrook is not given to that passive reverie more contemplative souls enjoy on the wild west coast of Vancouver Island. For those who live beside the Pacific Ocean's soothing lullaby, the cacophonous bang and clang of industry is another man's soundtrack. Islanders of the Pacific Rim enjoy the stress-free reverie that comes from living in an enchanted land of fog and fern, where misty mountain forests greet the sea and Green Party officials milk their unicorn herds in the magical meadows of Nevermore. Whereas in Cranbrook, there are no unicorns, but if there were, there'd be a two-bag limit on them during hunting season.

It was in Cranbrook that an old teammate from Halifax minor hockey–playing days said hello post-show. We played on the Bantam B Arrows the year we won our house league championship, after four periods of overtime. His callused handshake told me his life's labour had been different than mine. Raised in public housing by the railway tracks, his world growing up was a give-no-quarter corner of

Halifax. Some who left "the pubs" played a far better hand than the one they were dealt, while others fell hard in a world beyond the familiar that broke them lonesome. Not this dude, though. After going bankrupt with an unreliable partner running a pizza shop in Richmond, he met the woman who would become his wife and they headed for her hometown of Cranbrook.

Although we went to the same high school, we ran with different crowds, and other than a cursory nod in the hallways, our social circles were chasms apart.

In a thumbnail trajectory of his life until now, he said he'd quit school in grade eleven and made for Vancouver. I mentioned I'd gone to university after graduating, and he went quiet. Even growing up, the dude had the wary eye of a warrior about him, accompanied by a permanently tuned bullshit detector ready to deflate the first sign of pomposity. My mention of university turned the air around us tight. He was the one who read the room and broke the tension, though, not me.

"It's good you're funny, 'cause you never had much of a slapshot."

"Cripes, I still don't!" I said, and we laughed.

"Remember how those Civic Arena dressing rooms where we played always smelled like chickens?" I asked. He roared laughing. Suddenly, we were back. A memory shared of a seminal moment in time, teleported us back to an arena's dressing room circa 1972, thanks to the barnyard's worth of poultry kept caged there during the Atlantic Winter Fair.

This agricultural exposition always arrived after Thanksgiving, planting itself on the hallowed grounds of the Halifax Forum. For ten days, anyone who raised, rode or milked livestock came to compete and congregate among their own, while city-dwelling Haligonians

came to watch equestrians jumping, oxen pulling, farmers milking—
and some, I guess, to look at chickens sitting in cages, staring at the
wall, doing nothing at all.

The infamous Bill Lynch carnival tagged along too, setting itself
up in the parking lot to get that one last nickel from your pocket
before winter set in and they pulled out of Dodge. Bill's prime-time
appearance was during the waning days of summer, when August
arrived on swollen grey Atlantic clouds and the nights sat heavy and
still. That's when you'd hear the carny's haunting, nasal twang come
sailing down from Windsor Street for our bedtime ears to catch:

"Come see the Mini Horse! Come see the Mini Horse! The world's
smallest pony!"

Outside a circus tent hung a ten-foot tapestry depicting the star
attraction. This rendering inferred, in no uncertain terms, that the
Mini Horse was a holdout from the dawn of mammals, when ground
sloths weighed two thousand pounds and the equine genus we're
familiar with today could fit in a teacup. It stood Lipizzan stallion–
proud in the tapestry amongst a herd of its own, all grazing content-
edly on an imagined Cenozoic plain.

Bill Lynch's Mini Horse looked every inch the creature Doug
McClure and his band of cowboys chased through a crack in a wall
of rock, leading them to discover *and* capture a Tyrannosaurus rex,
in the film *The Valley of Gwangi*. (Spoiler alert: never lasso a T-Rex
and bring it back to a turn-of-the-century carnival being held in a
Western town, because the Gwangi will break its shackles, gobble
down an elephant, and then run amok and eat a one-eyed witch.)

After paying a full dollar, you stepped inside a dimly lit tent with
a dozen other gullible fools, only to witness a P. T. Barnum–level of
hucksterism whose audacity should have warranted applause—or

imprisonment. The Mini Horse was nothing more than a chihuahua with a little homemade saddle on its back!

"Look! It's prancing just like a horse," I heard someone say.

If it were a horse, I remember thinking, *but it's a chihuahua*!!

It was our own fault for believing the Mini Horse was real and not just an imaginative carny ruse. We should have known, given Bill's reputation for skirting round the rules. His midway flaunted safety standards. The Ferris wheel had bits of flesh and clothing hanging off it. For my money, it was and still is the scariest midway ride. You were seated in nothing more than a bucket that was totally open to the elements, with nothing but a rattling bar across the seats to wrap your fingers round in a death grip, while a million miles below, the controls were being operated by a chain-smoking carny with seven teeth, a grade eight education and a three-pack-a-day habit. They'd leave you at the top forever, too. I remember watching weather patterns change over the Gulf Stream. A family of miscreants excited their dad had finally been paroled would be seated with their felon father in the bucket in front of us, rocking it back and forth.

"You're not supposed to do that," one of us would yell way too loud. Expecting any help from the carny running the ride was futile . . . he was related to the people rocking the bucket!

One summer, the midway also featured a petting zoo. A more accurate description would be a *diseased animal* petting zoo. It was the Devil's menagerie! I saw a child pet a piglet with his bare hand, and it turned black and fell off! Bill advertised a real, live unicorn, too. In actuality, it was a blind pit pony with half a hockey stick taped to its head.

The Forum had a professional-sized ice surface that was removed for the run of the fair. Equestrians— rich girls from the South End in the Bengal Lancers—competed in jumping contests; big Dutch–German hybrids from the South Shore and their Eaton's catalogue "husky"-sized spawn cursed their oxen in feats of strength; dairy cows were milked in competition by meaty-handed, dairy-fresh maidens from farms in the Annapolis Valley; teamsters drove their quarter horses, with skills worthy of the Golden Horde, up the aisles at full speed into the Forum's arena. The Forum featured all the main attractions while the Civic Arena next door, with its smaller ice surface, housed stalls selling sundries, games of chance, miraculous household cleaning agents you couldn't find at Canadian Tire and, of course, chickens, in the dressing rooms.

I suppose the powers that be could justify stuffing avian livestock from floor to ceiling in the Civic's dressing rooms. You most certainly couldn't have that barnyard hum lingering in the dressing rooms of the Forum, because that temple of worship was the home ice of the Montreal Canadiens' Calder Cup–winning American Hockey League farm team, the Nova Scotia Voyageurs. Having future Stanley Cup winners like Yvon Lambert or Larry Robinson complaining their lockers smelled like chicken shit would never do. (Which, given that *chicken shit* in popular vernacular means "lack of courage," would smart even worse for a team's chosen goon, who weekly pulverized the snot out of opponents and even leapt over penalty box Plexiglas in full gear with skates laced to finish the fight they were in there for.)

In September 1970, NHL teams came to the Halifax Forum for an exhibition game. Kids at Chebucto School, where I went, had to attend morning shop class once a week at Bloomfield School, which sat much closer to the Forum than ours. This gave us the opportunity to catch a practice on our way home for lunch. The fancy name for shop class was "industrial arts," a form of gender-specific education where boys learned how to make metal cookie sheets while girls learned how to actually *make* the cookies in "home economics." A far more practical skill than the medieval one of metallurgy. When I moved out on my own at twenty-two, I could barely boil a can of soup without burning it, but give me three sheets of corrugated tin, metal-cutting shears and a can of red paint, and you've got yourself a weather-vane that looks like a lobster.

This particular weekday morning, we were watching the Boston Bruins practise. We had our autograph books out, when around the boards came their tough, scrappy right winger, Johnny McKenzie. I was leaning over as far as I could, yelling, "Johnny! Johnny! Gimme your autograph!" He stopped and turned toward me. It was the first NHL player's face I'd ever seen close up. The hockey card I had of him at home showed a player sporting a warm, welcoming, full-toothed grin from ear to ear. On this day, I learned real life is somewhat different.

Sweet Jesus! He had five teeth, and two of those were broken, sitting in a ferociously frightening visage. It was a face of great contusions, wrinkled folds of skin and lumpy scars earned from a million blueline collisions, high sticks, goal-crease battles and fists in the face. In actuality, Johnny's whole head was closer to a forgotten ball of suet, chewed over the winter by rodents that a spring thaw might reveal.

"Johnny," I pleaded louder, "gimme your autograph." He looked and said, "Piss off, you little red-headed prick." (Because I was once.) Another player skating close by overheard Johnny's rebuke and reprimanded him: "Johnny. Don't talk to the kid like that. He'll remember what you said forever."

And today, may I say, "Thank you, Derek Sanderson."

A week later, we got into the Forum during a Montreal Canadiens practice, when it was empty of onlookers. Even the ubiquitous Gollum-like Lusher, who we swore lived in the subterranean bowels of the building, was nowhere to be seen. Lusher doubled as a janitor and trainer's assistant, scurrying warily from behind the player's bench to the dressing room after every V's game, clutching the team's top-of-the-line Sherwood and Victoriaville hockey sticks, ready to run the gauntlet of kids asking those gods-who-walked-as-men for their game sticks.

Tough older kids, who'd soon be doing a stretch in juvie for pulling lunchtime B & E's, tried to snatch a loose one, but Lusher would give no quarter, for his mitts held a Gorilla Glue–tight grip on his bounty, protecting it with the same level of devotion a Benedictine monk would a Bible written by Saint Paul himself.

The Canadiens had just left the ice, save for defenceman Terry Harper, who was taking slapshots on an empty net. Beside him sat two buckets brimming with hockey pucks. Regina-born Harper would win four Stanley Cups and have a sterling career in the NHL as a solid "stay-at-home defenceman," a term reserved for those who played the position with more concern for protecting their goalie's crease than scoring goals. In fact, the man stayed at home so much, a "Terry Harper hat trick" wasn't scoring three times in a game, but three goals in a season! He was clearly a man not in it for the glory but for the game. Perhaps the morning we saw him taking shots on that empty net, he was daydreaming as to how great it would be to actually pop a few during a real game for a change.

One of us yelled, "Hey, Harper! How about a puck or two?" And I'll be damned if he didn't oblige! With a smile that lit up the Forum, he yelled, "Sure, boys!" and picking pucks from the bucket beside him, began flipping them over the boards to every corner of the stands, even pointing to where they'd be going, like cocky batters will do at home plate to let a stadium of fans know the next ball will soon be over the fence. High into the Forum they went, rattling off the seats and stairwells, as we, in unbridled grade seven Chebucto School rink-rat glee, chased our rubber bullion down, cradling them home in our arms much as Jack would have done those golden-goose eggs he'd stolen from the giant's kitchen.

And today, may I say, "Thank you, Terry Harper."

Life always came full circle during my travels. People from long ago showing up in theatre lobbies, waiting to say hello while I autographed the DVDs of my specials I'd be selling. Some faces who said hello at these signings belonged to those who'd not crossed my mind in forty-five years, save for a fleeting cameo appearance they'd made in a dream I had after eating Camembert cheese too close to bedtime. They'd stare with a knowing look, waiting for me to remember their names. Truth be told, I always did—and do—because I never really left the Maritimes. Do any of us from there? Does the melancholy tickle in our belly for back home ever really disappear? Meeting so many from there was most definitely due to the nomadic gene economic necessity has bred into a Maritimer's bones. After all, even Jesus had to leave home to find work. Yet even though the wind had carried us to different points of the compass, the necessity to regain a sense of "then" was tangible.

On occasion, the meeting was more than a cursory exchange of pleasantries and a wave goodbye with a wish for the best. Instead, it was one anchored to deeper water, held fast by the connective tissue of shared experience the struggle for a foothold in the wider world had not frayed.

Here in Cranbrook, on this pit stop on the road, I saw one man who'd found what he'd been looking for on the other side of the Great Divide. Standing beside his wife in their new home, we looked out through a bay window at a stunning panoramic view of the southern Rockies.

"Not a bad view for a kid from the ghetto, eh, Ronnie?"

"No, buddy. Not bad. Not bad at all."

Chapter Ten

CAR FROM AWAY

I'll never forget that summer a man walked on the moon—partly because I saw it on TV, but mostly because we were camping at the time, camping way at the northeastern tip of the continent, where Cape Breton's pretty green highlands fall to the sea.

As Dad's Plymouth Fury II drove over Cape Smokey, headed for our site in the national park, the scent of spruce, pine, ocean and field wafted through the open windows of that gas-guzzling dreadnaught of the highway. I'm willing to wager that every time we filled it up, Saudi Arabia dropped seven feet! His annual three-week parole from the airless towers of Maritime Telegraph and Telephone meant freedom for all, when we in great numbers of fun sang the night forever through, smothered in sunburnt arms and rum-toddy grins of family and friends, all of us illuminated by the softly hissing Coleman lanterns that cast our shadows into the evening road. Lobsters bound for the pot scratching in a box kept time to a guitar's strumming, while the cadence of a cribbage game danced along on the evening air, teasing its way in and out of conversation like lures in a trout pool.

Fifteen two, fifteen four, the rest don't score and your mother's a whore! (Not *our* mother; it's just the way the cribbage rhyme went. Had to clarify that.)

The drive from our home in Halifax took six hours. That's an eternity when you're eleven. My seven-year-old sister and I sat in the back seat while Mom rode shotgun. She was a traditional stay-at-home mom who, besides raising a family and doing *all* the cooking, lived for one thing: to clean house. It was her calling. She embraced the role as a sinner would the pursuit of salvation, scrubbing every corner, sink and baseboard, never missing a rogue dust bunny buried beneath the bed, or last summer's housefly, dead in a never-used wedding gift teacup relegated to the top shelf at the back of the cupboard.

"You don't have to clean back there, Ma. No one will see it."

"I don't care if someone else doesn't see it. I'll know it's there!"

Even today, her house is still so frighteningly spotless you'd be safer getting an appendectomy on her kitchen floor than in any hospital operating room in the country. A shrink would call it obsessive-compulsive, where she just called it "a clean friggin' house is what it is!" She took pride in what defined her. She enjoyed it. Preparing for three weeks of camping, not so much.

By the time we were ready to pull out of the driveway, she'd open the passenger-side door, exhale that world-weary sigh unique to mothers the world over whose home was their job but were finally scoring some R and R, then collapse in the seat, exhausted. In minutes, she was asleep against the window, her head wobbling in slumber, only to bolt upright an hour down the road screeching, "I forgot the friggin' towels!" We assured her she hadn't, holding them up in our hands—they doubled for pillows. She'd smile, blink and then say, "Anyone want a bologna-and-mustard-pickle sandwich?"

We camped in an Eaton's TruLine tent trailer we towed behind the car. It had a metal body and wooden cover that opened into sleeping platforms attached to the sides of the trailer, supported by rods attached to the lower chassis. A canvas covering acted as a roof and walls, held up by an abstract cat's cradle of aluminum poles that you practically needed a degree from MIT to construct.

The poles never seemed to fit together the same way each year, and the patronizing instructions, featuring an artist's shamelessly fraudulent rendering of a happy, smiling family on the box, was insulting. Our family never looked like the family from the instruction manual setting up their tent trailer . . . *ever*.

Clouds of mosquitoes from hell's fetid fields weren't draining the instruction-manual family dry of blood while the mom rooted frantically for repellent at the bottom of a box she swore she'd put it at the top of. Nor was there a conversation bubble over the dad's head, saying, "Sonofabitch bastard! Where in the name of Joe Jumping Jesus H. Christ on hockey skates is the other goddamn pole?!"

Once the tent trailer was up, there was one rule that had to be obeyed: never, *ever* touch the canvas walls when it was raining, or it would leak.

"But how bad will it leak?" I asked.

"Don't touch the canvas, Ronnie, and we won't find out," Dad said, staring at me like I wasn't his.

"Like, will it be a tidal wave of water?"

"Dad said just don't touch it," my sister put in, splatting another mosquito fat with blood on her arm.

"Or will it be a slow flood, like in the Bible?" I was a curious kid.

"Christ Almighty! Am I speaking Russian? Just don't touch it!"

"*Okayyyyyy . . .* "

No wonder my line of questioning got on his nerves. He didn't ask to be grilled about the consequences of touching wet canvas by his hyperactive kid. He just wanted his three weeks' vacation far from the airless tower where he worked, nostalgic for the days when he was on the road, installing phone systems, instead of shackled to a middle-management desk surrounded by professional engineers.

"Do you know why an engineer wears that iron ring on his finger, Ronnie?"

"No, Dad. Why?"

"It's to balance the lead in his arse."

Mom weighed in on his warning as she slathered calamine lotion on our mosquito bites, covering my sister and me in a chalky residue from tip to tail until we resembled primitive children painted in ceremonial pigment.

"Listen to your father and don't touch the canvas unless you want to wake up drowned," Mom warned.

"Don't be simple," Dad corrected. "You can't *wake up* drowned."

"Well, then, he won't *wake up* drowned, but we'll *see* him drowned when *we* wake up." Mom turned to me. "Don't touch the canvas when it's raining, he said."

That night, it rained. Hard. Dad turned to face me just before bedtime.

"What did I tell you?"

"Don't touch the canvas when it's raining. I heard you."

"So . . . don't."

"I won't."

He didn't believe me, because he kept staring. Did he see hesitation behind my eyes? Did he see a nanosecond of impertinence cross my brow that said, "Like hell I won't touch it"? I say this, because he said it again, only with an alliterative emphasis unique to his Burgeo-born pedigree that lent his profanity a poetic gravitas.

"By the lumped-up, woolly-eyed gentle German Jesus, don't touch the canvas walls when it's raining, or I will guaran-Goddamn-tee, there's gonna be a stranger in hell for breakfast by the Lord-snappin' arseholes!"

"I *heard* you. I'm not mental."

But I also heard the canvas beside my head, slick with moisture, beckoning.

"Over here. That's right, Ronnie. Look here. Touch me. Reach your finger out and touch . . . the . . . walls . . . of . . . the tent trailer. How bad can it be? It's not like it's going to drown you. But I bet you wonder if it will. Touch me."

Temptation began working its weird juju. My index finger was possessed of a will of its own.

I can't help it. Must . . . touch . . . the canvas. And just as my finger reached out, inches from satisfaction, a flashlight beam broke the night.

"Caught you, ya little Christer!"

Today, they call my condition ADHD. Back then they called it "Jesus Christ, there's something wrong with him."

When it did rain that summer, it fell heavily and consistently for several days in a row for a full week. Whatever sepia-toned nostalgia people might nurture of childhood days spent camping with family can be easily vanquished by simply remembering, "Isn't that the summer it poured rain so hard that the campground flooded, and a drunk guy almost drowned after passing out in a puddle beside his tent?"

At least we were off the ground in our tent trailer, and provided I never touched the canvas walls—*again*—it wouldn't leak—*again*—and we would not be forced to pack up and leave, like the tenting families we saw piling into cars headed for home. Their faces looked grateful with relief, like stranded victims of rising floodwaters suddenly plucked from their rooftops by rescue boats. Not us.

"We paid for three Jesus weeks and we'll camp for three Jesus weeks, by the Jesus," Dad said.

One particular morning, Dad decided we were going for a drive, because another family we'd been camping with had done it the day before. Only we'd go . . . "just a little bit farther." The drive was something to take the edge off our waterlogged cabin fever, even though it wasn't a cabin we were in, but a leaky Eaton's TruLine tent trailer I couldn't stop touching the canvas walls of.

Turning left from the campground, we headed north and just kept going. For some reason still unknown to me, Dad steered off the Cabot Trail proper and took, to quote Robert Frost, "the road less travelled." It was a secondary local road running by the small settlement of Dingwall, that went past an even smaller village of Capstick, towards the tip of the island where sat Meat Cove, the most northerly habitation in a destitute corner of a long-ago have-not province.

So bucolic is this knoll of emerald green today, you'd swear it belonged to some enchanted corner of Middle Earth. Besides the dozen perfectly groomed campsites scattered round the property, there's a charming gift shop and snack bar serving gloriously good clam chowder you'd truly go to war for. That's why it's particularly difficult to fathom the barefoot-hillbilly Hobbiton of tarpaper shacks and hillside dugouts we saw that summer when men walked on the moon.

The last time I drove there, twenty-seven years ago, there was still no guardrail to protect the absent-minded motorist from taking a deadly trip over the cliff to a beach of boulders far below. In 1969, the road was far deadlier and but a single dirt track where a shepherd could comfortably lead sheep, but a father could *not* comfortably manoeuvre a monstrous Plymouth Fury II with an engine bonnet "so Jesus big, if I hit a moose in this, you kids won't feel it in the back seat!"

The road ended where the shacks began. Meat Cove was a collection of rudimentary tarpaper hovels built of wood and cinder block. Save for the rusted skeleton of a 1950s-era Chevy sitting in a front yard, the scene was Neolithic.

We sat slack-jawed in our idling Plymouth, gauging the netherworld we'd driven into, when from nowhere and everywhere there suddenly arrived a swarm of filthy, snot-crusted, semi-feral urchins with rink-wide foreheads, clamouring round the car, exhibiting the dangerous curiosity of game farm simians, hell-bent on vandalism. That's when our mom began to curse.

"Jesus Christ! Jesus Christ almighty! Turn the car around, Bernie! Turn it around!"

Dad put the car in reverse and hit the gas. But instead of moving backward, we sank. In fact, we sank up to the wheel rims in a glutinous, thick gumbo that adhered with the conviction of the Krazy Glue that hadn't been invented yet. We were stuck in the muck of Meat Cove!

The pack had circled the vehicle by now, and although the doors were locked, our mother was frozen shell-shock still, her face contorted in primal fear worthy of a marmot trapped in a raptor's shadow, far from the safety of its cozy burrow.

As Dad gunned the gas, I turned to see a rooster tail of mud rising high behind us. Mom was starting to hyperventilate, and her usual voice was replaced by the feverish, high-pitched squeak of the afore-mentioned marmot. With eyes bugged out and loopy, she turned to me and my sister, shouting, "Don't open the fuckin' windows!"

We'd never heard our mom drop an f-bomb before. Ever. By the frenzied look in her eyes, though, we knew a switch had been flipped and she'd slipped into a dangerous valley of crazy all mothers are capable of falling into.

"Why would we open the windows?" we said.

Dad piped up, barking, "You touch the goddamn tent when I tell you not to; why wouldn't you open the goddamn windows, too?"

"But we're not in a tent now," I corrected.

"Don't talk back to your father," said Mom.

"I'm not. I'm just sayin' . . ."

"Then don't *just say* anything."

"I won't," I promised.

"Don't open the windows." The word *windows* became frighten-ingly elongated, ending in a high-pitched screech unique to an OCD-plagued sister whose piercing shriek could be heard in celes-tial orbits if you tracked dirt into her home, which was covered in more plastic than an autopsy table.

"I said I won't."

"Then don't."

"He won't!" My little sister said.

Like a lone prairie schooner crossing a cruel frontier, we sat help-less as the guttural hoots and raucous hollering of Meat Cove's barefoot denizens scurried to the back of our car and began, one at a time, to gleefully run through that rooster tail of spraying muck, as would Kool-Aid–drinking suburban children a backyard sprinkler.

"Ho-leee fuck," Dad muttered under his breath. He knew full well things had taken a bizarre and unsettling turn. Anything could happen now. Their blood was up, and that's when a mob is capable of anything. The car was surrounded by a brood of hilltop wildings of all ages, either half-naked or wearing tattered raiments perhaps pulled from the bodies of drowned sailors washed ashore. Their hair was either shaved to the scalp or a rat's nest of unkempt locks; they looked frighteningly similar to photos of those Rumanian children you'd see in the newspaper on occasion, the accompanying stories saying they'd been raised by wolves in the Carpathian Mountains and suddenly showed up one morning on a farmer's back porch, naked and filthy, chewing on a squirrel.

Perhaps fearing that should he continue revving the engine, the spinning wheels would drill all the way up to the chassis, Dad took his foot off the accelerator. The showering of mud stopped. So did the braying of the pack. They were flummoxed. Smeared in Meat Cove muck from tip to tail, they now looked lost and confused, much like a hyperactive two-year-old who's thrown a kitten against a wall and can't figure why it's not moving anymore. That's when the leader of the pack pressed his proscenium-browed, bucktoothed kisser against the driver's-side window and, scowling, pointed at my father, demanding he hit the gas again.

"We're only going to go deeper into the muck," Dad tried to say, but he couldn't, because he stuttered when he was nervous, and we knew his sentence was now an eternity short of completion. Dad was stuck spinning his own verbal wheels on the word *going*, and the poor man could not unstick them. When you stutter, it's bad enough trying to get a sentence out under pressure in an everyday social setting but having a menagerie of wildings laugh at you while you try does not work wonders in expediting the process. In his efforts to get past the dreaded *g*, his facial contortions tweaked the funny bone of the Meat Cove youngster, and he began to laugh at our father. Hearing this, the entire pack ran from behind the car and joined in—at what, they weren't certain, but their voices soon rose in a cacophonous imitation of their leader's guffaws.

Without warning, the pack backed away from the window and, parting, revealed a woman of fierce countenance. She wore a tattered cotton dress of simple design, and her skinny legs rose from a pair of green gum-rubber boots. In one hand, she clutched a stubby of Ten Penny, while in the other, a smoke dangled from nicotine-stained fingers. A gaunt face, chiselled sharp by the daily assault of the seasons, housed a hollow-eyed, thousand-yard stare born from isolation and God knows how many dark nights of the soul this woman had wrestled with during a lifetime's incarceration on this lonesome hilltop. She began yelling at the children, and although we couldn't hear the exact content, it seemed the eldest was getting the brunt of it. She kept pointing back and forth between him and the car. The woman walked towards us.

Dad rolled the window down, and our mother made that marmot sound again.

"We is gonna give you'se a push."

Dad stuttered a thank you. We stayed seated.

"That one's strong," she said pointing, "but he's not that strong. You'se'll have to get out," she said.

Dad, turning round to us in the back seat, tried to say, "Get out of the car," but judging by the way his eyes were rolling to the back of his head, we knew he'd never get past that troublesome *g* for at least ten minutes, so we just opened the doors and did what the poor man was desperately trying to tell us. Mom sat immovable in the passenger seat, trapped in a state of shell-shocked catatonia and making that weird marmot sound.

Standing outside the safety of our car in our clean-smelling summer clothes facing a pack of mud-covered children in their tattered raiments, we were the ones who suddenly felt dirty. Even though it was nothing but a sense of adventure that had taken us there that day, the woman's baleful stare said we'd come to take vicarious pleasure at the misfortune of others.

The leader barked orders to three of the bigger kids, and bending down, the four of them gripped the front bumper of that car and, with several mighty grunts, heaved it clear of its entrapment.

Our mom began to frantically wave us into the car.

Dad turned to the woman.

"Thank you," he said, and gave her five dollars.

She stared long at the fiver, so he gave her a twenty.

"That's better." And turning on her heel, she disappeared into a house lit only by candlelight, sitting on the edge of forever.

Pulling away, we saw the pack scurrying over the Meat Cove cliff for the beach—where, I assumed, they'd soon be picking the pockets of drowned sailors washed ashore.

We pulled away. The air inside the car felt close. Mom rolled a window down. Dad cleared his throat.

"Next time," he said, "we'll only go as far as Dingwall."

Dad always took his vacation the last week of July and the first two weeks of August, so being cursed with poor weather could scuttle what already was a laughably short summer.

"No harm with a little rain. The ocean's warmest then," Dad assured. I always wondered what measure of warmth he was referring to, because given the park's northern latitude, that stretch of the Atlantic Ocean never, *ever* got warm—and still doesn't in, say, a *Caribbean* sense of the word. Like, when you go to Cancún now, ten minutes after checking into the hotel you're neck deep in the Gulf of Mexico sucking back a tequila Slurpee and splashing in an ocean so tub-water-temperature perfect, you're as good as back in the amniotic yolk sac.

Warm water is not a luxury accorded summertime swimmers in "Canada's Ocean Playground." Other than a random two weeks at the end of August and a few fleeting days in September, taking a dip comes with a price: it stings your feet, softens your teeth and numbs your extremities, while a minion of whatever deity rules the deep squeezes your *cojones* in a vice-tight grip.

There are exceptions to the rule, however. On occasion, hurricanes, which once delivered a glancing blow to Nova Scotia but now come far too close for a homeowner's comfort, happen to come perfectly close for a swimmer's. The storms' tropical air warms the Gulf Stream to a euphoric degree of ideal bathtub temperature, when a week previous it was only tolerable for mackerel, seals and haddock. Three days before a hurricane makes landfall, suffering arthritics lucky enough to spend but a scant twenty minutes splashing about in the healing surf are rewarded such profound redemption from pain, they've been seen sprinting from the ocean and up the beach, doing backflips towards their towels, where they happily open jars of pickles for their family's picnic.

When it comes to that fleeting Maritime summer, the hospitality industry has basically four months to make the money they need to get through winter. Tourists are a course to be run full out, but come October, every grunt who's spent the season slinging trays of food and grog is suffering sore bunions, an aching back and a Tylenol habit, sporting that thousand-yard shell-shocked stare unique to the beaten and bloodied foot soldiers of their industry. They know every tip was a hard-won boon that came at the cost of catering to busloads of waddling, swag-happy travellers who spilled from a Carnival Cruise Line's gangplank for day trips hither and yon, to lay siege to every craft shop from Lunenburg to Corner Brook, where they'll load up on everything from jams and soaps and painted dories, to a replica of Joshua Slocum's johnson in a bell jar.

Anyway, back to my point. There's only so much of that service-with-a-smile a working stiff can take. Waitresses are the shock troops of the industry. They're the ones who take on the full-frontal barrage of surly patrons. I happened to be at a Nova Scotia South Shore restaurant late in the season when two busloads of cruise ship passengers took a diner hostage, and I watched a cranky customer complaining way too loudly for that late in the season that she'd "ordered my refill twenty minutes ago and it's still not here."

The waitress spun on her heel cornered weasel fast.

"You ordered your refill twenty minutes ago and it's still not here? Well, pardon me all to hell, but I was a slim eighteen-year-old queen of the sea twenty minutes ago, and now I'm not. I'm a forty-one-year-old, overworked single mother of two, running my hole off from dawn to double-shift dusk, hoping to scrounge enough from my savings to get four new snow tires on my Dodge Neon before winter comes or I shoot myself first. So, suck it up, buttercup—you'll get the tea when it's good and ready!"

Actually, I stand corrected. I believe she said, "I'm so terribly sorry. Coming right up, you horse-faced cow."

Like any perceived utopia, Nova Scotia does have its dark side. You're just not supposed to mention it. But hang around the wrong tavern on a Saturday night after the summertime postcard smiles are tucked away and replaced by winter's hard grimace. That's when a crusty, skunky-draft-drinkin' local with more attitude than teeth would cut your throat with a scallop shell just for beating him in shuffleboard.

About 150 kilometres outside Halifax, you lost radio contact with CJCH, which played the hits of the day. There'd be no decent reception for another few hours until you caught the signal coming from Antigonish. That radio station loved to play fiddle music. A *lot* of fiddle music. The instrument is fine in small doses, but as a soundtrack for life, it can test the tolerance of most mortal men. Fifteen years earlier, my father had been stationed in Antigonish for six months on a phone company job, and he woke to jigs and reels on the radio in the morning and went to sleep with jigs and reels at night. There are earworms and then there's "fiddle earworms": a pernicious brain invasion of uncompromising persistence. I'm certain that if fiddle music were piped non-stop into a black-ops interrogation cell from dawn till dusk, the most resistant captive would curl up in the corner, praying for a waterboarding session instead. (Note to self: never share this observation with a local audience in Mabou.)

On the other hand, my Cape Breton–born mother took issue with the bagpipes, a Maritime standard. Her justification for taking umbrage with the pipes was concise and to the point: "The sound gives me a headache, and I'm scared the people playing them with their faces turning purple are going to either have a stroke or shit themselves. I don't like them. No, I don't."

Once outside the radius of CJCH, there'd be no more singing along to "Bad Moon Rising," "These Eyes," or, yes, "Snowbird." Because Anne Murray hailed from Springhill, Nova Scotia, "Snowbird" hitting the top ten on Billboard in the US had everyone talking. I was partial to buddy who actually wrote the song, PEI's Gene MacLellan. His brilliant oeuvre includes "Put Your Hand in the Hand," recorded by a dozen artists as diverse as Elvis and Joan Baez, but outside of the Maritimes and musicians familiar with his work, he's largely uncelebrated by the general public. That's probably because he was never feted in the United States, unlike the songstress who made "Snowbird" famous. That American woman casts a long shadow.

"Car from away! Car from away!" I yelled as the licence plates zipped past.

"Don't yell in my ear when I'm driving!" Dad barked.

"But it's a game, Da. It's car from away."

"From away" meant anywhere but Nova Scotia. It especially meant *Americans*.

And there they were, driving road-hogging Oldsmobiles and Cadillacs, headed for the majestic Keltic Lodge that sat in Tudor splendour on a promontory of land jutting into the Atlantic above the town of Ingonish. Built by the provincial government in 1939 on property purchased from an Ohio rubber magnate, the hotel catered to high-rolling Americans come to golf its state-of-the-art eighteen-hole course and escape the summer heat of Florida, South Carolina and other lands of the imagination. Stepping from their Detroit-built land boats, sporting white shoes, Lacoste shirts and plaid pants, their perky blonde wives in tennis skirts bouncing beside them, the men strode with a high-noon swagger befitting those born to the world's post-war beacon of prosperity.

It was in the holy light of a purple gloaming that I first laid eyes on them, entering our national park in an avocado-coloured Oldsmobile and pulling a sixty-foot, chrome-plated, hermetically sealed Airstream living unit.

"Look!" I pointed. "It's the friggin' Jetsons!"

Here was the myth made manifest. Americans were here! In 1969, it was the country where a kid could order a two-man submarine from the back of a DC comic book. "Fires rockets and torpedoes," promised the ad. The claim seemed a stretch, but if it appeared in the back of an issue of *Sgt. Rock*, it must be true. Painful but also true, stamped on the ad was "Order Void in Canada." Did that ever suck, eh? The only thing I could get here in the winter was the flu. Not in America, though. There, you could get anything. Because America was the land of cool stuff!

Standing in the middle of the dirt road staring in slack-jawed wonder, however, was the personification of *un*cool: me, in ankle-high "floodwater" Tee Kay flares, a pair of Zellers-bought two-stripe North Star sneakers, a T-shirt and a too-goofy haircut courtesy of Lester and Earl, the gin-soaked barbers of our neighbourhood.

Lester and Earl's partnership consisted of a big, round, loud man and a soft-spoken thin one, who took turns falling on and off the wagon. When one was steady and drunk, the other was shaky and sober. Scissors whirred and snipped in reckless abandon around your head.

During that summer, long hair was *the* ticket to cool. It said you belonged to the side of history that mattered. The side that was taking the world in the right direction. The side that was fighting "the pigs" in the streets of Chicago, burning their draft cards and playing in bands.

Long hair was the ticket, but repeated pleas to let me grow mine fell on my father's stone-deaf ears. Instead, I was told to get my arse across the street for a sensible trim, or "By the Jesus, I'll chop it off with my garden shears!"

So away I went, peering back over my shoulder, hoping for a last-minute reprieve where I'd hear, "I'm joking! C'mon back. We're all going to be hippies, raise llamas and grow dope on a commune in the Annapolis Valley with Noel Harrison! Let's start by tie-dying my suit jacket!" Instead, I climbed the stairs to the sacrificial altar that belonged to the bastard sons of Sweeney Todd.

Perhaps in a long-ago, the notorious barbers had obliged customer requests for "a little off the top," "square back" or "just a trim" with professionalism and pride, competently wielding the tools of their trade in a two-chair shop redolent with the medicinal smells of Wildroot and Clubman Pinaud, which glowed translucent in iridescent blues and greens from neat rows of bottles. Their Dartmouth Barber Academy graduation certificates hung on the wall beside one of those ubiquitous calendars of a smiling woman in a bathing suit, cradling enormous breasts while standing beside a new Buick.

Lester and Earl formed their partnership not long after Europe fell to Nazi tyranny. With the port city of Halifax soon to be an embarkation point for thousands of troops bound for overseas, it's not hard to imagine Lester's voice booming with optimism: "The war is a gift, Earl! A gift! Sure, it might not be so good for the countries the Germans invaded, and everybody they killed and are still going to kill before they're killed themselves and it's all over, but for barbers . . . it's a gold mine, buddy, a gold mine! Because what do soldiers need most besides a rifle, smokes and a pack of French safes? Haircuts, Earl! Haircuts!"

The future lay plump with promise. After all, it was the beginning of their career, and beginnings are always rife with possibility. They had legitimate reason to be optimistic, what with the strategic location of their shop a few blocks north of a tent city housing hundreds of Allied troops. With army barbers overwhelmed by the sheer number of soldiers, headquarters put out a tender looking for civilian barbers to accommodate the overflow, which Lester bid for and won. All through the war, and for twenty years afterwards, both men were making the kind of living any barber would envy. That all changed forever the fateful day a deer ran into a clothesline full of washing in Earl's backyard.

Earl's wife, Doreen, had been hanging her bedsheets and undergarments out one crisp fall morning. Their house sat at the far end of Purcell's Cove Road, only a thirty-minute drive to the city. Earl preferred to live in what he considered the country. Lester could brag all he wanted about walking to work; Earl enjoyed the forest being so close to the house that "we can see deer in our field every morning after we screw."

As Doreen draped her sheets on the line, perhaps she felt the waning days of a summer sun warming her apple-bright cheeks and the chilly breeze of coming winter tickling the nape of her neck. Perhaps she heard the pounding of deer hooves as well. Did she hear the rifle shot, too? It's all conjecture. What is not, was the ten-point buck who burst from the forest in a blur of wide-eyed fear that made it oblivious to both the clothesline and Doreen.

One can surmise that on any given day other than this, an acuity bred in the bone would have made the buck very aware of any obstruction to its passage. But that day, running for its life, it did not. The deer hit the clothesline full sprint, and Doreen and the creature suddenly found themselves entangled in a bizarre *danse macabre*, feverishly trying to free themselves from the hanging sheets and underwear. Neighbours down the road said they heard a following shot and then quiet. By the time they arrived, there was no hunter to be seen, only poor Doreen and a ten-point buck draped in bedsheets, dead on the grass, a pair of panties hanging lazily on its impressive antlered head as if they'd been nonchalantly tossed there prior to their carnal tryst.

The hunter responsible was never found. It wouldn't have mattered to Earl anyway. No manner of vengeance could have soothed his broken heart, so a bottle of Tanqueray had to do the work instead. Although he arrived at the shop punctually each morning, dressed in his crisply starched barbershop tunic, he did so stewed, as he would be all day, floating half-aware of the world around him on a melancholy river of gin. His rheumy eyes threatened to spill into your lap from liquid sockets as his manicured hands, scrubbed to a waxy formaldehyde sheen, whirred a pair of scissors far too close to your face for comfort.

Earl's pièce de resistance was a truly heathen style of cut. Back when the Cowsills were singing that hair should be "shoulder-length or longer" and "shining, gleaming, streaming, flaxen waxen," mine was not. Earl shaved up the back of your head to the crown and around the sides, while the top was hacked with nicks and gouges to the porcelain smoothness of the skull. It was a Meat Cove trim, not a haircut. When the barber chair spun round to the mirror, mouths fell open with horror, marvelling at the audacity of Earl's butchery. Once you were outside the shop, your ears suddenly felt embarrassingly large and pink as they flapped, exposed and vulnerable to the hungry winds of winter.

Back at your kitchen table, you received nary an ounce of sympathy. Instead, you were told, "Don't worry. You're only eleven. It will grow back. And don't blame poor Earl, either. If your wife and a deer were found shot dead hugging each other with her panties on its head, you'd give bad haircuts, too."

As any good partner would, Lester tried his best to assuage Earl's sadness, offering a shoulder of support each evening after work as they closed Comeau's Beverage Room, their bellies full of skunky draft. Lester hoped Earl's depression would pass, but the hurt went too deep; time would not heal this. Meanwhile, Lester's marriage to Lois, a woman he'd met at a dance in Sambro after the war, ended childless when she left him for a carny who worked for Bill Lynch midways. During Lester's failed attempts to win her a large stuffed poodle at a game of skill, Lester swore he saw the spark of love ignite between his woman and the carny.

The point of the game was to roll wooden balls on what resembled an uphill bowling alley towards holes of ever-decreasing circumference, which increased in monetary value as they got smaller. If enough balls landed in the richest hole, you'd warrant a prize. As Lois stood tapping her feet with impatience, smoking Export As down to the filter, Lester spent a small fortune trying his best, to no avail.

Seeing his opportunity, the carny stepped from behind his booth and, with patronizing ease, effortlessly rolled the balls into holes of all the top denominations. Then, like a knight returning from a grail quest, he handed Lois the stuffed poodle, throwing a smug sideways glance to Lester that let him know his days were numbered.

Sitting with cold indifference at home in their living room, Lois would wistfully stroke the poodle's head reminding Lester of his inadequacy.

"I'm a barber," he'd plead, "not a bowler."

Lois was hearing none of it, and shortly thereafter, with promises of a life of adventure amongst his midway nomads, Lois followed her carny south to the Florida Panhandle, where his tribe whiled the winter away in sunny comfort, when they weren't doing time for petty theft.

That's when Lester started to drink more, and suddenly, Earl had company.

By the time of my visits, the darkest days of their tenure were upon them. Caring little for style or virtue of cut, they mowed into your scalp in a clear-cutting frenzy. Sometimes, your ears would almost be snipped by the tip of the scissors, and you'd jump with a fright, only to be reprimanded by Lester's whisky breath warning you to "stop squirming or I *will* cut ya!"

Time might not have healed Earl's broken heart, but it certainly worked wonders for haircuts. By the time 1975 rolled around, whatever issues had once polarized opinions regarding the length of your hair had disappeared with the last helicopter off the embassy roof in Saigon. The world had moved on. "Get your arse across the street for a trim" was replaced with "If you want my car on Friday night, you'll get your arse outside and shovel the Jesus sidewalk!"

Still, you kept a wide berth between yourself and that barbershop, just in case some malevolent force would magnetically pull you into one of those chairs for some butchery. I saw Lester's bulk from time to time, mowing white heads returned home after passing a winter's worth of kidney stones in Florida. On occasion, you'd see Earl standing on the barbershop steps, having a smoke and looking wraithlike in the sun. I'd pass by and nod, throwing up a "Hello, Earl," but he was elsewhere in thought, floating away on his dreamy river of gin, waiting for yesterday.

Little did I know the Americans' visit to our national park wasn't for basic summertime R and R. A war in Vietnam had forced their only boy to seek sanctuary in Canada. When his draft card arrived the previous year, he joined the legions of tie-dyed, knapsacked sons who threw their thumbs to the merciful hum of the highway. I guess Clyburn Brook in the Cape Breton Highlands had a healthier ring to the ear than the Mekong Delta.

His first winter there, the young man lived on the western side of the park, amongst the Acadians in Chéticamp. They know all too well what exile means, having walked *back* to Nova Scotia from the swamps of Louisiana, after the British gave these peaceful farmers of Norman blood the boot from their bucolic fields of Evangeline in 1755. The lonesome price of exile still haunts Acadian blood, and if anyone knows how to roll the welcome mat out for fellow travellers, it's them.

The American kid spent his year working in the woods and on the water, far from a war he had no faith in fighting, safe amongst a people who had hewn a home from Longfellow's "forest primeval" two centuries prior. Once summer came, he made his way over French Mountain and down to the squatter camps of his fellow draft dodgers, near to where a copper-coloured Black Brook gurgles into the sea. When his parents received the postcard from his home in exile, they too followed the road north from Baltimore, hoping to find him.

The father's change of heart had been a long time coming. I heard his story through the canvas walls of our trailer (on a rare night I wasn't touching them), as he sat with my father at our picnic table, weeping softly for the son he'd struck with his fist as a burning draft card turned to ash on a sidewalk two generations stood their ground on. Minutes later, the young man had walked away, holding his bleeding nose in one hand and his Boy Scout duffle bag in the other.

It was during that very summer that I saw men walk on the moon. The Americans in the Airstream trailer had invited several families over to watch the event on their TV. They gave the children grape Tang, too. *Grape* Tang—I hadn't even seen the orange kind yet! When they emerged from the back of that Airstream, carrying their portable TV, they actually *plugged* it into the side of what I figured was as close to an interstellar spacecraft as I'd ever get. But not only that—their TV was in colour! Colour! We didn't even have a colour TV at home. All we had was a little black-and-white Panasonic that sat on the kitchen counter. Its screen was so small, I think we had the first iPod and didn't know it. Dad got it for free from a stevedore neighbour after one of the Halifax dockyard containers "broke." Sporting a set of grape Tang lips from ear to ear, I sat wide-eyed, watching America take "one small step for man, one giant leap for mankind." How incredibly cool was that? They could plug a colour TV into the side of their trailer, and I wasn't even allowed to touch the walls of ours!

Several days later, bad weather roared in again, wreaking malicious havoc on the campground, blowing tent trailers over, trashing picnic tables and turning Black Brook from a gentle stream into a raging river that overran its banks. This was the very same storm that bereft of conscience, had drowned two local boys my age. They'd stolen a fisherman's dory for a joyride at the onset of the storm, only to disappear into the Atlantic's hungry maw.

Shortly after the storm's passing, we made our way to the beach, past the detritus of campground ruin and flooded sites. The beach was a battle zone of huge driftwood deadfall wound with monofilament nets, jellyfish, seagrass and seaweed ripped from the ocean floor and angrily strewn far inland by the gale's fury. Many campers were at the water's edge, scanning the grey horizon for some sign of the missing boys. Squinting through the drizzle and sea spray, I thought I saw things: a waving hand in a yellow dory, a flash of red baseball cap on the waves, anything other than the foreboding drone of the rescue boat moving back and forth across an empty point.

"There's something," I said too loudly.

A face turned towards us, all pale, streaked in pain and bottomless loss.

"Is he sure?" the man stammered.

I knew it was the father of one of the lost boys. Avoiding his eyes, I shook my head no and headed back to the campground, arms linked round my family. Looking back, I saw the Americans from the Airstream still staring out to sea.

That night in the cookhouse, someone started playing guitar, and before long we were singing again, the sadness of the day having given way to a few brews and good tunes. Requests were going back and forth, until the Americans asked for that Johnny Horton tune "Sink the Bismarck." No one knew the lyrics, so they started in alone: *In May of 1941, the war had just begun* . . . We all stopped cold, except the Americans, who saw nothing wrong with the lyrics. When told the war had started in 1939, they had no idea Canada had been in it for two years, alongside Britain, before the Japanese even knew where

Pearl Harbor *was*. Besides, they said laughing, we'd still be fighting it if they hadn't stepped in.

The guitar playing stopped. The night felt humid and close. People forgot the moon landing. "The astronaut's suits looked green," someone whispered. A guitar player started strumming "Farewell to Nova Scotia," and everyone joined in. Everyone except the Americans. They didn't know the words. After all, they were from away.

Chapter Eleven

VERNE

He was squatting on the asphalt beside the front door of the Petro-Canada station in Airdrie, Alberta, when I pulled in to fill up. Stepping out of my vehicle, I noticed this big fellow stand, cock his head and look my way.

Surrounded by a serpentine river of highways, gas stations are really isolated islands whose safety can be illusory at times. Despite being brightly lit, with strategically placed security cameras covering every angle, they can leave a person feeling somewhat exposed. A target. And I spook easily. It's an instantaneous full-body response, too, one that twists me into a wide-eyed wrestler's stance, hyperalert and ready to launch a litany of spitting profanity at my protagonist with the same religious zeal a Tourette's-suffering Quaker would direct at a spinning weather-vane.

This unfortunate reaction is bred in the bone. Not because I'm a Quaker, but because I'm descended from high-strung, high-blood-pressure-suffering, cholesterol-producing, poetically profane

Newfoundlanders and anxiety-prone Cape Bretoners. We also exhibit an equal predisposition for spontaneity and hospitality . . . provided you don't spook us. Spook us, and if we're holding something sharp, you could bleed.

Filling up the gas tank in my shirt sleeves, I thought how great it was not to be touring during winter for a change. Drifting into a reverie, I happily began butchering the lyrics to that old Seals and Crofts tune "Summer Breeze" and giving thanks that I hadn't suffered through the non-stop run of minus-40 days these flatlanders were still talking about a good month into an idyllic prairie spring.

In every town I'd visited, main streets were choked with strolling locals whose pale faces were lifted towards the warming sun. After six months locked in frigid incarceration, they were enthusiastically embracing a new-found freedom, much like hostages would who'd recently been sprung from some airless, dank dungeon where their captors had played nothing but Nickelback, fed them field mice and forced them to shit in a bucket.

"Summer breeze makes me feel fine," I sang as I turned to put the pump back. That's when a hand grabbed my shoulder . . .

I screeched. The fright had triggered the fight-or-flight response, releasing a tsunami of cortisol throughout my limbic system, trashing all sense of social restraint in its path. In a nanosecond, the happy man pumping gas singing an insipid pop song from the 1970s, was now crouched bug-eyed and frozen in a wrestler's stance that would look right at home on Billy and Eric's rodeo circuit but was oddly incongruous at a set of Petro-Can gas pumps.

"Ronnie James! Holy shit! I've been watching you since I was little."

I couldn't imagine this guy ever being little. He towered over me.

"Little? How old are you?" I asked.

"Fifty-seven."

"I'm sixty-one. You couldn't have been watching me since you were little."

"Whatever."

His dismissive indifference didn't bother me. Why? Because he knew my name!

After all, I'm in *Canadian* show business! No one knows our names. NDP backbenchers have more name recognition than Canadian performers. Oh well, with no star system here, we don't have as far to fall if the career takes a nosedive. We can take solace in knowing we'll never be Chubby Checker, bemoaning his lost mock chicken billions.

Most times when people meet you, it's "Hey! You're that guy from TV. What's your name again?" Then I say, "I'm Paul Gross," and they don't have a clue who he is, either. Name recognition from a stranger assures Canadian performers that we are not bound for obscurity faster than a 1960s child star who was put to pasture by Walt Disney at the onset of puberty.

The recognition also stroked my fragile self-confidence, which regularly vacillates between the existential despair of a forgotten refugee, standing on the beach without a toothbrush, and a delusional sense of destiny, where I envision leading the Israelites from bondage to the fertile valleys of Canaan.

"Are you gonna keep crouching, or what?" he asked.

I realized I was still locked in my wrestler pose.

"Sorry," I said, standing, "but you kinda scared me."

"You're not much taller even when you stand up," he said, and started laughing at his own joke. Everyone's a comedian.

He had a weathered jean jacket slung over one arm and wore a scruffy T-shirt that hung over a pair of torn and soiled grey sweat-pants. His arms and knuckles were marked with tattoos. At a glance, some looked as though they'd been legitimately inked by a professional in a parlour with a sterilized needle, while others could have been carved with a hot nail in prison. On his feet were running shoes of two different brands and colours, at which I chose not to stare. His hair was a dusty, matted mess in serious need of attention.

Fists of opponents had clearly built his flattened boxer's nose over the years, and the scars of those battles fought showed on dry, chapped lips he'd sometimes twist into a puckered grimace, while shutting one rheumy eye as he gauged my comments with a suspicion born to those whose trust in the world had long since been broken.

"Ha! Ronnie James! I can't believe Verne Cardinal is talking to a rock 'n' roll star from the radio!"

"I'm not a rock 'n' roll star. I'm a comedian. And I was on TV, not the radio."

"Whatever." There's that dismissive *whatever* again. I thought only teenage girls said this to each other in the hallways of junior high, but apparently not.

"What the hell are you doing here?" he asked.

"I'm headed for a gig in Leduc."

"Leduc? No shit! I'm headed for Leduc, too!"

Ah, Jesus. I saw his face brighten. Dollars to donuts, Verne was going to ask me for a lift. Something had registered behind his eyes— it was hope. My car was his salvation from this Petro-Can purgatory.

All the while, I was thinking, *Sure pal, I'd like nothing more than to share my vehicle for three hours with a stranger who's been sleeping by a dumpster at the back of a gas station for a week in decomposing sweatpants.*

He kept staring, waiting for me to offer a ride. I was cornered.

As mentioned in the first chapter, I'd been employed as an improviser in the Second City organization ten years prior to becoming a stand-up. Time spent in that company may have provided me the rudimentary stage skills needed to entertain suburbanites visiting downtown Toronto for a night of inoffensive satire, but in no way did it nurture the talent I'd need if ever I'd have to negotiate my way out of a tight corner with a casualty of colonialism at a set of gas pumps in Alberta.

Then the request came.

"Can you give me a lift to Leduc?"

The first rule of improvisation is to always "Yes, and—" the offering. Saying no will stall the scene, and the prime directive is to *always* move the scene forward. But this wasn't a scene, it was real life, and real life doesn't come with a script, so I did the next worst thing to saying no and asked a question. "Wha-what?"

How lame of me! It lacked gravitas. Why hadn't I at least come back with "As long as you don't mind travelling with someone being chased by alien bounty hunters, who will stop at nothing to get the Crystal Sphere of Zorlac I stole from the intergalactic warlord Slimy Jerry, during a trip to the Andromeda Galaxy. Hop in."

Another motorist had pulled up and was watching the scene unfold. Damn. An audience. I had to be on my toes. Can't suck in front of a potential reviewer. You never know when those career assassins will suddenly materialize out of the ether, ready to eviscerate you with their poison pen.

"Leduc! I'm headed to Leduc, just like you! My nephew works as a cashier at River Cree Casino and I need a place to crash."

This guy is good! He's furthering the scene by adding more information, and I'm just standing here like a stammering wannabe during a game of freeze tag in the Second City workshops.

(For those readers unfamiliar with the discipline's vernacular, freeze tag, or "switch," is an improv game where two actors start a scene based on an innocuous line of dialogue, while the rest of the cast stands onstage behind them. They watch the actors for body movements that spark inspiration. When one of the actors watching sees a physical position worth capitalizing on, they yell, "Freeze!" and then tap that actor on the shoulder, whereupon the new actor enters the scene, assuming the *exact* position of the one they've replaced. They, in turn, must justify the position they've taken with a line of dialogue, which hopefully takes the scene in an entirely different direction and elicits a big laugh—as opposed to the tedious explanation I've just given.)

"My nephew works as a cashier at River Cree Casino!" yelled Verne. So, in the parlance of my long-gone trade in improvisation, I chose to "Yes, and—" the unfolding scene by moving it forward with "I did stand-up at River Cree Casino! It's a great room!" A blatant repeat of what had already been said, that on a Second City stage would get an audience drifting into delirium looking for the exit sign.

Still, I had added something to the scene with Verne.

River Cree Casino, by the way, is a great gig as far as casinos go. Some of them have barns for theatres that are vast acoustic nightmares, designed more to house armies of gamblers who'd rather be blowing their children's university tuition at the blackjack table than watching you. I stand corrected. The term is no longer *gambling* but *recreating.* You have to love the audacity of that PR spin. If sitting in a diaper from dawn till dusk at a one-armed bandit hoping three lemons will line up so a fortune in nickels might land in your lap is recreating, then scratching your ass on the couch while binge-watching Netflix must be a triathlon.

With outstretched pleading hands and eyes moist with tears, Verne began his lamentation. "I lost the keys to my Kia, and this is where the bus from Worsley dropped me off. Been sitting here for two days. I'm trying to get to my nephew's place in Edmonton. It's true. I'm not shittin' ya."

I hadn't a clue where Worsley was, but judging by the wear on this man, it could have been Pluto and not a hamlet that, according to Wikipedia, is tucked into the western edge of Alberta's high plains Peace River Country, sixty kilometres shy of the BC border. In other words, it's a far point of frontier where one of the major food groups is still moose tongue.

Strange as it may sound, I believed him. The details were too specific to be fictitious. When you live in an urban centre, as I have in Toronto for the past forty years, you run a daily gauntlet of panhandlers. You learn to sort out the legitimately homeless from the junkies and drunks. To my trained urban eye, Verne was telling the truth. Besides, refusing to help the man would just kill the scene, and no one gets anywhere in improv unless they keep moving the scene forward. Kind of like life—and Verne's life at the moment was stuck, not going anywhere, at a Petro-Can station in Airdrie.

"All right, then," I said. "Hop in the back seat."

He stiffened at my suggestion and his tone sharpened.

"Why are you always putting Indians at the back of the bus?"

Pointing to the weeks' worth of potato chip wrappers, apple cores and banana peels on the passenger side, I said, "Because the seat is filthy."

"Filthy?" he said, pointing to his dirty clothes. "Like that's gonna matter. Don't you see what I'm wearing?! I'll be right back. I need to take a leak."

The other motorist had watched our scene unfold. His vehicle had one of those Christian stickers on the back window—the word *Faith* in the shape of a fish—that lets those of us who don't have the sticker know that the people who *do* have it are going to heaven and we're not. The man nodded his approval in much the same way Jesus might have a Good Samaritan whom He'd just seen handing a leper his last spoonful of baba ghanoush.

But I was alone, unlike peace-loving Jesus, who, when strolling the back roads of Galilee, performing miracles and keeping the wine flowing at a wedding, was always flanked by a posse of twelve bearded, sandal-wearing bros who looked like the opening act for the Oak Ridge Boys.

"What else could I do?" I said.

"It's the only thing you could do," the Christian replied, as he drove away with a smile and a wave worthy of Ned Flanders.

No, I thought, *there was another option.* When Verne was in the restroom, I could have called the cops and told them I was being harassed at the gas pumps by a dangerous-looking homeless dude. And what a giant prick move that would have been! The cops would show up and he'd be thrown in the paddy wagon, left to dry out in a cell, only to be swallowed by the penal system, and I'd be haunted by the knowledge I'd handed the poor guy over to the mercy of an institution that's been ridden with racial bias since the Mounties served the Cree Sir John A. Macdonald's eviction notice. Calling the cops just didn't seem right. Besides, shallow showbiz act that I am . . . Verne was a fan!

Another cardinal rule of improv is to always contribute—always offer something up to your fellow performer. It doesn't have to be perfect, so goes the theory, because once you make honest choices, there are no mistakes, only happy accidents. Right. Tell me another one.

Verne returned, grinning widely, and got in.

"I can't believe I'm driving to Leduc with a rock 'n' roll star from the radio," he said, getting into the back seat.

I pulled out of the station.

"I'm not a rock 'n' roll star. I'm a comedian. And it wasn't radio. I was on TV," I corrected . . . again.

"If you say so," he said and settled in for the drive.

It's one thing to know that Canada's Indian Act is a draconian document of colonial oppression responsible for the cultural genocide perpetrated by the paternalistic mandate of successive governments upon generations of Indigenous peoples. It's something else entirely to have a casualty of that patriarchy sitting in the back seat of your car, eating cashews whose chewed bits are hitting the back of your neck as he slaps the sides of his head, yelling, "I fucked up!"

On a canoe trip down the Nahanni River several summers ago, I met an enlightened couple from Pemberton, British Columbia, whose family had farmed eight hundred acres for several generations, not far from the affluent and internationally renowned ski resort of Whistler. The property was also close to a First Nations reserve suffering under squalid conditions, and this farmer employed as many of the residents as he could, making a point to give a lift to any he saw hitchhiking. "It's my contribution to reconciliation. It's every Canadian's moral duty to do what they can if given an opportunity," he said. Maybe giving Verne a lift was mine.

Canada's Truth and Reconciliation Commission has made Canadians aware of the generational impact our nation's unforgivably cruel residential school system has had on Indigenous people. Not many know the civil servant responsible for its implementation, though: Duncan Campbell Scott.

We like to think that the infamous Nazi war criminal Adolf Eichmann was the prototype of the cold-hearted bureaucrat who, with a total lack of conscience but a great degree of diabolical efficiency, orchestrated Hitler's "final solution to the Jewish problem." He personified, in the words of Hannah Arendt, "the banality of evil." Scott, on the other hand, never had that clipped German accent we heard watching every World War II movie growing up. As a kid, no fear was more primal than watching an SS officer demand to see "your papers!" That archetype has conditioned us to believe the Nazi evil was Germany's alone.

Well, Scott, as Canada's deputy superintendent of Indian affairs, had Eichmann beat with a chilling level of foreshadowing by thirty-five years. Ottawa-born Scott may not have performed his duties with an arrogant Prussian accent, but the darkness of the mandate was exactly the same. Check out this quote of Scott's from 1910:

> "It is readily acknowledged that Indian children lose their natural resistance to illness by habituating so closely in the residential schools and that they die at a much higher rate than in their villages. But this alone does not justify a change in the policy of

this Department, which is geared towards a final solution of our Indian Problem."

Gripping the wheel hard, I concentrated my energy on keeping the conversation on an even keel. The man who delivered a plaintive appeal at the service station had been replaced by one racked with confusion, sobs, torment and anger, whose stories veered into the fantastical. I stickhandled my way through our conversation, never knowing what comments might trigger the wrong reaction. Our ride was a high-wire act strung across the cultural divide between different worlds. I tried to find a common denominator.

"How about a few tunes?" I offered.

"Sure. Got any Doors? I played the Doors all the time in my DJ days."

"You were you a DJ?"

"At Brigham Young University," he said. "I was a Sixties Scoop kid. Ever hear of that?" In fact, I had. When Canada began dismantling the residential school system in the late 1950s, the practice of snatching Aboriginal children from their families didn't end with it. *The Canadian Encyclopedia* explains:

"[A]mendments to the Indian Act gave the provinces jurisdiction over Indigenous child welfare (Section 88) where none existed federally. By the 1960s, after nearly a century living under draconian and devastating federal policies, such as the Indian Act and residential schools, many Indigenous communities—particularly those living on-reserve—were rampant with poverty, high death rates and socio-economic barriers. With no additional financial resources, provincial agencies in 1951 inherited a litany of issues surrounding children and child welfare in Indigenous communities. With many communities under-serviced, under-resourced and under the control of the Indian Act, provincial child welfare agencies chose to remove children from their homes rather than provide community resources and supports."

Justified on the grounds of child neglect, instead of the true cause—poverty—up to twenty thousand children were taken from their families by government fiat and placed in foster homes to be raised by white people across North America, some of them sent as far away as New Zealand. Verne was one of those taken, and he ended up with a Mormon family in Utah.

"Yes. I was scooped. The Canadian government did that to me."

"I'm sorry."

"Whatever, though, eh? My Mormon father was really nice. So were my brothers and sisters. But they weren't my real family; my Indian family." With a yell, his mood shifted again.

"Hey, buddy, are you gonna play some Doors or what?"

Verne started to cry, filling the car with great, racking sobs that I most definitely did not have the skills to address in a confined space moving at 120 klicks.

"Don't cry, Verne. I'll find the Doors," I said, as I began to frantically scroll through my iPhone, secretly hoping I'd get stopped for distracted driving so the cops I didn't phone at the service station would appear and save me from what I was now thinking was a really stupid decision.

"I can't believe I fucked up! Hugh got me a good job at the community centre and everything. Hugh is a good man. He's my buddy. I gotta get in touch with Hugh to see what happened to my car keys and my wallet. I just can't remember his fuckin' phone number."

As if to loosen the number, Verne smacked his head—and more

cashews shot out of his mouth. Verne's flying cashews were starting to remind me of Uncle Ronald's flying peas, and for a second I wondered if anyone had ever given *him* a lift when he needed one.

Having a change of mind at this juncture of the drive was clearly a moot point. Nevertheless, my faith in the validity of Verne's tale had lapsed when, instead of seeing a vulnerable man down on his luck, I now saw a wily survivor of the mean streets who had cleverly played this gullible tool for a fool.

I found a Doors song: "Riders on the Storm."

Can't have that! No need to be singing along to that catchy lyric about a "killer on the road whose brain is squirming like a toad." I tell myself it's just my imagination working overtime. Verne's not going to whack me; he's just pissed off he can't find his car keys. I've been there. I just wish he'd eat with his mouth closed and stop spitting cashews on the back of my neck.

Indigenous activists, leaders and authors all confirm that the road to reconciliation depends on non-Aboriginals reaching across the racial divide to a people who can rightly claim, as the title of Arthur J. Ray's seminal history of Indigenous habitation in North America says, *I Have Lived Here Since the World Began.* It's a tall order to rectify five hundred years of occupation, but the country has to, or else heartless bastards like Duncan Campbell Scott will have won.

Douglas Knockwood, the revered Mi'kmaq elder and spiritual healer, knew this better than most. After a childhood spent suffering in the Shubenacadie residential school in Nova Scotia, he spent twenty years trying to erase the trauma, first by joining the army and fighting in the Korean War, seeing action on the infamous Hill 677, where seven hundred Canadian and Australian soldiers repelled five thousand Chinese regulars in close hand-to-hand combat. After being discharged, he disappeared into the darkness of Boston's skid row, until the day he stepped into an AA meeting and began wrestling his addiction to submission.

Returning to his Nova Scotia birthplace of Indian Brook, this warrior of the human heart dedicated the rest of his life to leading his people (and whoever else needed help) down the difficult and demanding road to sobriety. By the time he died at eighty-eight years of age, his rehab centres across Canada had helped thousands find freedom from alcohol.

The day I met Knockwood, he was receiving an honorary doctorate from my alma mater, Acadia University. Laugh lines wore deep grooves in his face. Grey hair hung long over his shoulders. His eyes twinkled with a mischievous enthusiasm capable of dissolving the hardest of hearts. I'd never met someone whose joy at being alive was so effusive. This healer of uncontestable achievement hummed with a tangible life force. We shook hands.

"You're that funny guy from TV," he said. "We watch you a lot. Comedy is good medicine."

"You've got to work with what you've been given," I said, "and since my math marks in high school were laughable, I figured I'd stay with what works."

He laughed hard. I congratulated him on his doctorate and the incredible contribution he had made in dedicating his life to helping others. His response was a humble understatement befitting this man of grace and fortitude: "I try and give people a road map to a better life is all, when the one they walk is hard."

"I can't remember my nephew's phone number, either!"

In frustration, Verne punched the headrest of the passenger seat, and I jumped. The car swerved.

"Jesus!"

"Relax," said Verne. "You're too jumpy."

Gripping the wheel harder and pressing my face closer to the dashboard, I thought the next punch, given Verne's agitation, could be upside my head. I was seriously beginning to doubt that the nephew existed. After all, despite only three years' difference in our ages, Verne *did* say he'd been watching me since he was little. Impossible . . . unless I'd guest-starred on *The Friendly Giant* as a three-year-old, which I did not, but that's not to say I didn't want to. It was the CBC's iconic morning show, one that every Canadian-born baby boomer was glued to during their preschool years. For those readers not born to my era (or born to it but raised by wolves who never had a TV), *The Friendly Giant* featured, well, a giant. He wasn't a real giant, though, just a guy in a costume who played a recorder and conversed with Jerome, a talking giraffe whose buddy, Rusty the Rooster, lived in a bag nailed to the castle wall. And they wondered why my generation did mind-altering drugs!

Right now, I was wishing I'd played a shrink on TV so I could use some second-hand psychology skills I might have picked up in the role to calm Verne down. Unfortunately, all I had to work with were very dormant improv skills. Comedy has its limitations in the real world. I realized I hadn't been breathing. That would help.

"When I can't remember a phone number, I start doing something else and eventually it pops in my head," I suggested.

"Do something else?" said Verne. "I'm sitting in a car. What else can I do? I was doing something when I was eating cashews, but they're all gone."

Not all *gone*, I thought. *Half the bag is still stuck to the back of my neck.*

Then I made a choice—a strong choice, I figured. One that would move the scene forward and hopefully take Verne to a calmer place where he didn't want to punch things. So, on this sunny spring day, surrounded by a waking Earth freed from winter's grip, I decided to extol the virtues of the country I've had the good fortune to embrace, while stringing my trapline from coast to coast across the peaceable kingdom whose benevolent ways and standard of living are the envy of the world.

"What a day we're having, Verne! God, I love touring Canada!"

"Love Canada? *Love Canada?!*" And that's when Verne, his lips twisted in a hateful grimace, launched half his body over the back seat and growled in my ear, "Have you ever woken up an Indian?"

Not the reaction I'd been hoping for.

I wished Viola Spolin had been in the car with me now. So much for improvisational theatre and its bogus promise that there's no such thing as a bad choice, only happy accidents. Happy accident, my ass! Given the head-on collision that was Verne's reaction to my choice, it's a wonder the car's airbag didn't explode.

In improv, a location, a situation, an emotion and a profession are the only components you're given to construct a reality. In the current scene that I was trying to orchestrate to its happy conclusion, a lone cast member might introduce it to the audience by saying something like, "Based on your suggestions, we now take you to a very scared comedian's rental car on a highway in Alberta."

Have you ever woken up an Indian?

How could I answer that? That one question contained the full weight of Canada's treatment of Verne's people and our complicity in it. The systemic racism; the never-ending battle over land claims; the hundreds of places like Grassy Narrows, where the only ones who ever pay for the corporate malfeasance are the poisoned; the 1,400 cases of missing and murdered Indigenous women our government promised to solve and hasn't; the high rate of teenage suicide in dead-end boreal gulags strung along the treeline, where clean drinking water is a rumour and tuberculosis is not. You can bet that if brown water were coming out of the taps in some tony corner of Canada, like Westmount, Rosedale, Tuxedo Park or Kitsilano, it would be fixed faster than a horny horse in the Mounties' Musical Ride.

No, I thought, *I've never woken up an Indian and I never will*. I've enjoyed a white man's privilege in a white man's nation. No priest flanked by a couple of Mounties ever snatched me from my mother's arms when I was watching *The Friendly Giant*.

Have you ever woken up an Indian?

The question sat between us with the dead weight of history. How could I ever answer that to his satisfaction without coming off as a patronizing prick? Then I did what every comedian does to defuse a bomb when things get tense. I took a chance and went for the laugh.

"Have I ever woken up an Indian?" I replied. "No. But I *have* given one a lift to Leduc."

Verne's face pulled back. He got that look I spoke of earlier. The one where he squinted one eye and twisted his lips the way you do when you're trying to solve a math problem—or figure out whether the person who just made a joke has done it at your expense, and if they have, where in their face you'll be punching them. The quiet was broken by a thunderclap worthy of heavenly intervention.

"*Ah-hahahahahaha!*" he roared. "That's fuckin' funny! *Bahahahaha!* 'But I *have* given one a lift to Leduc!' Good one! I can't believe I'm driving in a car with a rock 'n' roll star from the radio! This is my lucky day!"

No, Verne, I thought as my sphincter unclenched and I began to breathe again, *it's* my *lucky day, buddy.*

With the music blaring, two men crossed a cultural divide in an Avis rental car, singing "Break on Through (to the Other Side)" while hitting the kind of odious notes that guaranteed neither of us would ever be the front man for a Doors tribute band.

"There's a service station," Verne pointed out. "I gotta take another piss."

We pulled in, and he went inside. I got out of the car to stretch my legs. *I could leave right now,* I thought. *Just pull away.* Anyone would. Things had gotten scary back there. The dude is bent out of shape. He's carrying the kind of weight no amount of singing along to the Doors can lift. Just pull away and leave. But what a douchebag move that would be! Gutless. It would be the height of cruelty. I was embarrassed for even entertaining the thought. Imagining Verne walking out of that pit stop and not seeing my car was a thought I just could not entertain. Besides, if I learned one thing during my days at Second City, it's that you never, *ever* bail on a scene.

Verne ran from the station, shouting. "I remembered my nephew's phone number! Let's go!"

"That's fantastic, Verne," I said, wondering why he was in such a rush.

"It just came to me in there," he said, smiling and ripping into a package of beef jerky sticks.

"I thought you lost your wallet?" I said.

Verne bit into a stick.

"I did," he said with a wink. "Want some jerky?"

I punched into my phone the number Verne gave me. A recording answered.

"Hi. It's me. Eric Buffalo. Leave a message."

With a good three hours left until showtime in Leduc, I decided to drive
Verne thirty minutes farther, to his nephew's house in Edmonton. He
was lucid now. Happier. Things had turned around. I had a reasonable
suspicion he'd been drinking prior to our meeting at the Petro-Can
station, but it appeared the drive had sobered him up somewhat. An
enthusiasm had lifted his dark spirit. He bobbed around in the back
seat, looking out the windows at familiar landmarks.

"See that hospital there? It's where we had our daughter. She's so
beautiful. So is her mother. She's a Navajo. Have you ever met a
Navajo woman?"

"No," I said.

"You should. And if you marry her, don't fuck it up like I did."

Having forsaken the woman who had my back during many lean
years of struggle, I knew what he meant.

"I'm just gonna drink a lot of water and sleep for two days. Did I
tell you my brother runs a sweat lodge? He keeps it too hot, though.
You're supposed to heal in there, not drop dead," he said laughing.

His life began to spill from him now. All the years estranged from
his three children. A passing reference to prison time he waved off
with an obvious reluctance for detail. His buddy Hugh, who hired
him to work at the community centre way up in Worsley. He remembered *that* phone number, too.

We dialed it. A voice came on the line—a recording sounding
measured and sure. Verne's story was true. Like Douglas Knockwood
said, some people just need a road map.

As we pulled up beside his nephew's house, a teenage kid on roll-
erblades was busy stickhandling an orange ball up and down the
driveway. Vern got out.

"Hey."

The kid stopped.

"Hey, Uncle."

"Where's Eric?"

"Working at the casino."

"Oh."

I got out of the car. Verne pointed at me.

"Do you know who this is?"

The kid looked at me as if he was supposed to.

"No."

"He's Ron James. A rock 'n' roll star from the radio."

"I'm not a rock 'n' roll star, Verne. I'm a comedian, and I was on TV, not the radio."

"If you say so."

And with that, Verne turned and headed for the house.

Chapter Twelve
WHAT NIETZSCHE SAID

For a comedian used to performing in an intimate club setting, nothing could've prepared me for the first time I stepped on the flagship stage of Just for Laughs International Comedy Festival: the intimidating 1,700-seat Théâtre St-Denis. This was the setting for the televised gala performances the country would be seeing on the CBC the following winter. Your set had to come in at a tight eight minutes, which I always found daunting. Given my long-winded runs, it took me that long just to set up the joke! I guess that's why it took me six failed showcases to make their cut.

My problem was, I always tried to fit in *way* too much content. I was always too far down the road before the words got out. The performance was too frenetic. Marry my overtly Canadian content to that kind of energy, and it's clear why a critic once called me "Stephen Leacock on Benzedrine." Bull's eye! You'll get no argument here.

Watching some of those earlier sets, it's a wonder I didn't self-combust. I never gave myself time to enjoy the moment. It took until

2009, after a substantial ten-year learning curve, to deliver a set at the Théâtre St-Denis that pleased me as much as the audience. Being comfortable in my own skin on *their* stage had everything to do with learning to be comfortable in *mine*.

Every comedian has their own way of getting in the zone. Lining up the night's script from end to end on three banquet tables in my dressing room helped me. Touring with Shantero Productions provided this luxury, allowing me the time alone backstage to visualize the performance to come without interruption. Getting your pre-show game face on right is imperative. But no such luxury existed at comedy festivals. Whether Montreal, Winnipeg or Halifax, during those pressure-packed nights you'd be in the company of a dozen other comedians strung tripwire taut, pacing a backstage electric with tension. It was absolutely necessary to do time in those trenches, but once I found a way of working that suited me, I stayed with it. Performing back-to-back dates nurtured a confidence that allowed me to deliver the kind of show I'd been trying to grow into: one where the rhythm of words and respect for language painted a picture that worked in tandem with the joke. Eventually, my previously frenetic stage energy was replaced with a comfort level onstage which allowed for pauses and the content that I'd worked so hard to craft to finally breathe.

The first five CBC specials helped tremendously as well. Having to deliver a new one-hour special each year, along with the subsequent shooting and editing of them, provided an exponential leap in my learning curve. During the shooting of *Quest for the West* (the second, and my favourite, of the first five regionally themed specials) at the Jack Singer Concert Hall in Calgary, I received this note from network executive Anton Leo: "Don't forget to have fun. Even if you're not, look like you are." That advice was a definitive turning point. Prior to that special, I approached every live performance with the aggressive energy of a boxer about to enter the ring. With seven cameras, a packed house and eighty pages of script memorized, I was literally going from the page to the stage. Thanks to that note, I did have fun that night, and it changed my approach forever.

Anything worth doing well takes time, and in this particular craft, as George Carlin once said, it's "stage time, stage time, stage time." *That* is fundamental. Becoming competent in anything demands repetition. Just as the first hammer a carpenter picks up doesn't build him a mansion, neither does a comedian's first great set land him a television special. You have to fail first . . . and fail repeatedly.

The adage "That which does not kill us makes us stronger" comes from the pen of the nineteenth-century German philosopher Friedrich Nietzsche. He also said, "These shoes feel too tight in the toe, Herr Klinghoffer," but that quote never stuck. It clearly lacked the gravitas to warrant a place in the zeitgeist.

Why? Because innocuous comments have a short shelf life. To last, a comment has to *say* something. On the other hand, sage wisdom, with its Windexed clarity into the human soul, never has a best-before date. (I'm pretty sure "Windexed" is not a verb but as I've said before, "What odds?" It's my book.)

A good joke lacks an expiry date, too. Certain ones stand the test of time. "They smoke in Quebec like it's a cure for cancer" happens to be one of mine.

Sometimes you work hard for a good joke. Its gestation period can be as long as a blue whale's, rolling and lolling in the amniotic fluid of your brainpan until its eventual birth. At other times, a joke is born standing up, with strong legs that will last a lifetime. It will also provide, for its creator, a definitive memory of the moment it stepped into this world.

For instance, while driving back to Nova Scotia one summer, I happened to miss the turn-off to the Champlain Bridge in Montreal and decided I'd stay in Old Quebec, three hours farther east instead. I remember feeling fine about my oversight and not bothered in the least. After all, it was July and I was bound for Canada's Ocean Playground, whose waters wouldn't warm up enough for a five-minute swim until the last Saturday in August anyway, so why rush?

I imagined waking to the smell of fresh croissants in a charming eighteenth-century hotel overlooking the Plains of Abraham, where General Wolfe met his maker, General Montcalm met his match *and* his maker, France got the boot, and Britain got the continent. Once up and about, I'd pick up a copy of *Le Devoir*, then kick myself for never having learned French beyond *ouvre la porte*, grab a cappuccino to go and hit the road.

And it would have been nice, had I not missed the turnoff to Quebec City as well. That's because I was listening to an audiobook read by a Buddhist scholar who was telling me how to "stay in the moment," and I forgot to . . . but mostly because I have a PhD in ADHD that hadn't been diagnosed yet.

Pushing well past a reasonable hour to still be at the wheel, I drove onward and stopped for the night in Sainte-Anne-de-Beaupré. This corner of La Belle Province is home to an infamous Roman Catholic basilica named for St. Anne, grandmother of Jesus and patron saint of sailors, that attracts devout pilgrims from all over the world who come to worship at this place of recorded miracles. Had I known back then I'd drawn a genetic card for ADHD, I could have dropped some coin in the plate, lit a candle and prayed for some divine deliverance— but I'm a lapsed Anglican, and saints don't smile on the heathen.

The original recipient of St. Anne's benevolence was an arthritic local stonemason, Louis Guimond, in 1658. (I'm not sure why the stonemason received St. Anne's first miracle when it's sailors she's fond of, but such points are lost to history.) Apparently, after laying three stones for the foundation, Louis was miraculously cured of his affliction, and immediately went from walking with the posture of a peddler carrying a kingdom's worth of bricks on his back to exhibiting the agile grace of a man who just scarfed a mittful of extra-strength Robaxacet and downed a couple tequila shooters.

That's not why I stopped in Sainte-Anne, though. I stopped because, after ten straight hours on the road, my eyes wouldn't stay open, and I've heard that's bad for driving.

There was only one motel with a vacancy sign, and when I entered the lobby, it was clear why. It was a hole. This wasn't a chain motel. No lucky franchisee had a piece of this action. I felt sticky just standing there.

A bell sat on the counter. I rang it. Five minutes later, the proprietor appeared, rubbing his sleep-crusted eyes. He was a short troll of a man wearing boxer shorts and a wifebeater undershirt who grunted at me in a surly Gaspé patois known only to him and three Franciscan friars from Opus Dei. You'd get a warmer welcome at a halfway house. Thankfully, he had manners enough to scratch his nuts with his left hand as he passed me the room key with his right.

I turned on my heel and headed across the parking lot. Opening the door to my room, I entered a twenty-by-twenty-foot hovel, rank with the smell of stale tobacco and carnal sin, where truck-stop hookers no doubt turned their tricks and Rock Machine enforcers broke thumbs of opponents. In this tiny room sat seven ashtrays. *Seven!* On the bureau, on the nightstand beside the bed, on the toilet, beside the broken TV, the sink and even the tub. That's when I wrote the joke, "They smoke in Quebec like it's a cure for cancer."

Where was I? Right. My trip to Edinburgh in 1996.

After a short but successful run in Toronto and a national CBC radio broadcast of that one-man show I'd written, I naively decided to perform at the most competitive fringe festival in the world.

The minute my feet hit Scottish soil, I started to doubt the intelligence of my choice. The flight attendant had graciously given me a full bottle of Scotch on the plane, saying, "I've seen you many times at the Laugh Resort in Toronto. You always kill! You'll do great over here. Great!"

(In its prime, the Laugh Resort was a great comedy club. With a seating capacity of 175, it catered to a wide demographic and was home to an accomplished and supportive community of comedians. Each brought to their craft a definitive point of view and a style that was all their own. Along with the pugnacious Tim Steeves, comedy lifer Simon Rakoff, LGBTQ trailblazer Elvira Kurt, the indomitable Harry Doupe, thrice-published novelist and former fighter pilot Barry Kennedy, multiple-award–winning writer Mark Farrell, and the irascible Irish rebel, stalwart friend and creative collaborator, Ottawa-born Chris Finn—who, like Tim and Mark, would write for *This Hour Has 22 Minutes* and *Rick Mercer Report*—the club also hosted the likes of Ray Romano, Louis C.K., Rich Hall, Kevin James and Ellen DeGeneres. This club was instrumental in revitalizing my comedic mojo. After hitting the wall in Los Angeles and souring on the fleeting rewards of improvisational theatre, at thirty-six I'd finally found the place I felt I belonged. People say improv and stand-up are similar. Not. At. All. An improvisational comedy troupe is closer to half a dozen Bolsheviks trying to decide the colour of a tractor on a communist farm, while stand-up is an enlightened dictatorship.)

A full bottle of Scotch! Bonus! Great Scotch, too, it was. Scotch distilled in the sacred, peat-sweet waters of Islay that Merlin the Wizard was baptized in.

For some reason lost to time, we disembarked not by the usual walkway leading directly into the airport, the one that ground crews attach to the plane upon landing, but the old-fashioned way, down a set of stairs they'd rolled to the door of the plane, leading to the tarmac. Soon as the doors opened, I thought we'd landed in Ecuador. Scotland was in the throes of an unholy heat wave, and a country synonymous with flushed faces and short tempers was living up to the stereotype. I saw two baggage handlers arguing in the guttural tongue of my forefathers and thought, *I bet this is what Robbie Burns sounded like drunk.*

As I turned to look, the bottle of Scotch I'd irresponsibly tucked between my chest and right arm slipped from its grip and, falling to the ground in slow motion, violently exploded at my feet. The baggage handlers saw it too, and for a moment a look of pity crossed their clinically sunburned faces, then they turned back to poking each other in the chest and cursing.

First step I took on Scottish soil and my free bottle of single malt was bleeding out in a puddle of amber liquid on the hot tarmac. This was the kind of omen that would have turned an Iron Age army back. Not me. I was here for a three-week run.

The opportunity to play the fest had arrived in a roundabout way. The artistic director of a small theatre in Toronto (where I'd originally performed *Up and Down in Shaky Town*) offered me a 50 percent discount on a performance space in Edinburgh after a cancellation by a troupe of actors who'd placed a $5,000 down payment. They'd cancelled because they couldn't afford flights for their cast of twenty-five. That's right: *twenty-five* actors. Not sure what kind of scratch those thespians would pull down from a night's performance, but I'm willing to wager none was eating pheasant under glass after the gig. I understand that suffering for your art is noble, but starving for it was never in my wheelhouse, especially with my squirrelly metabolism. (If I don't eat every two hours, my blood sugar goes squirrelly and I'm taking hostages.)

Scrounging up a rogue five thousand dollars, I matched what was already deposited, bought a plane ticket and, like the architects of the ill-fated landing at Dieppe in 1942, girded myself for battle, blind to the possibility of failure. Plus, along with the theatre space came the troupe's substitute stage manager. I assumed he'd be a professional—say, someone who could co-ordinate elementary lighting and sound cues. Simple. Not advanced calculus. Not transplanting the living brain of an ocelot into a rhesus monkey. It turned out, though, that he was slumming in the theatre as a hobby.

A *hobby*? A hobby involves airplane glue and a model kit, doesn't it? Or singing in a barbershop quartet. Hunting. Gardening. Train sets. Needlepoint. *Those* are hobbies. Stage managing is *not* a hobby.

Maybe he saw it as an opportunity for employment after graduating with a PhD in his chosen field of folklore. *There's* money well spent. What do you do with a degree in folklore? Unless there's a paying gig somewhere for a translator fluent in the Elvin tongues of

Tolkien, I expect the best option with a folklore degree *is* stage-managing for a twenty-five-person cast who aren't making a living, either.

Someone in charge of the University of Edinburgh's real estate department saw an opportunity for a quick cash grab by renting mothballed study halls to festival productions. The troupe had rented an ancient study hall with seventy-five seats that reeked of the gloom of the tomb. I'll wager good money the last time the doors were opened John Locke was in there, writing a mid-term.

However, over on the other side of town it was another story. There, the brightly lit flagship theatres such as Assembly Hall and the Gilded Balloon were festooned with banners of beer sponsors that catered to round-the-block lineups for sold-out performances every single night. No ghostly stench of eighteenth-century cholera victims in those theatres. No, sir. They were filled with joyful, chortling patrons come to laugh the night away, happily quaffing pints of Stella Artois while nibbling bags of haggis-flavoured crisps.

These beautiful venues were featured in the glossy tome of a program that provided biographies, places, dates and times for all performances. Every festival patron carried a copy under their arm. Those programs stood in stacks at every newsstand, restaurant and bar. It was the bible of the festival. Every performer needed to be in *this* program in order to be seen. I was not in it. I was in another one. I was in the program nobody saw, and if they did, never used.

My contact in Edinburgh, the person who'd been hired by the troupe to ensure the details of my show made it into the main program, was a small, ferret-faced grifter who, I would later learn, had done time for petty fraud. I mailed him all my materials from Toronto well ahead of the deadline, but he missed it. Perhaps he had to meet his parole officer that day? Maybe he was at the greyhound races, or forging old ladies' signatures on stolen cheques? His former criminal status was revealed well into the run and at least went some way toward explaining his trouble with deadlines.

As a result of not being in the real program, my show rarely had more than five paying customers at a time. Sometimes none. Sometimes three. Actually, the average *was* three. It's difficult to get an audience on a roll of laughter when there are barely enough people in the house for a game of backgammon. The presence of a rare dozen paying customers stoked my hope that sales had picked up momentum but I found myself the following evening staring into an empty theatre space looking for laughs but instead hearing echoes.

I recall a particular matinee when the theatre held only a pair of exhausted Fringe-goers, collapsed in their front-row seats. One was asleep, while the other wasn't paying attention. They'd come to see *Waiting for Godot* performed by a Bangladeshi puppet troupe but got the wrong address. Suffering from that thousand-yard stare unique to exhausted festivalgoers, once in my space they stayed put, optimistic that they were about to witness that diamond in the rough everyone hopes to discover among 1,500 Fringe acts. Instead, they were stuck watching a Canadian man's monologue about three years of struggle in Los Angeles, whose words didn't sound remotely close to anything ever written by Samuel Beckett.

The comedy gods had it in for me, and their contempt was righteous. The first morning of rehearsals I'd placed a poster on a sandwich board outside the theatre. Besides featuring the title, it had three different photos of my face each representing a different phase of my three-year sojourn in LA: happy, hair-pulling insanity, and resignation. After two frustrating hours spent trying to co-ordinate lighting cues with someone who should have been back in the folklore faculty club discussing the mating rituals of Rivendell over a pitcher of mead with Bilbo Baggins look-alikes, I stepped outside for some fresh air before I suffered an aneurysm.

Standing beside the poster were a couple of Scottish stagehands having a smoke. One of them pointed his cigarette, and in a brogue thick with matter-of-fact understatement, said, "Aye. Someone's puked on your poster." And indeed, sliding down my middle face was a softball-sized dollop of human honk. The other stagehand looked closer at the poster just to be sure. "Aye. That's puke, all right."

Some wandering inebriant had not the decency to duck into an alleyway for their noontime hurl and decided to aim for my poster instead. Lovely. I wouldn't need to see the Oracle of Delphi to know this run was going to suck.

After the first week I wanted to bolt for home. But quitting was for losers . . . and people who had more money than me. See, I'd arrived on a charter flight, and to buy another ticket at full fare would have exhausted a meagre bank account *and* next month's rent in Toronto. Then why did I even go you ask? All these years later, I know exactly why: I thought I was better than I actually was.

In retrospect, my impetuous decision was clearly due to the conceit of a rookie, not to mention a display of glaring disrespect for a craft that takes a lifetime to master, if one ever does. I'd heard stories about Canadian comedians breaking into Britain and doing well, so why not me? After all, I'd had three good reviews for my one-man show and had served two years in the clubs. Twenty-five years and a thousand gigs later, I find it hard to fathom what bade me hop the pond for Edinburgh. A day of reckoning was due, and mine had started with the busted bottle of free Scotch the day before.

I convinced myself the lack of attendance had nothing to do with my show, but more to do with the inordinate number of attractions in Edinburgh that summer. Besides the monster of a fringe festival which featured everything from a Swahili-speaking Shakespeare company to the sold-out-for-their-entire-run-in-minutes Tokyo Shock Boys, an X-rated acrobatic troupe from Japan that twisted and tumbled from trapeze to trampoline—naked—while shooting lit firecrackers out of their asses, there was a military tattoo in the imposing medieval castle on the hill, an international book fair and a film festival catering to the thousands of tourists choking the cobblestone streets of Old Town, which doubled as the summertime home for every balloon-twisting, stilt-walking, juggling busker from Belgium to Tangmalangaloo. Every street corner was filled with one of them doing something. I watched a rummy take a shit in a hat before I realized it wasn't a show!

Compounding it all was the heat: the insufferable, oppressive, stultifying heat. Air conditioning was non-existent in most places, and chain-smoking was still embraced with enthusiasm in every bar.

One morning after celebrating a three-out-of-five-star review from a national newspaper, *The Independent*, that did nothing to increase my sales, I woke with a five-star hangover. It was one of those head-pounding assaults on the system that gets you making pacts with Jesus. My head felt hydrocephalic and so clinically large, it rivalled a gigantic balloon in the Macy's Thanksgiving Day parade, in need of being held down by metal guy wires.

I've always found the best cure for a hangover (besides not drinking in the first place) is to stretch your legs and walk it off. So, I headed out very gingerly for a saunter downtown on a blistering-hot Sunday afternoon, knowing that beneath my feet were ancient catacombs where befouled and semi-conscious junkies lay in cool repose . . . the lucky bastards. I hoped I might find some shade and rest beneath the branches of a healing willow, but there was nary a tree to be found. The last one in Old Town was chopped down in 1310 to burn a witch.

What there were plenty of on that day the mercury was busy breaking records across Great Britain were bagpipers. In fact, Old Town was choked—from the city square and all the way to the Orkney Islands, I'll bet—with the largest gathering of pipe bands in the free world. Did I mention the bands were tuning up their instruments? We are all familiar with the sound of one bagpipe being played. Given my Maritime upbringing, it was hard to attend any function when I was growing up without hearing "the pipes." From funerals to weddings to hockey games, there was always a kilted piper playing some melancholy lament or goosebump–raising battle hymn written for longgone rebels marching to slaughter on the fields of Culloden that could stir the hardest of Scottish hearts to pudding. Perhaps you yourself have heard their haunting notes echoing over the hills while summering in the countryside when some local kid but six weeks into lessons decides to break out his pipes and play a whining dirge at close of day? *I hope he's only playing one song*, you think, *because cats screwing on a winter's night sound better than that.*

I think it's one of those instruments that takes quite a bit of time to master.

On the cobblestones of Edinburgh that day, scarlet-faced pipers sweating like the damned swayed in the draconian heat. Every one of them was bedecked in a mind-boggling array of tribal finery and tartan kilts, whose matching sashes were held in place by tribal crests, buckles, pins and sporrans. Some even had the skins of leopards and lion manes draped over their shoulders—peeled, no doubt, from the backs of the big cats during a long-gone empire's supremacy, when Africa was ripe for the plunder.

Some held sceptres and sported daggers stuck in woollen socks, rising knee high from spit-polished boots. The ones who weren't constantly adjusting their bags (their *pipe* bags, that is) were strapped into gigantic drums from chin to crotch and wore on their heads fur hats whose chinstraps were yanked tight as a tourniquet, pinching their volcanically purple heads into stroke-inducing, lock-jawed grimaces. Surely there's a better way to spend a sweltering Sunday afternoon than standing in woollen tartan, laden with forty pounds of tradition, under a blistering sun, watching your buddies take a face plant to the pavement?

Recreation during a summertime heat wave in Canada means cracking a cold one and then jumping in the lake—unless you're in a pipe band, of course. Then, I expect, you're marching under a hellacious hot sun at some meeting-of-the-clans just one B-flat away from heatstroke wishing you'd studied piano.

Struggle provides its own unique epiphanies, and in Edinburgh, I had mine. Besides ripping the guts from the show daily, reworking the running order, punching up jokes, writing new ones and trying my best not to buckle under the soul-sucking weight of rejection, it was imperative that I showcase at whatever open-mike venues existed in town. I hoped the sterling response to the five minutes allotted every performer would have the doors of my venue swinging off the hinges with cheerful crowds of festivalgoers, tired of seeing Japanese acrobats fart exploding firecrackers. One space in particular stood out. Its name was synonymous with that quaint European medieval pastime of turning hungry hounds on baited omnivores: the Bear Pit.

Its stage sat floor-level to the audience and was leered over by a balcony packed to the rafters with drunken revellers who'd come to satiate their blood lust in an arena where bedlam ruled. It had a reputation of being, in the parlance of our trade, "an unforgiving room." That's not to say I hadn't been warned. When I signed up, the festival organizers in charge of booking the place did everything short of draping themselves in garlic before uttering the venue's name, as if protecting their souls from a curse. "The room is very cruel," they whispered. I remember thinking, *It can't be any crueller than someone puking on my poster.*

Yes, it could.

On the evening of the performance I stood at the back of the room, feeling a bad case of amateur-night tongue take hold. Biochemical secretions in the hypothalamus had sent raiding parties of cortisol and adrenalin to hijack my nervous system, sucking my mouth so clean of moisture, I'd have sold my soul for a thimble of spit. The fight-or-flight response had been activated. This early-warning system evolved in the human brain countless millennia ago, when bands of early *Homo sapiens* roamed a cruel and harsh savannah, falling prey to hungry carnivores who stalked, ate and then shat this prey in steaming heaps of scat on lonesome hills beneath the eye of a nameless god. Back in a day when we were dinner, it was best to be aware of your surroundings when you were out picking berries.

My heart was beating deer-in-the-headlights fast as I watched each act ascend the stage and get chewed up alive by that meatgrinder of a crowd. From singers to poets to actors to clowns, each did their time to an accompaniment of catcalls, boos and profanities yelled from the room's dark recesses, until a real warrior of my calling took the stage. He strode through the crowd, and as soon as he hit the spotlight, grabbed that microphone, stared those piss tanks square in the eye and delivered . . . in spades.

It was a Canadian comedian by the name of Mike Wilmot, who has since become a household name in Britain but was an unknown on that sweltering Edinburgh night twenty-five years ago. Watching him *own* that room of ornery, raucous liquor pigs stood as a shining example of what I was not: fearless.

It would take several years before I'd be able to work a room with the level of confidence I'd just witnessed in Wilmot. Breaking the imaginary fourth wall, so sacred in theatre, is paramount in stand-up. Separation is not the goal; integration is. Moving fluidly from scripted set to spontaneous, off-the-cuff improvisation creates a symbiotic—and, most importantly, *personal*—relationship between the act and an audience. Harold Pinter didn't work his pauses into a play so an actor could randomly go off script and start riffing with the room. Stand-up, on the other hand, encourages that. It's why it's such an unusual art form. Stand-up is a metaphysical tennis match, where the serve is the joke, and its return the laughter. Each cannot exist without the other. A play can exist whether or not the audience is entertained. Stand-up comedy, on the other hand, exists only *with* laughter; otherwise, you're Rupert Pupkin in his mother's basement.

Following Wilmot is something few seasoned veterans would willingly do even today, but that night, I was next. Never one to tolerate the pretensions of the one-man show with its musical cues and lighting effects, this battle-hardened hit man of the smoke-choked club circuit uttered nary a word as he left the stage to explosive applause. He walked past, wearing the war face of a comedian who's just killed, knowing he's left nothing but slippery viscera on that stage.

Still held captive to the script, and not yet skilled enough on my feet to link the best jokes from the show into a litany of one-liners, get my laughs and get off, I opened with the first paragraph of *Shaky Town*. In a one-person show, you set the tone for the story to come, but here, in this asylum, that decision merely stirred the rage of the inmates.

I began with the earnest delivery Toronto critics had praised me for: "Three years ago with family in tow, I hopped a 747 Conestoga wagon to follow well-worn trails of the jet stream west, like so many other beaming pilgrims before me . . ."

I heard a rustling from the balcony, as though grumpy trolls were waking from an afternoon nap.

". . . we settled on the Western edge of a vast and mythic valley in the City of Angels whose inhabitants felt immune from the ravages of time. It was a pistol-packing Brigadoon . . ."

And then it came, a bellow from the balcony's recess: "Who gives a fuck?!"

Soldiers in a firefight see the world around them move in slow motion. So it was for me as I watched a can of beer sail from the balcony over the audience's heads some and land on that small stage, where it splashed its contents all over my feet. I'd barely had enough time to admire the thrower's accuracy when a loud voice worthy of Luciano Pavarotti bellowed, "You suck!" The crowd took its cue, and in unison began their chant: "You suck! You suck! You suck!" I remember thinking, *Sweet Jesus. I'm here for three weeks.*

Nietzsche definitely had a point.

If you're questioning whether or not Canada is still two solitudes as literary lion Hugh MacLennan so aptly depicted it in his classic 1951 novel of the same name, a night spent watching French comedy at Just for Laughs *(Juste pour rire)* will allay those doubts for good. Québécois comedy is orchestrated insanity. Traditional joke structure is thrown out the window. The French like their comedy loud, zany, prop-heavy and verging on bedlam.

I followed one of the more famous French prop acts once during a corporate show in a convention centre ballroom filled with every Toyota dealer in Canada. About a dozen Japanese executives who'd flown in from Kyoto were seated in the front row, wearing headphones for translation purposes. For the French act they were about to see none were needed, because that act could be universally appreciated from Uzbekistan to Kuala Lumpur: a man wearing a fluorescent orange flight suit *covered* in fifty-seven old-fashioned bicycle horns, on which he played Tchaikovsky's *1812 Overture* . . . while riding a unicycle. How do you follow that?

I didn't have to worry because . . . it wasn't his closer! For that *coup de grâce*, he wriggled into a giant yellow prophylactic, inflated it with an air pump, held the neck closed from inside, then bounced around the stage in his balloon. I watched hopelessly from the wings as the Toyota executives were overcome with laughter, providing him with a level of tectonic applause a comedian following a prop act never wants to hear. By the time I finished my act, they were still laughing . . . at him.

The late, great comedian Mike MacDonald used to tell a story about opening for West Coast militant vegan and musician Bryan Adams. Mike had booked the gig six months prior, when Adams was an unknown. Standing backstage the night of the gig, hearing fifteen thousand people chanting, "We want *Bry*-an! We want *Bry*-an!" made it very clear to Mike that Bryan was now most definitely very *much* known. As the chanting rose to a deafening roar, a grizzled old janitor who'd seen it all tapped Mike on the arm and said, "I hope Bryan's *your* name."

I crossed paths with this trail-blazing icon one Winnipeg winter's night at Rumor's Comedy Club. Mike's two-week headlining run was starting just as mine was wrapping up. I'd first seen this comedian of legendary prowess in 1980, during his incendiary prime, at the original Yuk Yuk's location on Bay Street in Toronto. I was struck by his conviction and confidence standing alone in the spotlight, watching him channel the anger that fuels our funny into a cohesive piece of killer comedy.

That was around the first time I'd ever signed up for an amateur night. I was doing a nerd character at the time, born during those heenie-headed hot-knife sessions in the shadow of Blomidon, when brothers from another day inspired a faith that my funny might one day pay. Playing a character covers you in a sheath of armour that straight stand-up never does. After eight minutes, I stepped off that stage to enthusiastic applause. I was invited to a local diner with Mike and several other comics afterwards and made the mistake of making a joke. No one laughed.

Mike turned to me and said, "You have to be here a year before you're allowed to make a joke." By the reaction of those other comedians, he meant it. About to take a bite of his sandwich, he caught himself in mid-thought, turned back to me and said, "By the way. What I just saw you do was the birth of the Beatles." Then he went back to eating his sandwich and never said another word.

I went back the next week and bombed. Miserably. Then a few more Mondays in a row after that and bombed some more. I never had the guts to suffer the quiet that the learning curve calls for at that stage of a career. Folding up my tent after six weeks' effort, I headed for Second City's improv classes, never going near a stand-up stage again for another fifteen years.

I didn't see Mike again until I had a few years under my belt in the clubs. I mustered the guts to ask this battle-hardened veteran if he'd watch and critique my set. He obliged. I'd hear his unmistakable laugh from the back of the room. More a caw than a guffaw, and it seemed to escape reluctantly from his chest despite himself. But when it did, I knew I was on to something real and right.

When my set was over and the audience gone, we sat at a table in the empty club. With the owner, Ross Rumberg, perched gargoyle-silent beside us, this supposedly hard-headed taskmaster who did not suffer fools—this stellar comedian of ferocious talent, bedevilled by clinical haunts compounded by an American dream unrealized, who, at the peak of his powers, delivered such room-destroying, incendiary sets they're burned into the retinas of every comic who witnessed them—patiently delivered what were, hands down, two hours of the best notes I've ever received. Don't get me wrong: it's not like the Mormon Tabernacle Choir backed them up with stirring harmonies. When that obsidian-sharp comedic mind of his got down to business, I was bleeding! With a reformed addict's respect for a higher power, Mike fought the black dog with GlaxoSmithKline as his wingman, continuing to mine the terrain where comedy gold might lie while marshalling an iron will in pursuit of it.

The fact this skilled road warrior of exemplary pedigree and perseverance took the time to show a greenhorn during his first foray in-country where to ford the river, stands as testimony to his generosity. In an arena the uninitiated consider cutthroat, Mike personified everything but.

He passed far too soon and remains, for me, a totemic figure in Canada's comedic pantheon.

When it comes to giants, the biggest reward of performing at JFL was, hands down, being in the company of them. The card I drew for that boon was the "Merchant of Venom" himself, Don Rickles.

"Mr. Warmth" hosted the Théâtre St-Denis gala I took part in along with half a dozen other acts in 2003. With that jovial bulldog of a noggin poking out of a tailored tuxedo, Rickles entered the theatre to a host of trumpets playing theme music worthy of a matador's entrance to the bull ring, and with his arms spread wide, he drank in the spontaneous, rapturous applause.

This comic god, World War II navy veteran, pal of Sinatra, bang-the-table, funny-as-hell Dean Martin roast guest and Johnny Carson favourite, who honed his craft in the clubs of 1960s Las Vegas playing to pug-nosed wise guys come looking for laughs after dumping a body in the desert, was seventy-five years old at the time and absolutely *owning* that room . . . and he hadn't yet said a word.

Gathered round the monitors backstage with the other comics, I stood slack-jawed with admiration. My mind drifted back to that night on the ninth floor of Crowell Tower at Acadia University in 1976, when half a dozen of us were losing our minds watching this free-form wizard put Frank Sinatra in stitches on Carson's *Tonight Show*.

It's a classic bit. On those days when gravity seems to be pulling harder than usual and the mid-winter blues have your spirit pinned to the mat, do yourself a favour and Google this clip: "Rickles/ Sinatra/Carson 1976."

Rickles walks onto Johnny's set unannounced, surprising Frank. He takes his applause, crosses to the Chairman of the Board, takes a knee—as one would in front of any mafia don—then . . . kisses his ring. That's the set-up. Frank yanks his hand away, laughing. Taking a seat beside a man whose underworld connections were never a secret, Rickles leans in and says, "Marco Mongonanzo was hurt. Fumbino Bombatso . . ."—he puts a finger against his temple—"two bullets in the head . . . Thursday."

Sinatra loses it with laughter, just like we did that night in university and again in Montreal, standing round the TV monitors backstage, watching Rickles claim his place.

When it was our turn to work, he gave everyone an excellent off-the-cuff introduction, and although I don't remember the content of it, I certainly remember his reaction after my set was finished. I'd done a bit about camping beside some Germans: "Camping's fun . . . in the daytime. But soon as the sun goes down, everything that eats meat wakes up. I was pretty safe, though. I camped beside some Germans. God love 'em, but their accent will scare off anything." Then I launched into shamelessly stereotypical World War II–movie German, building into a crescendo worthy of the Führer wrapping up a tight set at Nuremberg. Then I tagged the bit with "and they were only trying to set the tent up." Rickles came right up to me, grinning that trademark grin, and said, "Great set, kid."

I was stunned. *Stunned.* My hero had just complimented my work. He grabbed me by the shoulders and stared me square in the eyes, comic to comic. "I never got my first break in show business until I was thirty-eight." I assumed he was insinuating we shared the same trajectory, and it was only a matter of time before I, too, would have my breakout role as he did with *Kelly's Heroes.*

"How old are ya?" he asked.

"Forty-two."

Without missing a beat, his smile morphed into a face you'd use to greet a widow at a closed casket. With eyes full of pity, he gently slapped the side of my cheek, saying, "You're finished," and then walked away.

Eh? Complimented *and* burned by Don Rickles in under thirty seconds. Pretty sweet.

That night, he generously signed my Just for Laughs poster and wrote, "Funny is as funny does, and you are." That's what I remember the most about JFL. Being able to see and sometimes meet the best acts of our generation. Whenever the road got old, and it certainly did, I reminded myself that Don Rickles let me know I chose the right one to roam.

Even though most professional comedians have been performing stand-up for a lifetime, there's still the occasional set that sends you right back to amateur night. We owe that experience to the Faustian bargain of the much-wanted, well-paying 'corporate gig.'

Ninety-five percent of the time, the suits are a great audience. Having made a company or organization laugh, you were in and out in an hour with five times the scratch in your pocket that you were normally paid. Oh, and it always helped if the clients weren't too rich. Rich people hate to give up status, and the comedian needs that investment in order to get laughs. A recognition of your own imperfections helps, too, but no one ever got rich thinking they weren't the smartest one in the room.

Certain professions are tough. Lawyers are the worst. I once did a benefit at Osgoode Hall in an ornate room full of high-rolling Toronto barristers, raising money for cystic fibrosis. Never took a dime for the gig, and in forty minutes, I never got a laugh, either. A $750-an-hour legal assassin came up to me afterwards and said, "You were funny, but we're lawyers. We laugh on the inside." I bet. Especially when you're crucifying some poor bastard for every nickel they're worth.

Lesson learned: no good deed goes unpunished.

Once you sign on the dotted line, they've got you. Corporate gigs have simple rules: no political content, no religious material and no sex jokes. So, you follow the rules, play it safe and pay the mortgage, just like people do in the real world, even though not wanting to toe the company line in the real world is what made you become a stand-up in the first place. In my experience, the sweeter-sounding the corporate booking, the higher the price that is paid in self-worth. And when corporate gigs go south, they do so in spectacular fashion.

I once had a gig in Cancún, where a company had flown their five hundred managers. You rarely get the opportunity to do the same quality of act for a corporate crowd that real fans pay to see in theatres, because the businesspeople you're performing for never dropped a penny to see you—their entertainment committee did, hoping the same performance they might have seen on TV or in a packed thousand-seater will be effortlessly replicated. In Cancún, though, it proved hard to recreate that magic in a cement-walled echo chamber on a night sticky with humidity, in which I fought to be heard over the eight gigantic fans blaring inside and the Yucatán surf crashing outside.

Over half a dozen planeloads of audience, who'd come from different towns and cities all across Canada, had suffered a fierce bitch-slapping at thirty thousand feet, battling stratospheric winter storms trying to get there and by now were punchy, hungry, exhausted and cranky. Not the ideal conditions for comedy. All they wanted was a tequila-fused cocktail, and sleep. The last thing they wanted was to sit through an hour of stand-up.

Besides being funny, a comedian needs a few simple things to succeed. Steve Martin noted in his stellar autobiography, *Born Standing Up: A Comedian's Life*, that "distraction is the death of comedy." The man must have done a few corporate gigs. All you want is an audience to see and hear you with no interruptions. Simple. It's hard to accomplish that when there's a five-foot ice sculpture of a prancing unicorn blocking the view of the stage you're standing on, and a microphone from a karaoke machine plugged into a scratchy sound system.

Getting laughs from a corporate crowd hasn't changed since the Middle Ages. That's when someone in authority saw the local Fool standing on his stool during market day, doing a tight ten minutes on the price of turnips, and whisked him up from the muddy street to perform for the lord and lady of the manor. If he killed, he'd get a bath, be fed cabbage soup and kept as a halfwit stable pet for their amusement during dinner parties. A definite perk, considering his life up to that point amounted to sleeping in a dry corner of the moat on a bed of urine-soaked straw.

Stepping onstage, I knew the night would be a challenge when I noticed everyone in the first two rows had their backs to me, while the remainder of the room were walking around, chatting. The first few opening jokes dropped stone-dead fast to the floor. I launched quickly into the heavy artillery and surefire road-honed gold that had been killing in every venue I'd just played on tour, that I naturally assumed would surely win them over in the vast cinderblock warehouse of a room I couldn't stop imagining as a temporary morgue during a natural disaster. Much to my surprise, the material elicited the same reaction I'd have received *were* the floor actually covered in corpses. There was absolutely no way to corral this audience into a cohesive whole, where they'd laugh en masse as one living, breathing entity—the way people do when they actually *want* to see you.

All the moisture in my mouth fled to my palms. The professional act I prided myself on delivering to paying audiences was dangerously close to taking a dark turn. I was but a synapse away from turning on the audience, the stage, the company and even the country of Mexico itself by launching into a profane and unprofessional tirade that would have made the darkest devils in the bullring of Hell blush.

But I didn't. Why? Because no matter the vicissitudes of a room filled with an audience who did not give a rat's ass whether I did my act or set my balls on fire, I "screwed my courage to the sticking-place," to quote the Bard, and as every comedian does who is getting paid, *I . . . did . . . my . . . time.*

When I was done, there was no applause. I heard a woman say, "Thank God he's done."

I couldn't agree more.

Then there's a once-in-a-lifetime gig that places you in the middle of a maelstrom.

One day in 2008, I emceed a party for the 99th Grey Cup and the Canadian Football League Alumni Association. That was the event where ex–BC Lions quarterback Joe "The Toughest Chicano" Kapp decided to settle a score for a dirty hit on his wide receiver, Willie "Will o' the Wisp" Fleming, by Angelo "King Kong" Mosca . . . in 1963.

That's right. *Forty-five* years before.

Angie, as he was known (an affectionate but incongruous moniker for a 245-pound bruising assassin) had delivered that career-ending hit after the play was whistled down, and incredibly, it was not seen by the referee.

(Perhaps the guy was related to Kerry "I Didn't See It" Fraser, the NHL referee who missed Wayne Gretzky's infamous high stick that opened up Doug Gilmour's face like a sardine can during the 1993 play off series against the Los Angeles Kings and Toronto Maple Leafs. With blood running down Gilmour's face but no penalty called, the Great One went on to score the winning goal in overtime for LA, eliminating the Leafs from playing the Montreal Canadiens for the Stanley Cup and forever guaranteeing that Fraser's name, if spoken at all by those who bleed blue, would be done so only in the company of blistering profanities.)

Angie's hit knocked Willie out of the game, causing Joe's Lions to lose the Grey Cup to Angie's Hamilton Tiger-Cats. Once again—that would be forty-five years previous, when these titans were in their mid-twenties. Do the math. And you thought the Israelis and Palestinians could hold a grudge?

The intention was for me to interview these CFL Hall of Famers onstage after my stand-up set. Clearly, the organizers hoped these icons would reinforce faith in a league given its last rites far too often, and that, softened by the wisdom of age, the former combatants would reminisce fondly about battles won and lost, soothing old wounds as old warriors should, letting bygones be bygones. Think again.

The Delta Hotel ballroom was packed with CFL fans, drinking beer and happily eating rubbery hotel chicken, their faces flush and eager with expectation, all of them sporting jerseys of their favourite teams. There were assorted CFL alumni of good standing, lifetime achievers, local dignitaries, families, feted guests and armed forces personnel on hand to piggyback our patriotism onto the last bastion of professional sports that is still exclusively ours.

There were also a couple of threatening-looking army tanks parked out front. Vancouver had just experienced a Stanley Cup playoff riot, so, given its recent orgy of liquor-fuelled anarchy, perhaps they stood as a warning to the first drunk punk from Surrey who might want to chuck a beer bottle at a cop car: try it, and you'll wake up with a shaved head in Kandahar, cleaning latrines.

I finished my set, which had been rife with Canadiana . . . surprise me . . . and everyone was in a good mood. Mosca was seated at a table in the front row, stage left. He was the biggest human being I'd ever seen. This mountain of meat and muscle who once wielded a fierce and frightening rage on the field, was now a seventy-one-year-old gentleman seated quietly amongst family members and clutching a cane.

After my lengthy introduction which lauded a lifetime of accomplishments on the gridiron and in wrestling arenas across North America, this Goliath carefully rose and, on wobbly knees, ascended the stage. When we shook hands, my small, freckled paw was swallowed by a Neanderthal-sized mitt belonging less to a twenty-first-century human, than a time when men sat around a feeble campfire in a chilly cave snapping mammoth bones in two at suppertime. It was a monstrous appendage of bone, gristle and callused skin, once used to serious effect in turning strong men in cleats into useless puddles of floppy cartilage.

Kapp, on the other hand, was still a lean, mean, lithe competitor with the coiled energy and athletic grace of a predatory cat. After an equally long introduction by me, in which I touted him as the only man to quarterback in the Rose Bowl, Super Bowl and Grey Cup, he rose from his seat and spontaneously picked a sprig of what looked like heather from the centrepiece on his table and joined me onstage. I said hello, and although he acknowledged me, he never really *saw* me. His eyes were fixed instead on that stolen victory of 1963, when poor Willie hobbled off the field, lost and incoherent after Angie's two-ton hit.

They stood at opposite ends of the stage as a screen lowered and archival footage of the 1963 Grey Cup began to play. It was a grainy black-and-white film of football players wearing helmets so lame in their protective capability, they seemed made of papier mâché. We saw Willie, with the football, get tackled by a linebacker. He was down when from nowhere came the six-foot-six, 245-pound Mosca, who plowed into him with the fury of a runaway train. Standing just to my left was Joe. I heard him whisper between clenched teeth the words he had no doubt barked from restless sleep these past forty-five years: "Dirty prick." I thought, *This can't be good.* Once the pin was pulled on that live grenade of this septuagenarian Chicano, it was primed for maximum impact.

I'm sure the result would have been just as explosive had German and Russian World War II veterans standing on the same stage been entertained with scenes from the Battle of Berlin. Doors to darker days that should have stayed closed forever would open, old hauntings would stir, and like reveille echoing down the halls of time, the room would erupt in a spontaneous contagion of grievance, with ancient scores being settled as the former Russian commando, an eighty-three-year-old Yuri planted a fork in the temple of Helmut the former German commando.

With the benefit of hindsight, I suppose it would have been best for all involved if the CFL alumni had shown a Looney Tunes cartoon instead.

It's been said that one can feel the barometric pressure drop before a battle, that the quiet is all-encompassing. After my introduction, the CFL fans who'd been laughing along to my set only moments earlier fell silent. Their eyes were glued to the stage. Carrying the bulk of age, Angie tentatively ascended the three steps to the stage, cane in hand. Joe was standing onstage, looking every inch a spring-loaded weapon of war. His coal-black eyes, furious with memory, stared Mosca down, while his left hand absent-mindedly fingered the heather in his right.

Three chairs sat empty onstage, waiting for their occupants: a pair of former grid-iron titans weighing in collectively at over 400 pounds, carrying an Old Testament level of hate for an ancient grievance, and a non-sportscaster comedian whose premonition of pending doom had his "Spidey sense" tingling.

Instinct is peculiar. It's hard to quantify. It's something that lives in the realm of the supernatural. Nevertheless, it's something one learns to trust after thirty-five years onstage—like when it's telling you to get *off* it. Then again, sometimes I can't shut up, especially when it's imperative that you follow the unwritten rule of the calling and, despite the response to your funny, always do your time!

There was one last chance to turn down the temperature in the room. Turning to face Kapp, I acknowledged the heather in his hand and said, "I see you're bringing a peace offering to Angelo, Joe."

He seemed to hear me, if just vaguely. Perhaps my remark echoed down the halls of time where he was standing, staring across the field at that clueless referee who missed a notorious late hit half a century ago.

"What?" he grunted.

"The heather in your hand," I repeated. "A peace offering to Angie?" That's when I saw my statement find purchase. He looked at the heather, then back at me, and with a predatory twinkle in his eye reserved for a puma stalking a meal—not a septuagenarian stalking another septuagenarian with a cane—hissed, "Exactly." He had a plan, and I saw it formulating behind a malevolent smirk.

An arthritic Angie lumbered towards his chair and sat down, holding a corded microphone in his right hand and a cane in his left. Joe, on the other hand, strode to centre stage with the determined confidence of an avenger and, looking his nemesis in the eye, flicked the heather he was holding in Angie's face. Angie, taken aback, growled, "Shove it up your ass." Seventy years old or not, if you've been raised in a Boston ghetto, as the big man had, those street skills never leave you.

Joe flicked Angie's face with the heather again, and this time, Angie swung the microphone, barely missing Joe's face. That's when things moved fast. Joe shot the sprig of heather out a second time, and Angie, his ire up despite being a millennium away from the reflexes he once had, lashed out with his cane. Instead of connecting with the hand holding the heather, the cane connected with Joe's head, sending his glasses flying across the stage. (It's not every day you see a septuagenarian behemoth go all Jack Sparrow on another septuagenarian's noggin with a walking stick.)

Joe, in turn, doubled up his street-fighting fist and delivered three rabbit punches to Angie's face. Angelo "King Kong" Mosca, taking the blows full on the beak, teetered backward and toppled downstage right in a plaster-cracking collapse to the floor. I'm sure tectonic plates in the deepest Pacific took a seismic shift that day, for when he dropped, the structure shook.

Although not seen in the video that went viral on YouTube, the bottom half of Angie lay prostrate on the floor, while his massive dome and shoulders hung behind the stage curtain. Only half of him was visible, which was an apt enough encapsulation of the former King Kong Mosca, victim to the ravages of time.

Just because Angie was down for the count didn't mean the fight was over. Remember, this was happening in a matter of seconds. It's already taken me ten times longer to tell this story than the time it took me to witness it. Sure, there was a collective gasp from the room when Mosca fell, and I'm sure whoever might have been choking on a piece of the hotel's poultry was quietly turning blue, but no one had moved.

They were transfixed, particularly the half dozen hard-core veterans of the Afghanistan conflict seated in the front row, sporting jarhead haircuts, stone-cold stares and chests festooned with medals. Perhaps, like the men we'd come to honour, they too were trapped in the past and still in the fray somewhere up in the Panjwayi, chasing the Taliban down some dusty arroyo.

Joe cleared the stage in two determined strides and, as if punting a pigskin for the end zone, wound his leg back and laid three vicious boots to Angie's midsection, barking, "And stay down, you piece of shit!"

Soon as Angie fell, that instinct I spoke of earlier kicked in . . . and I bolted from the stage. In the video clip, there's a short man in a suit making a beeline for the exit, looking more like a circus performer escaping a fire in the Big Top than an emcee. That's me. What else could I do? If I'd got between those angry bulls, the only way I'd have walked away with my life would've been with rodeo clown training.

Truth be told, watching Angie topple over struck me as the saddest thing I'd ever seen. He looked so confused, as if gravity itself had conspired with his assailant and pulled him to the mat. Rushing from their seats, the soldiers helped Angie to his feet. Joe, too, looked lost, standing in the middle of the stage, holding his now-broken glasses while appealing to the audience with outstretched arms, his left hand still holding the heather.

"Sportsmanship!" he said, as he looked back and forth from the audience to Angie. "Sportsmanship."

Clearly, the suppurating wound of grievance had not healed over time. Whatever atonement was expected—and quite frankly, needed—went AWOL that afternoon.

A woman's voice rose from the silent crowd, sounding tired and sad, saying, "Let it go, Joe. Let it go."

Writing this book twelve years later, after what feels like three lifetime's worth of battles won and lost in the comedy trenches, that woman's words resonate with a wisdom worth embracing. Let. It. Go.

Those of us who stand in the solo spot know that anger fuels the funny, and we have all worn the shoes of Joe and Angie one time or another. Haunted by lost moments in the sun. Burdened by professional jealousies and trivial resentments. Personal wounds incurred a thousand lifetimes ago still suppurate. Holding grudges is like holding a thousand-pound bag of bricks: it cripples whoever carries it.

It's best to lighten your load on the road, not add another brick to your back, especially at a point in the journey where mortality is no longer just another man's worry.

By the way, while we're talking mortality, I don't want to go out strapped to a machine in the sepulchral gloom of the hospital room. I want to go standing up, with a take-no-prisoners final charge of adrenalin. If you have the luxury of knowing *when* you go, it's *how* you go that matters most. So, chopper me to the Barrenlands and drop me near the treeline buck naked, smeared in bacon fat . . . just to facilitate predator interest. As the whine of helicopter blades recedes in the distance, you stand alone and exposed, feeling nothing but nature's frigid kiss. Alone you came into this world, and alone you will leave it, *but* you're going to have some company first.

From the forest, there comes a howling. *Wolves! Wolves!* If you want to live, you'd better run, you old bugger! *Run! Run for the life that's left in you.* Clutch your shrunken junk and run!

A burst of fur from the treeline, and Pow!—out across the wasteland the pack sweeps, pink tongues lolling, canines shiny in the morning sun with hungry eyes the colour of a blue, cruel moon.

Your spindly legs, which once moved when you wanted them to, are now taking umbrage with the brain's directions. Still, you do your best to stretch those alabaster pins free of Earth's gravitational pull . . . and will you look at that! You. Are. Running!

With a quick glance over your shoulder, you see the pack moving full tilt towards their prey and think, *Boy, are they ever pretty!* And that's when *Canis lupus*, with jaws agape, flies perpendicular for your jugular and, in a rat-tat-tat of final heartbeats, you step into the eternal. In minutes, what's left of your mortal coil lays on the lap of Mother Earth, where ravens and whisky jacks will come to tug on spare scraps of flesh, the wind your only witness.

One thing's for certain, you'll be the talk round the shuffleboard game at the old folks' home.

"Hey, Earl, did you hear what happened to ol' Ron?"

"No, Archie. What?"

"He got eaten by wolves."

"For the love of God, he *what*?!"

"Got eaten by a pack of wolves. On the tundra. Smeared buck-naked from tip to tail in bacon fat, too."

Earl, holding his shuffleboard stone, will pause in quiet contemplation as the totality of Archie's statement sinks in. He will gauge his surroundings and see this generic, sterile and antiseptic purgatory, ruled by a repetition of soul-sucking sameness that will be his life until the Reaper makes a house call.

That's when Earl will turn to Archie and ask, "Out of curiosity Archie, what do you think a trip like Ron's cost?"

ACKNOWLEDGEMENTS

Thanks to Scott Sellers, associate publisher, Penguin Random House Canada, and Tim Rostron, senior editor, Doubleday Canada, for their patience and encouragement. Thanks to freelance copy editor Lloyd Davis for his gimlet eye. Thanks also to my eldest daughter and old soul Cayley, whose enlightened and thorough suggestions on content throughout the rewrite were very helpful and to my youngest, the irrepressibly irreverent red-haired force of nature Gracie, whose progressive vision keeps her father moving to the right side of history. Much praise for my parents, Bernie 'n' Joyce James, a pair of sterling originals from the Greatest Generation, who gave my sister and me a work ethic, unconditional love and a sense of humour in a home that, once upon a time, was forever filled to bursting with a pantheon of friends and family during good times and bad. A big high-five to all those theatres, both big and small, in every province across the Dominion, whose stage doors have opened with a welcome for my producer and me these past twenty years and whose perseverance during the dark days of the pandemic stands as testimony to their resilience and commitment in maintaining the cultural health of our nation. Finally, I'd like to express my deep gratitude to those Canadian audiences whose faith in my funny has been feeding me and mine for a lifetime. A person telling jokes to a room full of people is a comedian. A person telling jokes to no one is just talking to themselves. We need each other.

© David Leyes

RON JAMES launched his comedy career in the early 1980s as a member of the internationally renowned improvisational troupe The Second City in Toronto. After appearing in dozens of commercials, movies and television series, he moved to Los Angeles with his young family in tow to chase the American dream. His three-year struggle bore far more successful results when he returned home and launched his critically acclaimed one-man show *Up and Down in Shaky Town*, which led to a solo career in stand-up comedy. Over the last twenty-five years he's created and starred in two TV series and a record-breaking nine one-hour network comedy specials, which became a New Year's viewing tradition for millions of Canadians. When not filling theatres from coast to coast, he splits his time between the Toronto he's called home for over forty years and the "back home" where he was born and raised, Nova Scotia.